Software Quality

Theory and Management

Second Edition

Software Quality

Theory and Management

Second Edition

Alan Gillies

Department of Business Information Management
University of Central Lancashire

INTERNATIONAL THOMSON COMPUTER PRESS
I(T)P™ An International Thomson Publishing Company

London • Bonn • Boston • Johannesburg • Madrid • Melbourne • Mexico City • New York • Paris
Singapore • Tokyo • Toronto • Albany, NY • Belmont, CA • Cincinnati, OH • Detroit, MI

Software Quality: Theory and Management, Second Edition
Copyright © 1997 International Thomson Computer Press

A division of International Thomson Publishing Inc.
The ITP logo is a trademark under licence.

For more information, contact:

International Thomson Computer Press
Berkshire House
168–173 High Holborn
London WC1V 7AA
UK

International Thomson Computer Press
20 Park Plaza
Suite 1001
Boston, MA 02116
USA

Imprints of International Thomson Publishing

International Thomson Publishing GmbH
Königswinterer Straße 418
53227 Bonn
Germany

International Thomson Publishing Asia
60 Albert Street #15-01
Albet Complex
Singapore 189969

Thomson Nelson Australia
102 Dodds Street
South Melbourne, 3205
Victoria
Australia

International Thomson Publishing Japan
Hirakawacho Kyowa Building, 3F
2-2-1 Hirakawacho
Chiyoda-ku, 102 Tokyo
Japan

Nelson Canada
1120 Birchmount Road
Scarborough, Ontario
Canada M1K 5G4

International Thomson Editores
Campos Eliseos 385, Piso 7
Col. Polenco
11560 Mexico D.F. Mexico

International Thomson Publishing South Africa
PO Box 2459
Halfway House
1685 South Africa

International Thomson Publishing France
Tours Maine-Montparnasse
33 avenue du Maine
75755 Paris Cedex 15
France

Products and services that are referred to in this book may be either trademarks and/or registered trademarks of their respective owners. The Publisher/s and Author/s make no claim to these trademarks.

Whilst the Publisher has taken all reasonable care in the preparation of this book the Publisher makes no representation, express or implied, with regard to the acccuracy of the information contained inthis book and cammot accept any legal responsibility or liability for any errors or omissions from the book or the consequences thereof.

British Library Cataloguing-in-Publication Data
A catalogue record for this book is available from the British Library

Library of Congress Cataloging-in-Publication Data
A catalog record for this book is available from the Library of Congress

First printed 1997

ISBN 1-85032-312-7

Typeset by Saxon Graphics Ltd, Derby
Cover Designed by SPY Design, London
Printed in the UK by T.J. International Ltd.

Contents

Preface   ix
Preface to the first edition   xi
Acknowledgements   xiii

Part 1: The theory of software quality   1
1 Introduction   3
    1.1   What is quality?   3
    1.2   Software quality   5
    1.3   Views of quality   7
    1.4   The author's view: quality is people   14
    1.5   Questions for discussion   14
    1.6   Further reading   15

2 Hierarchical models of quality   16
    2.1   What is a hierarchical model?   16
    2.2   The hierarchical models of Boehm and McCall   18
    2.3   How the quality criteria interrelate   22
    2.4   A practical evaluation   24
    2.5   Questions for discussion   27
    2.6   Further reading   28

3 Measuring software quality   29
    3.1   Measuring quality   29
    3.2   Software metrics   31
    3.3   Metrics cited in the literature   33
    3.4   The problem with metrics   36
    3.5   An overall measure of quality   38
    3.6   Questions for discussion   42
    3.7   Further reading   44

4 Developments in measuring quality   45
    4.1   The work of Gilb   45
    4.2   The COQUAMO project   53

4.3   Recent work on metrics   56
4.4   Quality profiles   58
4.5   Questions for discussion   66
4.6   Further reading   66

Part 2: The management and improvement of quality   67
5 The CASE for tools and methods   69
5.1   The growth of software engineering methods   69
5.2   Methodologies based upon the waterfall lifecycle   73
5.3   CASE tools   84
5.4   The contribution of methods and tools to quality   89
5.5   Alternative approaches to software development   92
5.6   Standards based on the software engineering lifecycle   98
5.7   Questions for discussion   99
5.8   Further reading   101

6 Quality management systems   102
6.1   A historical perspective   102
6.2   Terms   106
6.3   Elements of a QMS   109
6.4   The key to quality management: a human quality culture   117
6.5   Quality in software: the current situation   124
6.6   The problem of user requirements   127
6.7   A QMS for software   130
6.8   Quality assurance or quality improvement?   137
6.9   Questions for discussion   140
6.10 Further reading   141

7 The ISO9000 series of quality management standards   142
7.1   The purpose of standards   142
7.2   The ISO9000 series: a generic quality management standard   144
7.3   ISO9000-3: notes for guidance on the application of ISO9001
      to software development   152
7.4   The impact of ISO9000 and TickIT   155
7.5   Questions for discussion   166
7.6   Further reading   166

8 Models and standards for process improvement   167
8.1   Chapter summary   167
8.2   The Capability Maturity Model   167
8.3   Individual levels of the CMM   171
8.4   The role of the CMM   174
8.5   SPICE   175
8.6   Conclusions   179
8.7   Questions for discussion   180
8.8   Further reading   181

9 Case studies: from kitchens to software   183
    9.1   Introduction to case studies   183
    9.2   Total quality in the kitchen   183
    9.3   A software house: Sherwood Computer Services   188
    9.4   Does quality deliver benefits?   195
    9.5   Discussion   201
    9.6   Questions for discussion   202
    9.7   Further reading   202

10 Trends in quality: the future   203
    10.1 Four key issues in quality   203
    10.2 Are CASE tools addressing the right issues?   203
    10.3 Is process improvement appropriate for software development? 208
    10.4 What is the likely impact of standards?   211
    10.5 Beyond software quality: the need for a strategic view 214

Answers to selected questions   217
    Chapter 3   217
    Chapter 6   218

References   219
    Further reading   226

Index   229

Preface

Since the first edition, there have been a number of developments in the field. In particular, process improvement standards such as the Software Engineering Institute's Capability Maturity Model (SEI CMM) and the international SPICE standards have become much more significant. The inclusion of these standards will make the text more relevant to readers outside of the UK. Standards in general have become much more important as purchasers of software have insisted that accreditation is a prerequisite for bidding for contracts.

The second edition provides the opportunity to bring the material up to date, and some major surveys have been included which examine the uptake of methods and standards amongst the practitioner community. They show that there is a long way to go to convince many organizations of the benefits to be derived.

More case studies have been included in the text, again in the attempt to make the text more international in appeal. The new material is largely included as mini-studies in the main text, although another major case study is included in the case study chapter together with an update to the Sherwood case study.

The chapter on tools and methods has been extensively revised in the light of readers' comments. In addition, Chapter Five from the first edition has been deleted. Much of this chapter reflected personal research of the author. With the additional material to be included, it was felt preferable to delete this material to prevent the inexorable growth which has characterized many second and subsequent editions of other titles. The material formerly presented there is thoroughly referenced in the bibliography and can be read in the original reference sources if required.

In recognition of the use that has been made of the book in teaching, each chapter concludes with a set of questions relating to the content of the chapter. Some are suitable for discussion, others are quantitative in nature. Solutions are provided for the numerical questions.

Through these changes, I have sought to address concerns raised by readers and ensure that the material presented is up to date. In a book of this size and purpose, it is not possible to cover all the issues within the area of quality. For example, readers seeking a quantitative view will find Norman Fenton's book on Software Metrics, now also in its second edition, provides much more detail in this area. This book has not tried to reproduce a poor imitation. The purpose of this book remains to provide an overview of the subject for practitioners and students. The further reading sections and bibliography are recommended reading for all.

Finally, as always, I would welcome comments on the book, and my email address is appended for the purpose.

Professor Alan Gillies
Preston, October 1996
a.c.gillies@uclan.ac.uk

Preface to the first edition

The need for quality in software should be self-evident. Our dependence upon computers in all spheres of life is continually increasing. It is therefore essential that computers operate reliably and effectively. There are still those who scoff at the need for quality and dismiss it as another 'flavour of the month'. However, this is a short-sighted and dangerous approach. Whilst we may disagree about the means to the end of good quality, the achievement of good quality software cannot be ignored.

The purpose of this book is to present a rounded view of the subject, bridging the gap between software engineering and quality management. Software engineering tends to suggest that quality may be achieved solely as a product of good engineering practice. Total quality management (TQM) emphasizes the importance of people, culture and process management. It does not, however, take account of the peculiar nature of software. Software is unusual because it does not have a physical existence. Unusually, errors once corrected, stay corrected.

The consequence is that an effective treatment of the subject must consider both engineering and management aspects of quality. It must also reconcile the theoretical models provided by the research literature with the practice of IT professionals. Increasingly, with an emphasis upon 'hybrid' management, there is a need to consider the 'fitness for purpose' of software in its support for the business objectives of organizations. This is particularly the view from the IT Institute where we have been educating hybrid IT graduates since 1986.

The book is organized into two principal Parts, the theory of software quality and the management of software quality. There is also a final section entitled 'Beyond Software Quality', which looks at the future of the subject in terms of 'fitness for purpose' or 'effectiveness'.

Chapter 1 is an introduction dealing with the thorny issue of the nature of quality, examining current and classical definitions and the specific issue relating to software. In Chapter 2, the classical hierarchical models of quality provided by McCall and Boehm are described. These models form the basis of most subsequent work. Chapter 3 considers the use of metrics to measure quality within the hierarchical models. It examines the criteria for a good metric and concludes that the current picture is not too encouraging. Details of some of the more recent research by Kitchenham, Gilb and Fenton are considered in Chapter 4. The Japanese perspective is also considered and the 'software factory' concept examined. Part I concludes with a study carried out by the author. It examines the current view of software quality, found in six UK companies. The LOQUM modelling process, evolved during the study is described and an overall picture is drawn.

A consideration of CASE tools and methods and their impact upon quality begins Part II. Chapter 6 draws upon experience gained during the recent Salford/DTI Solutions programme. The methods considered in detail are SSADM and IEM. Chapter 7 considers classical total quality management and describes the needs of a quality management system to be applied to software development. The chapter compares the different philosophies of three principal 'gurus': Deming, Juran and Crosby. The next chapter describes the role of standards in the field of quality management. The chapter focuses upon the ISO9000/EN29001/BS5750 series of standards. The standards are described and their relevance to software is discussed. The new (1991) notes for guidance for the application of ISO9001 to software development are also described, together with standards for software and hardware; for example US DoD STD2167A. Two case studies which illustrate many of the points raised in earlier chapters are found in Chapter 9. The two examples are a kitchen firm who have BS5750 accreditation and a software house who are moving towards accreditation and have adopted many working practices intended to improve quality. By way of conclusion, Chapter 10 considers three questions:
'Are CASE tools addressing the right issues?'
'Is TQM appropriate for software development?'
'What is the likely impact of standards?'

Finally, Part III provides an epilogue to the main sections by considering the question of IT effectiveness. Ultimately, software only represents a quality solution if it is effective in enhancing the user or organization's capability. This is a complex issue and this chapter merely sets out some of the principal issues.

The book is primarily aimed at IT professionals and postgraduate courses. It is being used on the MSc programme at Salford. It may also find some use on final year undergraduate courses. It is intended to be readable and interesting. Any comments would be gratefully received by the author.

Alan Gillies
IT Institute
Salford

Acknowledgements

Many people have contributed to this book in its two editions. I would like to thank my wife Jenny and friend Dave Walker for their endless corrections to the first edition. I would like to thank the editors and production staff who have been associated with both editions. I am particularly grateful for comments received during publication and also during the life of the first edition. Finally, I would like to thank all the companies and individuals who have contributed experiences, and Helen Tague for compiling the index.

The following trademarks are acknowledged:

Ada is a trademark of Department of Defense, Ada Joint Program Office
C and C++ are trademarks of AT&T Bell Laboratories, Inc.
DEC is a trademark of Digital Equipment Corpoation
Excelerator is a trademark of Index Technology Corporation
GEM is a trademark of Digital Research, Inc.
IEF is a trademark of Texas Instruments, Inc.
Ingres is a trademark of Ingres Corporation
MS-DOS and Windows/3 are trademarks of Microsoft Corporation
Turbo Pascal and Turbo Pascal for Windows are trademarks of Borland International, Inc.
UNIX is a trademark of AT&T Bell Laboratories, Inc.

The use of other trademarks without acknowledgement is unintentional, and will be acknowledged at a future date if notified.

PART I
THE THEORY OF SOFTWARE QUALITY

Chapter 1

Introduction

1.1 What is quality?

It is always important to define terminology at the start of a book. So let's start by considering just what we mean by quality. It would be helpful if quality was an easily defined and unambiguous concept. Regrettably, quality is 'hard to define, impossible to measure, easy to recognise' (Kitchenham, 1989a). Quality is generally transparent when present, but easily recognized in its absence, e.g. when a new car falls to pieces, or a computer program fails to perform properly.

To explore the nature of quality further, consider the motor car as a product. In particular, we shall examine three examples which have all been highly successful products and, therefore, presumably represent some sort of quality solution. The three cars in question are a Rolls-Royce, a Ford Escort and a Mini.

The name Rolls-Royce is synonymous with quality in the mind of the general public. The name is used to describe other high quality products, e.g. 'the Rolls-Royce of ...'. Here, high quality is associated with a very high level of specification, a fast smooth ride, a high quality of finish on the paintwork, a great deal of hand craftsmanship, and a degree of perceived quality, otherwise known as 'snob-appeal'. The other key feature of the type of quality represented by the Rolls-Royce is that cost is no object. The aim is to produce the best possible car irrespective of price. Quality considerations related to economics are irrelevant. Criteria such as fuel economy, servicing intervals and costs and the price of insurance premiums are all irrelevant in this case. If you can afford the car, you can afford the rest. The Rolls-Royce represents quality in terms of excellence, unconstrained by cost considerations.

The Ford Escort, on the other hand, is an example of a quality solution which epitomizes a mass-produced product. Quality is still associated with the level of specification, quality of ride, quality of finish on the paintwork and so on, but expectations are lower and it is recognized that the product is designed to a price. Criteria connected with economics such as fuel economy, servicing intervals and costs and the price of insurance premiums are now some of the critical factors. Such cars are designed to provide the maximum quality at given cost.

The Mini may not be regarded by some as a quality solution at all. It is unashamedly designed with cheapness in mind. All quality considerations are compromised by the cost factor. In absolute terms, the ride is poor, the comfort is poor, the speed performance is poor, but the car is cheap. Further, the car is cheap to maintain. Quality is compromised in areas such as comfort and ride and this may be acceptable. However, if quality is compromised in the areas of reliability and maintainability, longer-term costs are incurred and the overriding attraction of the car is lost. A cheap car with a limited specification is acceptable, but a cheap car that involves compromises that incur longer-term expenditure is not a quality solution under any terms.

This illustration provides some insights about quality which may be usefully examined further:

(a) Quality is not absolute. It means different things in different situations. The Mini and the Rolls-Royce both represent quality in different ways. Quality cannot be measured upon a quantifiable scale in the same way as physical properties such as temperature or length.

(b) Quality is multidimensional. It has many contributing factors. It is not easily summarized in a simple, quantitative way. Some aspects of quality can be measured, such as maximum speed, fuel economy; some may not, such as quality of paint finish. The most easily measured criteria are not necessarily the most important. People are irrational beings, and the acceptability of a product may depend upon criteria which are very hard to define.

(c) Quality is subject to constraints. More people buy Ford Escorts than Rolls-Royces because most people's quality assessment is constrained by cost. Assessment of quality in most cases cannot be separated from cost. However, cost may be wider than simple financial cost: it refers to any critical resources such as people, tools and time. Some resources will be more constrained than others and where there is a high demand for a resource that is heavily constrained, the availability of that resource will become critical to overall quality.

(d) Quality is about acceptable compromises. Where quality is constrained and compromises are required, some quality criteria may be sacrificed more acceptably than others; e.g. comfort should be sacrificed before reliability. Those criteria that can least afford to be sacrificed may be regarded as critical attributes. They are often a small subset of the overall set of quality criteria.

(e) Quality criteria are not independent, but interact with each other causing conflicts. For example, fuel economy is generally adversely affected by the speed at which a car is driven. Thus, if a quality car is one that may be driven fast and one that shows good fuel economy, then a conflict exists between the two desirable attributes.

There is a bewildering range of formal and informal definitions available. Some of the most significant are summarized in Table 1.1.

The problem with all definitions is the context-dependence of quality.

For example, the Oxford English Dictionary (OED), states that quality is 'the degree of excellence' (OED, 1990). This is an attractive definition but is insufficient for our purposes. The nature of 'excellence' must be considered in more detail to make the definition more effective. However, there is a more serious problem with this definition.

Table 1.1 Definitions of quality

Source	Definition
OED, 1990	The degree of excellence
Crosby, 1979	Zero defects
ISO, 1986	The totality of features and characteristics of a product or service that bear on its ability to satisfy specified or implied needs
Frühauf, 1994	Quality is when the customer comes back, not the product

Within a commercial context, it is necessary to consider the constraints upon excellence. A commercial organization pursuing excellence for its own sake without regard to customer requirements will not prosper. Customers generally require acceptable performance at a particular price point, rather than absolute excellence. This is why more customers buy Ford Escorts than Rolls-Royces. However, a company ignoring quality issues for the sake of short-term financial advantage is equally unwise. The Japanese manufacturing industry, which has long been upheld as a paragon of virtue in the quality area, has regarded the pursuit of quality as the path to long-term profitability. In commercial terms, quality may be associated with taking a longer-term view than the immediate situation. Many quality initiatives will take time to reap commercial benefits.

An alternative formal definition of quality is provided by the International Standards Organization (ISO):

'The totality of features and characteristics of a product or service that bear on its ability to satisfy specified or implied needs.'

(ISO, 1986)

The standard definition associates quality with the ability of the product or service to fulfil its function. It recognizes that this is achieved through the features and characteristics of the product. Quality is associated both with having the required range of attributes and achieving satisfactory performance within each attribute. These features of quality may be applied to software as well as to motor cars. We shall, therefore, now consider the specific quality issues associated with software.

1.2 Software quality

The definitions provided thus far may all be applied to software. However, some definitions have been suggested which specifically refer to software quality. Kitchenham (1989b) refers to software quality as 'fitness for needs' and claims quality involves matching expectations. This definition specifically recognizes the two features of a piece of quality software: conformance to its specification and fitness for its intended purpose. These may be summarized as:

- Is it a good solution?

- Does it address the right problem?

The Department of Defense (DoD, 1985) in the USA defines software quality as 'the degree to which the attributes of the software enable it to perform its intended end use', which neatly combines the need to provide a good solution with the requirement to answer the right question.

Software quality does appear to be particularly problematical when compared to an arena such as manufacturing. At a workshop (Gillies, 1990), a group of IT professionals were asked why software quality was different from other types of quality. It was suggested that each type of product made its own quality demands but that computer software was particularly problematical for the following reasons:

- Software has no physical existence.
- The lack of knowledge of client needs at the start.
- The change of client needs over time.
- The rapid rate of change in both hardware and software.
- The high expectations of customers, particularly with respect to adaptability.

Consider the comparison with a car. There is no expectation that a motor manufacturer will keep your car up to date with the latest specification. If the latest specification is required, then a new model must be purchased. This is also the case with packaged software, such as the word processor used to produce this book. It is the bespoke nature of many systems which raises the expectation of complete adaptability and flexibility. The aim of a bespoke solution is to provide an exact match to user needs. This can be a frustrating process, beset with problems such as:

- The question of 'Who is the client?' Is it the DP department? The departmental manager? The whole collective organization? The end user?
- The need to reconcile different user needs, for example, 'experts' and 'novices' who may be the same person at different points in time.
- The need for the system to evolve with the organization.

There is an ambiguity arising within the software development process from the need for design and production techniques. Within the software quality area, the need to provide a solution that matches user needs is often considered as 'design quality', whilst ensuring a match to the specification is considered as 'manufacturing quality'. The classic software development waterfall lifecycle tackles this ambiguity by addressing design and production in different stages of the process (Figure 1.1).

The implementation and testing phases are closely related to manufacturing. This analogy is taken to its logical conclusion in the 'software factory' approach pioneered in Japan. The aim of such a software production process is to ensure that the product meets the design specification. Within this process, the design specification is a reference point against which conformity and therefore the quality of the product may be assessed.

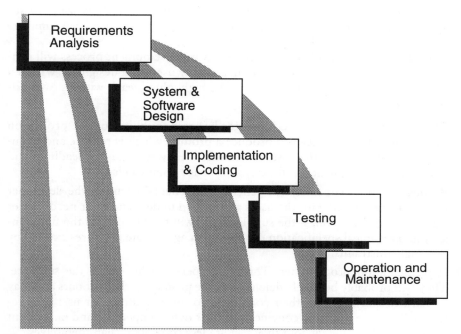

Figure 1.1 The traditional waterfall lifecycle model.

At the requirements analysis and design phase, no such reference point exists and the quality of the design is much harder to assess. The quality of design may only be measured subjectively and indirectly. Many apparently attractive quality initiatives focus upon improving the implementation of software from an already established design specification. However, this will prove ineffective where the critical stages in determining overall quality lie at the design stage. Further, the rigid division of 'design' and 'manufacture', although attractive to system developers, can place significant constraints upon the effectiveness with which the final system meets the users' requirements.

1.3 Views of quality

Quality is a multidimensional construct (Figure 1.2). It may therefore be considered using a polyhedron metaphor. Within this metaphor, quality is represented by a three-dimensional solid. Each face represents a different aspect of quality such as correctness, reliability, efficiency.

Therefore, it is perhaps inevitable that it has been classified according to a number of 'views' or perspectives (Figure 1.3).

Within our metaphor, these views may be regarded as external observers looking down at our polyhedron. These views are often diverse and may conflict with each other. Each view comes from a particular context, and any single view tends to give us only a partial picture. The views identified tend to be stereotypical. For example, a distinction is commonly made within software quality between the 'user or client' and the 'designer or supplier'.

The views are generally presented in adversarial pairs such as users versus designers. The different perspectives of designers and users have been summarized in terms of a list of objectives (Table 1.2).

In practice, the stakeholders within a software development process will generally form a much broader spectrum than simply users and designers. Within a software project, the following roles may be highlighted, each with its own priorities and concerns:

- Project manager. The project manager has responsibility for the project on the supply side. He is keen to produce a product which is reliable and maintainable and will keep the customer satisfied. However, he has deadlines and budget constraints which will exert a force for compromise.

- Business analyst. The analyst is generally the clients' friend in the developer camp. He has liaised with the users and should understand their needs better than anyone else amongst the suppliers. He will tend to defend the functionality and technical specification of the system against the pressures exerted by external constraints.

- Implementation programmer. This is the person who writes the software. They will probably be highly defensive of the product of their labours and may be hard to convince that their code does not meet technical or user requirements. They are probably convinced of their own competence and may resent interference by others whom they feel are less competent than themselves.

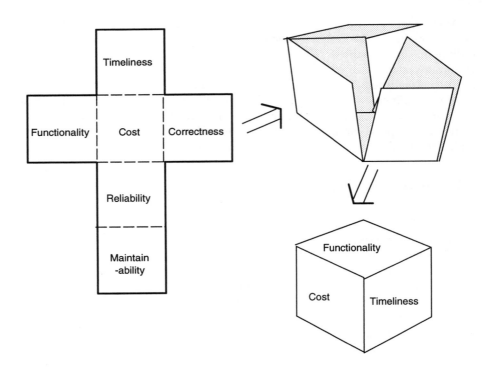

Figure 1.2 Polyhedron metaphor for quality.

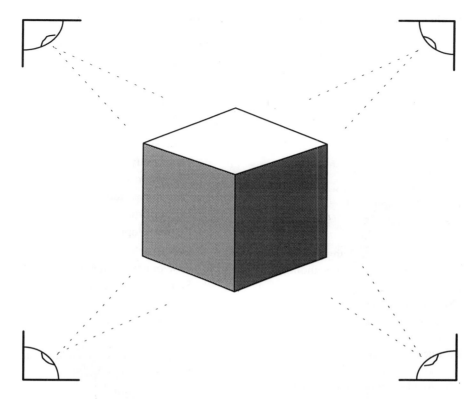

Figure 1.3 Views of quality within the polyhedron metaphor.

- Quality auditor. Within an organization, it is the job of the quality auditor to detect departures from a quality solution, whether it is technical defects or a poor match to requirement. The auditor cannot win. Any action on his/her part increases the workload of the programmer and adversely affects the time scales and budgets of the project manager, and any inaction is likely to lead to dissatisfaction expressed by the user camp.

- End user. This is usually a junior person who often has very little input into the development process, but has to use the system in the end. If the end users' ideas are taken on board by developers ahead of their superiors', then the developers risk the wrath of the people who pay the bill. Yet it is the end users' reactions which will determine the acceptability of the system in the medium and long term.

- Line manager. The line manager is the end user's boss and may be the instigator of the project. The manager will try to find a solution that appeals to the workers under them, but must also justify time scales to senior management.

- Project sponsor. The sponsor is the one who pays the bill. They will often be remote from the day-to-day implementation issues and will want a successful outcome to boost their prestige and justify the expenditure. A successful outcome is likely to be judged by on-time delivery within budget as much as on broader quality issues.

Table 1.2 The conflicting views of users and developers

Views Of Quality

User	Designer
What I want	Good specification
Fast response	Technically correct
Control information	Fits within systems structure
Easy to use help menus	Easy to maintain
Available as required	Difficult for user to damage
Exception data	Fast development
Exception reporting	Low maintenance
Reacts to business change	Ease of development
Minimal technical understanding	Standards across all systems
Input data once	Well documented
Common definitions	Modern approach
Single terminal and keyboard	Correct data
No errors	High level of user involvement
Fast development	User managed
Access to all systems	Users well trained
Minimal lead time for developments	User trials of full system
Graphics	Simple menu structure
Ad hoc analysis	Simple recovery
Accurate time and cost estimate	Structure for future IT path
Idiot proof	Integrated systems
Easy to correct mistakes	Common hardware base
Effective feedback from technicians	Secure from hacking
Reliable/well tested	Auditable
No unplanned downtime	Stable systems
Minimum maintenance	
Cheap to run	
Contains all foreseeable requirements	
Standard keyboard functions	
Adaptable	
Meets business objectives	

Each stakeholder has his or her own objectives from the project. Many of these objectives will conflict with each other. The overall quality may be judged in terms of how well each stakeholder is satisfied at the end of the day. The most likely personnel to lose out in a conflict are the people nearest the coal-face: the implementation programmer and the end user.

In an attempt to classify different and conflicting views of quality, Garvin (1984) has suggested five different views of quality (Figure 1.4):

1. The transcendent view
    This view relates quality to innate excellence. Another word for this might be 'elegance'. This is the classical definition of quality, in tune with the dictionary and the Rolls-Royce. It is impossible to quantify and difficult to apply in a meaningful sense to a large software project. An attempt to build in a high degree of innate excellence to a software project is likely to be constrained by resources. Large software projects are inevitably expensive,

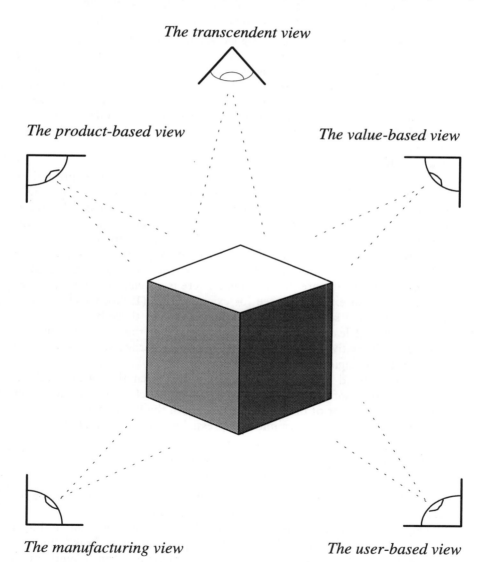

Figure 1.4 Five views of quality (after Garvin, 1984).

and this tends to emphasize the value-based view (described below). Where an 'all singing, all dancing' solution has been attempted in the past, it has often proved unpopular with users because of its complexity.

2. The product-based view

    From this perspective, the higher the quality, the higher the cost. The basis for this view is that it costs money to build in quality. Quality of this type may be added to a product in two ways:

    (a) greater functionality, such as increased security through built-in functionality;

    (b) greater care in development leading to a higher quality solution, such as through the introduction of a quality management system.

    The likes of Crosby (1979) have argued against this view, saying that 'quality is free'. They are referring to the fact that improvements in quality at the manufacturing stage lead to fewer defects and greater reliability in use, with a reduction in the cost of wastage and maintenance. This view finds support amongst software economists who point to the fact that 80% of software development costs are in maintenance. However, it may be difficult to prove a conclusive link between investment and return due to the time lag between the two.

3. The user-based view

    This can be summarized as 'fitness for purpose', a view first expressed by Juran in the late 1940s. It is an important view of quality that has often been sacrificed in software engineering in the past in favour of technical correctness. Thus the aim of ensuring that the software solution addresses the right problem is a noble one. The practical attainment is not simple.

    These aspects of quality are often very hard to quantify in a satisfactory way. The complexity and fuzziness of the problem have often led to neglect of such issues in software development. There is a wealth of literature concerning practical experience; see for example Gilb (1988), which suggests that conventional sequential methodologies such as those based upon the waterfall model lead to inadequate solutions from the users' perspective. Uptake of alternatives is slow, and they are still regarded with suspicion by many software engineers.

    Quality defined in terms of giving the users what they want tends to intimidate some software designers who, having watched computing power walk out of the door of the DP department with the PC, may take refuge in criticizing the users. Some opinions expressed to the author include:

    'People out there can't get it right!'
    'They don't understand about software quality!'
    'They certainly don't know what they want!'

    Whilst there may be some truth in some of these statements in some applications, it is the developers' responsibility to correct them.

    Let us return to the car analogy again. When a customer wants to buy a car, they may not know anything about compression ratios, brake fluid viscosities or brake horsepower. The customer looking for a small family car is likely to express his or her requirements in terms of a cheap reliable car which will go as fast as possible on as little petrol as possible. Does this constitute knowing what is required? The customers know what they want in terms of quality criteria: speed, economy, comfort, cost. It's up to the salesman to point out that it's not feasible to expect a 100 mph, 100 mpg car for £100. But there's a nice little runner for £4,000 over there, sir ...

Users do have ideas of what they want. They may express them in ways that designers find difficult to quantify. It is the job of the design and requirements analysis process to turn users' ideas on the subject into a requirements specification and then a design. The user will also take some requirements for granted. Generally these will be the technical requirements, e.g. they expect a computer system to work reliably and efficiently. The user-based view of quality will be determined by the quality of the match between their requirements and the design.

4. The manufacturing view

The manufacturer's view measures quality in terms of conformance to requirements. A simple example might be the dimensions of a component. The specification will state both the required dimension and the tolerance that will be acceptable. As the requirements are laid down in a specification, this is referred to in this book as 'match-to-spec.' quality. This view of quality is the most common amongst software engineers and lies at the heart of sequential development methodologies of the traditional waterfall type. It is currently being promoted through the use of methodologies, computer-aided software engineering (CASE) tools and total quality management (TQM) schemes as proposed by Crosby (1979). It is attractive because it is the easiest view to quantify.

Within manufacturing, the zero defect approach to quality is growing in popularity. The principal philosophy behind such a view is that errors are avoidable, but expected. However, whilst error-free software is highly desirable, high-quality software involves more than this. If this is all that quality is about, why do people buy Rolls-Royces when there are reliable cars at much less cost? The manufacturing side of software is already better served by quality techniques than the design stage. Further improvements to manufacturing may not be cost-effective.

In addition to this, the zero defect approach faces barriers to acceptance. There is a story told of a contract programmer (apocryphal, I hope) who arrived at a site belonging to a large computer company to find a prominently displayed poster announcing 'Days to Zero Defect'. Underneath, the figure 332 had been crossed out and replaced with 331. Impressed, he went about his business. The next day, he was surprised to see that the poster still read 'Days to Zero Defect: 331'. He went about his business. And the next day ... and the next ... and the next ... and the next. After six weeks, he asked someone about it. The employee replied, 'Well, have you noticed any improvement?' The moral of this story is that any procedures and quality models are only as good as the people who implement them. And if quality is about believing that zero defects are really possible, there's a big job on to convince people.

5. The value-based view
    This is the ability to provide what the customer requires at a price that they can afford. This is critical in the automotive industry for products such as the Ford Escort or the Mini. Within software development, this view of quality as constrained by cost is better suited to a wider view of resources than simple financial cost. People, time and tools may all act as constraints upon the attainment of the desired level of quality. In addition, there may be internal conflicts between the user and technical requirements of the system.

1.4 The author's view: quality is people

There is a tendency amongst writers in the software quality area to emphasize procedures, tools and systems. This appears to stem from their background in computer programming and the origins of quality management ideas within the manufacturing area. However, this author takes the view that, fundamentally, software quality is about people. This is what makes the subject both complex and interesting. We have already seen the diversity of personnel with a stake in the development process. Quality is determined by people because:

- It is people and human organizations who have problems to be tackled by computer software
- It is people who define the problems and specify the solutions
- It is still currently people who implement designs and produce code
- It is still people who test code
- It is people who use the final systems and will make judgements about the overall quality of the solution.

Tools, processes and quality management systems are all aids to enhancing quality, provided that the people are capable and motivated towards their effective use. The largest barrier to the effective introduction of CASE tools, with their promise of higher quality systems, remains the impact upon human working practices (see for example Gillies and Smith, 1994). Whilst parts of the development process, such as implementation of designs to produce code, may be improved by automation, most tasks remain in the human domain, although tools and systems may provide effective aids.

This book therefore focuses upon the human or 'people' aspects of quality. Where tools, methods and processes are discussed, they are seen in the context of assisting people and enabling people to carry out their function effectively. In the next couple of chapters, we consider the theoretical models proposed in the past and evaluate their usefulness.

1.5 Questions for discussion

The following questions are intended for group discussion. Although based on this chapter, they will benefit from wider research of the issues as preparation.

1. Name five companies that you associate with quality products or services. What characteristics do these companies share? Are these characteristics demonstrated by software suppliers in your experience?
2. Software is intangible. How does this affect our perception of the quality of software systems? The Federal Aviation Authority in the USA insists that all systems must be fully tested before a certificate of air-worthiness can be awarded. Is this possible in the context of software systems?
3. Garvin's five views (section 1.4) are not intended as exhaustive. What other views of quality might one consider? Are all views of equal importance?

1.6 Further reading

Frühauf, K. (ed.) (1994) Software Quality: Concern for People, *Proceedings of the 4th European Conference on Software Quality*, VDF, Zurich, ISBN 3 7281 2153 3.

Garvin, D. (1984) What does product quality mean? *Sloan Management Review*, 4.

Gillies, A.C. and Smith, P. (1994) *Managing Software Engineering*, Chapman & Hall/International Thomson Publishing, London.

Chapter 2

Hierarchical models of quality

2.1 What is a hierarchical model?

In order to compare quality in different situations, both qualitatively and quantitatively, it is necessary to establish a model of quality. There have been many models suggested for quality. Most are hierarchical in nature. In order to examine the nature of hierarchical models, consider the methods of assessment and reporting used in schools. The progress of a particular student has generally been recorded under a series of headings, usually subject areas such as Science, English, Maths and Humanities.

A qualitative assessment is generally made, along with a more quantified assessment. These measures may be derived from a formal test or examination, continuous assessment of coursework or a quantified teacher assessment. In practice, the resulting scores are derived from a whole spectrum of techniques. They range from those which may be regarded as objective and transferable to those which are simply a more convenient representation of qualitative judgements. In the past, these have been gathered together to form a traditional school report (Table 2.1).

Table 2.1 A traditional school report

Subject	Teacher's comments	Term grade (A–E)	Exam mark (%)
English Maths Science Humanities Languages Technology			
OVERALL			

The traditional school report often had an overall mark and grade, a single figure, generally derived from the mean of the component figures, intended to provide a single measure of success.

In recent years, the assessment of pupils has become considerably more sophisticated and the model on which the assessment is based has become more complicated. Subjects are now broken down into skills, each of which is measured and the collective results used to give a more detailed overall picture. For example, in English, pupils' oral skills are considered alongside their ability to read; written English is further subdivided into an assessment of style, content and presentation. The hierarchical model requires another level of sophistication in order to accommodate the changes (Figure 2.1). Much effort is currently being devoted to producing a broader-based assessment, and in ensuring that qualitative judgements are as accurate and consistent as possible. The aim is for every pupil to emerge with a broad-based 'Record of Achievement' alongside their more traditional examination results.

Many of the points raised within the context of pupil assessment are paralleled in the assessment of software quality. A similar hierarchical approach, considering quality under a series of headings, is adopted by many authors. The resulting models are therefore known as hierarchical models of software quality.

The idea of a hierarchical model of quality in software dates back to the 1970s. It is worth considering the state of the art in computing at the time. The IBM PC was not yet born, computing was still centralized within the all-powerful DP departments. Two principal models of this type, one by Boehm *et al.* (1978) and one by McCall *et al.* (1977), are still cited today.

A hierarchical model of software quality is based upon a set of quality criteria, each of which has a set of measures or metrics associated with it. This type of model is illustrated schematically in Figure 2.2.

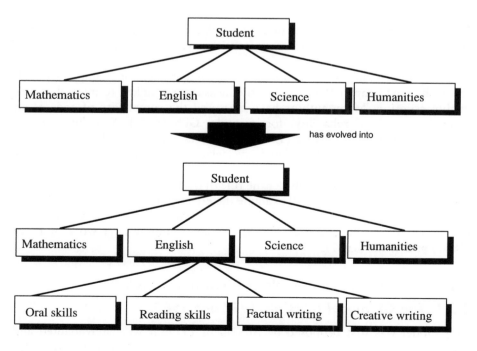

Figure 2.1 A more sophisticated model has evolved.

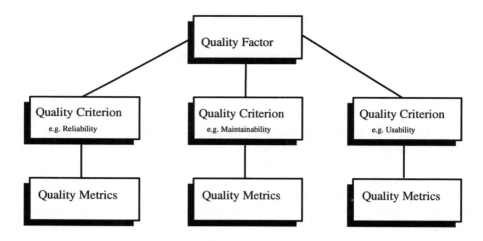

Figure 2.2 A schematic hierarchical view of software quality.

Examples of quality criteria typically employed include reliability, security and adaptability. The issues relating to the criteria of quality are:

- What criteria of quality should be employed?
- How do they inter-relate?
- How may the associated metrics be combined into a meaningful overall measure of quality?

As an example of the metrics linked to each characteristic, the metrics associated with reliability include accuracy, consistency, error tolerance and simplicity (Figure 2.3).

Unfortunately, life is rarely as simple as we might like. For example, we shall see in the next chapter that many of the measures are linked to more than one quality criterion. Many authors have measured the complexity of code as an inverse measure of reliability, for example, Gilb (1977), Woodward *et al.* (1980), Chen (1978), Myers (1976), Thayer *et al.* (1977), Hansen (1978). However, complexity is also related inversely to other criteria such as correctness and maintainability.

In this chapter, we shall consider the role of quality criteria within these models. In the next chapter we shall examine the effectiveness of the associated metrics. We shall first consider these issues in terms of the models of McCall *et al.* (1977, 1980) and Boehm *et al.* (1978) and incorporating later work by Perry (1987) and Watts (1987).

2.2 The hierarchical models of Boehm and McCall

2.2.1 The GE model (McCall, 1977 and 1980)

This model was first proposed by McCall in 1977. It was later adapted and revised as the MQ model (Watts, 1987). The model is aimed at system develop-

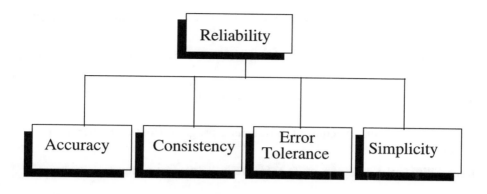

Figure 2.3 Metrics associated with reliability.

ers, to be used during the development process. However, in an early attempt to bridge the gap between users and developers, the criteria were chosen in an attempt to reflect users' views as well as developers' priorities. With the perspective of hindsight, the criteria appear to be technically oriented, but they are described by a series of questions which define them in terms acceptable to non-specialist managers.

The model, illustrated in Figure 2.4, identifies three areas of software work: product operation, product revision and product transition. These are summarized in Table 2.2, and the criteria are defined in Table 2.3.

Table 2.2 The three areas addressed by McCall's model (1977)

Product operation	requires that it can be learnt easily, operated efficiently and that the results are those required by the user.
Product revision	is concerned with error correction and adaptation of the system. This is important because it is generally considered to be the most costly part of software development.
Product transition	may not be so important in all applications. However, the move towards distributed processing and the rapid rate of change in hardware is likely to increase its importance.

Table 2.3 McCall's criteria of quality defined

Usability is the ease of use of the software.

Integrity is the protection of the program from unauthorized access.

Efficiency is concerned with the use of resources, e.g. processor time, storage. It falls into two categories: execution efficiency and storage efficiency.

Correctness is the extent to which a program fulfils its specification.

Reliability is its ability not to fail.

Maintainability is the effort required to locate and fix a fault in the program within its operating environment.

Flexibility is the ease of making changes required by changes in the operating environment.

Testability is the ease of testing the program, to ensure that it is error-free and meets its specification.

Portability is the effort required to transfer a program from one environment to another.

Reusability is the ease of reusing software in a different context.

Interoperability is the effort required to couple the system to another system.

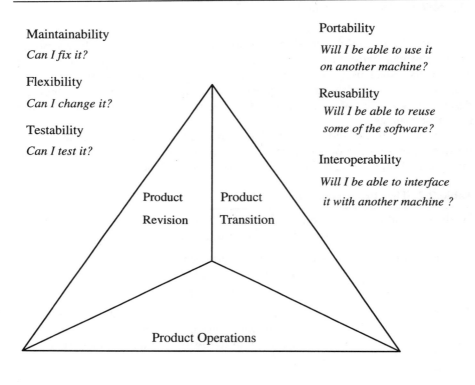

Maintainability
Can I fix it?

Flexibility
Can I change it?

Testability
Can I test it?

Portability
Will I be able to use it on another machine?

Reusability
Will I be able to reuse some of the software?

Interoperability
Will I be able to interface it with another machine ?

Product Revision

Product Transition

Product Operations

Correctness	*Does it do what I want?*
Reliability	*Does it do it accurately all the time?*
Efficiency	*Will it run on my machine as well as it can?*
Integrity	*Is it secure?*
Usability	*Can I run it?*

Figure 2.4 The GE model after McCall (1977).

McCall's model forms the basis for much quality work even today. For example, the MQ model published by Watts (1987) is heavily based upon the McCall model. This study carried out by the National Computer Centre (NCC) in the UK and GMD in Germany provides a more recent assessment of the metrics which are associated with the criteria outlined in McCall's model.

2.2.2 The Boehm model (1978)

Boehm's model (1978) was defined to provide a set of 'well-defined, well-differentiated characteristics of software quality'. The model is hierarchical in nature but the hierarchy is extended, so that quality criteria are subdivided. The first division is made according to the uses made of the system. These are classed as 'general' or 'as is' utility, where the 'as is' utilities are a subtype of the general utilities, roughly equating to the product operation criteria of McCall's model. There are two levels of actual quality criteria, the intermediate level being further split into primitive characteristics which are amenable to measurement.

The model is summarized in Figure 2.5.

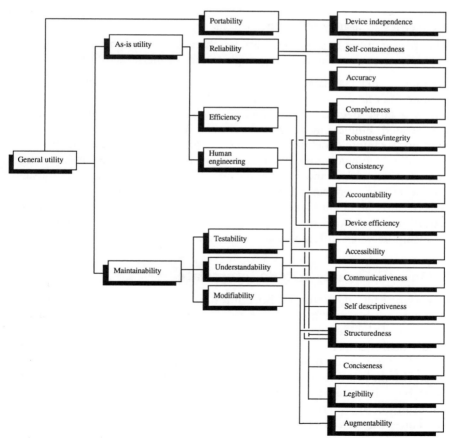

Figure 2.5 Boehm's model (1978).

This model is based upon a much larger set of criteria than McCall's model, but retains the same emphasis on technical criteria.

The two models share a number of common characteristics arising from their hierarchical nature and also from their origins in the computing culture of the 1970s:

- The quality criteria are supposedly based upon the user's view. In practice, they represent a designer's subset. There are some curious definitions provided for the criteria, for example some are defined in the negative: maintainability is the absence of effort required to fix a bug in the software. The metrics discussed in the next chapter represent the designer's attempts to measure these criteria.

- The models focus on the parts that designers can more readily analyse. For example, the criteria included are all connected with technical aspects of software quality. Further, the distribution of metrics is not uniform amongst the quality criteria cited. There are many measures associated with maintainability and reliability, but other characteristics are not measured by any existing metrics.

- Hierarchical models cannot be tested or validated. It cannot be shown that the metrics accurately reflect the criteria.

- The measurement of overall quality is achieved by a weighted summation of the characteristics. The resulting single 'figure of merit' is of limited value.

Neither model claims to be universal nor exclusive. The application will determine the relative importance of these characteristics. In practice, the models show a large degree of commonality and many of the characteristics are closely related. Fine distinctions may be useful in some applications, and not in others. For example, Boehm talks of modifiability where McCall distinguishes expandability from adaptability. Conversely, Boehm separates usability from documentation, understandability and clarity. From the lofty perch of hindsight, the models show more similarities than differences. Discussions with IT professionals recently highlighted the issues of measurement, the technical bias and the question of representing overall quality. The latter depends critically upon the relationship between different quality criteria.

2.3 How the quality criteria interrelate

The work of McCall, Watts and Boehm results in hierarchical models, comprising quality criteria and quality metrics. The individual measures of software quality provided do not provide an overall measure of software quality. For this, the individual measures must be combined. The individual measures of quality may conflict with each other, and compromises may have to be reached. The solution sought is an optimum balance of factors rather than an ideal solution. This problem has been considered by Perry (1987). He summarized the interrelationships between criteria as direct, neutral or inverse. The relationships he defined are summarized in Figure 2.6.

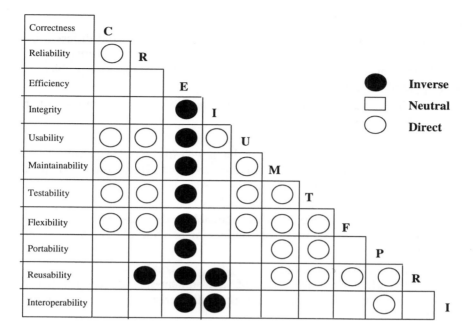

Figure 2.6 Relationships between criteria, after Perry (1987).

Some of these relationships are described below:

- Integrity vs. efficiency (inverse)
  The control of access to data or software requires additional code and processing leading to a longer runtime and additional storage requirements.

- Usability vs. efficiency (inverse)
  Improvements in the human/computer interface may significantly increase the amount of code and power required. Rector (1989) recently suggested that in the case of medical systems the interface may require considerably more power than the program itself.

- Maintainability and testability vs. efficiency (inverse)
  Optimized and compact code is not easy to maintain. Inevitably, well-structured, well-commented and modular code is less efficient. This well-structured code is also easier to test.

- Portability vs. efficiency (inverse)
  The use of optimized software or system utilities will lead to a decrease in portability.

- Flexibility, reusability and interoperability vs. efficiency (inverse)
  The generality required for a flexible system, the use of interface routines and the modularity desirable for reusability will all decrease efficiency.

- Flexibility and reusability vs. integrity (inverse)
  The general and flexible data structures required for flexible and reusable software increase the data security and protection problem.

- Interoperability vs. integrity (inverse)
  Coupled systems allow more avenues of access to more and different users. The potential for accidental access is increased as well as the opportunity for deliberate access. Systems sharing data or software bring extra problems.
- Reusability vs. reliability (inverse)
  Reusable software is required to be general: maintaining accuracy and error tolerance across all cases is difficult.
- Maintainability vs. flexibility (direct)
  Maintainable code arises from code that is well structured. This will also assist any modifications or alterations that are required. Thus a direct relationship exists between these properties.
- Maintainability vs. reusability (direct)
  Similarly, well-structured easily maintainable code is easier to reuse in other programs either as a library of routines or as code placed directly within another program.
- Portability vs. reusability (direct)
  Portable code is likely to be free of environment-specific features. It is also likely to be well structured. Both these characteristics will assist the reuse of code.
- Correctness vs. efficiency (neutral)
  The correctness of code, i.e. its conformance to specification, does not influence its efficiency. Correct code may be efficient or inefficient in operation.

Perry's analysis, although very helpful, suffers from two drawbacks. The first is the assumption that the relationships are commutative. This is not always the case. Secondly, the relationships are sometimes obscured by their application dependency; because of this, some of them may defy classification.

2.4 A practical evaluation

In a study of software quality in six large organizations, Gillies (1992) looked at the problems highlighted in the previous sections. The author elicited six hierarchical models of quality, in terms of criteria used by both users and developers of software. The following findings emerged.

Correctness was seen as an umbrella property encompassing other attributes. Two types of correctness were consistently identified. Developers talked in terms of technical correctness, which included factors such as reliability, maintainability and the traditional software virtues. Computer users, however, talked of business correctness, of meeting business needs and criteria such as timeliness, value for money and ease of transition.

This reinforced the existence of different views of quality as outlined in Chapter 1. It suggests that these developers emphasized conformance to specification, whilst users sought fitness for purpose. There was remarkable agreement between the different organizations as to some of the basic findings. In particular:

- A basic distinction between business and technical correctness.

- A recognition that different aspects of quality would influence each other.
- The study confirmed that the relationships were often context and even project dependent.
- The studies demonstrated that the relationships were often not commutative. Thus although property A may reinforce property B, property B may not reinforce property A.

A schematic model based upon the results of this research is shown in Figure 2.7. Tables 2.4 and 2.5 show the results of a specific study within a large manufacturing company.

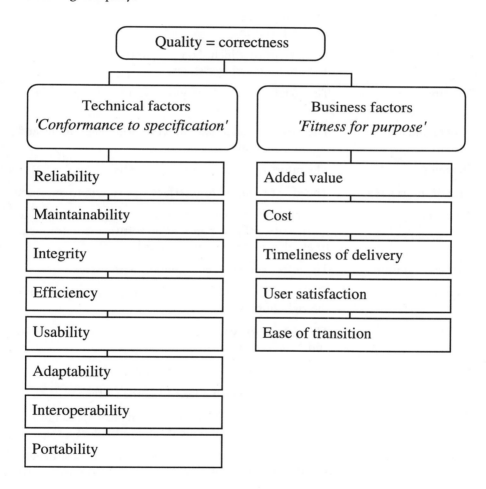

Figure 2.7 A schematic hierarchical model of quality based upon practical studies.

Table 2.4 Software quality criteria elicited from a large manufacturing company

Criteria	Definition
Technical correctness	The extent to which a system satisfies its technical specification.
User correctness	The extent to which a system fulfils a set of objectives agreed with the user.
Reliability	The extent to which a system performs its intended function without failure.
Efficiency	The computing resources required by a system to perform a function.
Integrity	The extent to which data and software are consistent and accurate across systems.
Security	The extent to which unauthorized access to a system can be controlled.
Understandability	The ease of understanding code for maintaining and adapting systems.
Flexibility	The effort required to modify a system.
Ease of interfacing	The effort required to interface one system to another.
Portability	The effort required to transfer a program from one hardware configuration and/or software environment to another or to extend the user base.
User consultation	The effectiveness of consultation with users.
Accuracy	The accuracy of the actual output produced, i.e. is it the right answer?
Timeliness	The extent to which delivery fits with the deadlines and practices of users.
Time to use	The time for the user to achieve a result.
Appeal	The extent to which a user likes the system.
User flexibility	The extent to which the system can be adapted both to changes in user requirements and individual taste.
Cost/benefit	The extent to which the system fulfils its cost/benefit specification both with regard to development costs and business benefits.
User friendliness	The time to learn how to use the system and ease of use once learnt.

The full details of the study are given in Gillies (1992), referenced below.

Table 2.5 Relationships elicited between the criteria in Table 2.4

Criteria B	Criteria A															
	R	E	I	S	U	F	EI	P	U	A	T	T	A	U	C	O
Reliability		O	+	+	O	O	O	O	O	O	O	O	O	O	O	O
Efficiency	O		–	–	–	–	–	–	–	O	–	+	–	–	O	–
Integrity	+	–		+	+	O	–	–	+	+	–	O	O	–	O	+
Security	+	–	+		+	O	–	–	+	+	–	O	O	–	O	–
Understandability	O	–	O	O		+	O	O	O	O	–	–	O	O	O	O
Flexibility	O	–	O	O	+		O	O	O	O	–	–	O	–	O	–
Ease of interfacing	O	O	+	+	+	+		+	+	–	–	O	O	O	O	O
Portability	O	–	O	O	O	+	+		O	O	–	O	O	O	O	–
User consultation	O	O	+	O	+	O	O	O		O	–	O	O	O	O	O
Accuracy	+	O	+	+	+	O	O	O	+		–	O	O	O	O	O
Timeliness	–	O	–	–	O	–	–	–	–	–		–	–	–	O	–
Time to use	+	+	O	O	–	–	–	O	O	O	+		+	–	O	–
Appeal	+	+	O	+	+	+	+	+	+	+	+	+		+	+	+
User flexibility	O	–	O	O	O	+	O	+	+	+	O	–	O		O	O
Cost/benefit	+	+	+	+	+	+	O	O	+	+	+	+	O	+		+
User friendliness	+	O	O	O	O	O	O	O	+	O	–	O	+	+	O	

O indicates that there is no relationship or that the relationship is heavily context-dependent.

+ indicates that if criteria A is improved, then criteria B will also improve, or that if A is degraded, B is also degraded.

– indicates that if criteria A is degraded, then criteria B will also be degraded, or that if A is improved, B is also improved.

2.5 Questions for discussion

1. McCall's and Boehm's models are supposed to represent a user perspective. Do you agree with this? If not, justify your conclusion by considering what criteria are important to users. (You may like to refer back to Chapter 1.)
2. McCall's and Boehm's models were developed in the era of batch processing and mainframe computers. How far are they affected by the move to interactive personal computing? As organizations move towards networked group working systems, what new criteria of quality will be needed?
3. How far does Perry's analysis of relationships tally with your own experience of computer systems? Has it been overtaken by advances in technology?

2.6 Further reading

Boehm, B. *et al.* (1978) *Characteristics of Software Quality*, North-Holland, New York.

Gillies, A.C. (1992) Modelling software quality in the commercial environment, *Software Quality Journal*, 1, 175-191.

McCall, J.A. *et al.* (1977) Concepts and definitions of software quality, *Factors in Software Quality*, NTIS, 1.

Perry, W. (1987) *Effective Methods for EDP Quality Assurance*, 2nd edn, Prentice-Hall.

Watts, R. (1987) *Measuring Software Quality*, NCC Publications.

Chapter 3

Measuring software quality

3.1 Measuring quality

In a recent study, the author found that the most frequent problem highlighted by IT practitioners concerned the measurement of quality. In this chapter we look at some of the problems, and in the next we examine some solutions. Many IT personnel have come from engineering or physical science backgrounds. They are used to measuring properties precisely and unambiguously. Galileo is supposed to have said, 'What is not measurable, make it measurable', and this has set the tone for scientific and engineering measurement ever since. However, in making things measurable, we must ensure that we are not distorting the situation and that the figure derived does indeed reflect the property under scrutiny.

Quality measurement, where it is considered at all, is usually expressed in terms of metrics. A software metric is a measurable property which is an indicator of one or more of the quality criteria that we are seeking to measure. As such, there are a number of conditions that a quality metric must meet. It must:

- be clearly linked to the quality criterion that it seeks to measure
- be sensitive to the different degrees of the criterion
- provide objective determination of the criterion that can be mapped onto a suitable scale.

However, metrics are not the same as direct measures. Consider the traditional fairground trial of strength (Figure 3.1). It does not measure strength in a direct, absolute and verifiable way, but rather gives an indication of strength in terms of the height reached up the column. The height reached is proportional to the force exerted upon the plate at the bottom, but this is affected by factors other than strength, such as swing technique. The height attained is, therefore, like a metric of strength, that is a measurable property which is related to the criteria under investigation. We must establish that the metric (height) provides an accurate representation of the measurable property (force exerted upon the plate), which in turn should correlate well with the property under investigation (strength). Social scientists are comfortable in dealing with messy multivariate problems. Engineers and computer scientists are often less so.

Figure 3.1 A traditional metric for strength.

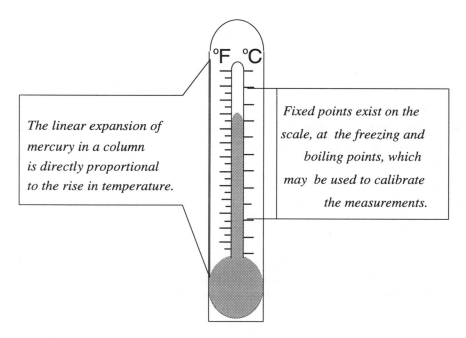

The linear expansion of mercury in a column is directly proportional to the rise in temperature.

Fixed points exist on the scale, at the freezing and boiling points, which may be used to calibrate the measurements.

Figure 3.2 Temperature may be measured in terms of linear expansion.

Contrast this with the use of the expansion of mercury to measure temperature in a thermometer (Figure 3.2). The relationship between linear expansion and temperature rise is direct, linear and verifiable by experiment. Expansion depends only upon temperature and calibration points exist at the freezing and boiling points of water to establish an absolute scale. Quality criteria are never dependent upon a single property in this way and no reference points exist to establish an absolute scale. Many IT people find it difficult to adjust to consideration of the quality of software, which cannot be measured in terms of simple, absolute and unambiguous scales.

Measurement techniques applied to software are more akin to the social sciences, where properties are similarly complex and ambiguous.

A typical measurable property on which a metric may be based is structuredness. The criteria of quality related to product revision, maintainability, adaptability and reusability are all related to the structuredness of the source code. Well-structured code will be easier to maintain or adapt than so-called 'spaghetti code'. Structuredness, at its simplest, may be calculated in terms of the average length of code modules within the program.

$$\text{Structuredness} \propto \text{modularity} \propto \frac{\text{lines of code}}{\text{number of modules}}$$

More sophisticated measures of structuredness have been based upon the path through the code, taking account of the entry and exit points within each module. Well-structured code is characterized by only one entry point to, and one exit point from, each module.

3.2 Software metrics

Metrics are classified into two types according to whether they are predictive or descriptive. A predictive metric is used to make predictions about the software later in the lifecycle. Structuredness is used to predict the maintainability of the software product in use. A descriptive metric describes the state of the software at the time of measurement, e.g. a reliability metric might be based upon the number of system 'crashes' during a given period.

Different authors have taken different approaches to metrics. The two pioneers of hierarchical models, McCall and Boehm, adopted different approaches to metrication. Boehm advocated methods based upon checklists requiring 'yes/no' answers. For example, structuredness is 'measured' by questions such as:

- Have the rules for transfer of control between modules been followed? (Y/N)
- Are modules limited in size? (Y/N)
- Do all modules have only one exit point? (Y/N)
- Do all modules have only one entry point? (Y/N)

A well-structured program will produce positive answers to such questions.

McCall's approach is more quantitative, using scores derived from equations such as

McCall's structuredness metric $= \dfrac{n_{01}}{n_{tot}}$

where: n_{01} = no. of modules containing one or zero exit points only
$\quad\quad\quad n_{tot}$= total number of modules

Generally, in this approach, scores are normalized to a range between 0 and 1, to allow for easier combination and comparison. This appears attractive, but may give unjustified credibility to the results obtained. For example, it may be acceptable on an intuitive basis to assert that there is a relationship between structuredness and product revision criteria such as maintainability; however, it is impossible to validate this relationship and determine whether it is a linear relationship or more complex in nature. It is also impossible to validate whether the dependence of maintainability on structuredness is identical to that of adaptability or reusability.

3.2.1 What makes a good metric?

Almost ten years after the initial work of McCall and Boehm, Watts (1987) published an analysis of the multitude of metrics that had been suggested in the intervening period. He suggests seven criteria of a good software metric (Table 3.1).

Table 3.1 Seven criteria for a good metric, after Watts (1987)

Objectivity	The results should be free from subjective influences. It must not matter who the measurer is.
Reliability	The results should be precise and repeatable.
Validity	The metric must measure the correct characteristic.
Standardization	The metric must be unambiguous and allow for comparison.
Comparability	The metric must be comparable with other measures of the same criterion.
Economy	The simpler and, therefore, the cheaper the measure is to use, the better.
Usefulness	The measure must address a need, not simply measure a property for its own sake.

A further important feature is consistency. Some measures appear to combine quite different factors. A measure should not be based upon a combination of apples and oranges, i.e. it should be dimensionally consistent.

Automation is also desirable. A measure that lends itself to convenient automation is clearly at an advantage. Such a measure is, by definition, objective, and automation boosts both economy and convenience.

The criteria of a good measure suggested by Watts (1987) eliminate many of the measures that he himself cites from the research literature. Many metrics are still based upon subjectivity. IBM, for example, measure the usability of software products by surveys of their users. Many measures of usability are based upon user judgements and it is difficult to see how an effective measure of usability can be made wholly free of subjectivity. Part of usability is simply down to issues such as 'Does the user like it?'

The question of validity is also problematical. Validation together with comparability and standardization suffer from the lack of an absolute standard. There is no reference point for quality and no absolute quality, unlike simple physical quantities such as length, time and mass. The goals set by Watts for metrics are laudable, but appear to be unrealistic in practice.

3.3 Metrics cited in the literature

Watts cites 40 metrics from the software engineering research literature. This might appear to be a healthy selection. However, a look at the distribution of the metrics across the criteria reveals that the metrics are not evenly distributed. Three quarters of the 40 measures are concerned with just two criteria: reliability and maintainability. Four criteria are not metricated at all, and three more have only one metric associated with them. The criteria are ranked in Table 3.2 according to the number of metrics cited.

Table 3.2 Metrics available for each criterion (after Watts, 1987)

Quality criteria	Number of metrics cited
Maintainability	18
Reliability	12
Usability	4
Correctness	3
Integrity	1
Expandability	1
Portability	1
Efficiency	0
Adaptability	0
Interoperability	0
Reusability	0

This uneven spread of metrics is exacerbated by the fact that many of the metrics are based upon the same fundamental measurable property, and may therefore be considered as variations upon a theme. For example, complexity is used as a handle on both reliability and maintainability, and 13 measures are described as based upon complexity. The metrics cited depend to a very large extent upon just seven distinct measurable properties: readability, error prediction, error detection, complexity, mean time to failure (MTTF), modularity, testability. We shall, therefore, classify the metrics cited according to the fundamental property on which they depend.

1. Readability as a measure of usability

   Readability may be applied to documentation in order to assess how such documentation may assist in the usability of a piece of software. Two specific measurement methods have been proposed. The Flesch–Kincaid Readability Index forms part of the US DoD Standards for user manuals. It works at a syllable level and can be calculated using the formula:

   Grade level $= 0.39a + b - c$

   where:

   $a =$ the number of words in the sentence
   $b =$ the mean number of syllables per 100 words
   $c = 15.59$.

   The score relates to school grades in the USA. Standard writing averages 7 to 8. The other method is the Fog Index (Gunning, 1968):

   Fog index $= 0.4a + b$

   where:

   $a =$ the number of words in a sentence
   $b =$ the percentage of words with more than two syllables.

2. Error prediction as a measure of correctness

   Halstead (1977) has suggested a number of basic parameters such as the number of operators and operandi in a program. Using these basic parameters, Ottenstein (1981) predicts the number of errors to be found during validation and the total number of errors found during development.

   This measure is based upon the assumption of a stable software development environment. This assumption lies at the heart of the COCOMO (Boehm, 1981) and COQUAMO (Kitchenham, 1989a,b) models, and is discussed further in the next chapter. The practical requirement is for a bank of statistics about current programming performance.

3. Error detection as a measure of correctness

   Remus and Zilles' model (1981) of defect removal uses the number of detected errors and a measure of error detection efficiency to predict the number of errors remaining undetected. This treatment is based upon a number of assumptions, principally that the number of defects is proportional to the length of the program and that the rate of defect removal can be predicted. This model, to be used with confidence, requires the same statistical information as error prediction in order that the basic assumptions may be verified in the environment under scrutiny.

4. Mean time to failure (MTTF) as a measure of reliability

   MTTF is given by

   $$MTTF = \frac{t_{TOT}}{R_t}$$

   where:
   $t_{TOT} =$ the total time period,
   $n_t =$ the number of failures in t_{TOT}.

It may be assessed by measurement, estimation or prediction. Predictive measures suggested thus far have failed to take account of the development process.

In Musa's execution time model (Musa, 1975), reliability is calculated in terms of the execution time, the total number of possible failures and the MTTF at the start of the test. Using these parameters, he calculates the current MTTF (t_F) and calculates reliability (R) in terms of the length of the operation phase (t_{OP}):

$$R = \exp\left(\frac{-t_{OP}}{t_F}\right)$$

5. Complexity as a measure of reliability
   The assumption underpinning these measures is that as complexity increases, so reliability decreases. Complexity is to be measured in several different ways. McCabe (1976) proposed a cyclomatic number, based upon graph theory, that seeks to estimate the number of linearly independent paths through the program. Variants have been suggested by Gong and Schmidt (1988) and Myers (1976). Other measures of complexity have been suggested by Gilb (1977), Woodward *et al.* (1980), who proposed a measure dedicated to FORTRAN, Chen (1978), Thayer *et al.* (1977) and Hansen (1978).
6. Complexity as a measure of maintainability
   Complexity is also indicative of maintainability. Its use as a measure of maintainability has been suggested by McCabe (1976) using his cyclomatic number, McClure (1978), Oviedo (1980), Yin and Winchester (1978), Zolnowski and Simmons (1979), Gilb (1977).
7. Readability of code as a measure of maintainability
   Readability has also been suggested as a measure of maintainability. Three authors have suggested ways of measuring readability of source code. DeYoung and Kampe (1979) measure readability in terms of the number of statement lines, the average length of variable names and the total number of program branches. More complex alternatives have been provided by Gordon (1979) and Jorgensen (1980).
8. Modularity as a measure of maintainability
   Increased modularity is generally assumed to increase maintainability. Four measures have been suggested. Yau and Collofello (1979) measured 'stability' as the number of modules affected by program modification. Kentger (1981) defined a four-level hierarchy of module types:

   - control modules
   - problem-oriented modules
   - management modules for abstract data
   - realization modules for abstract data.

   The model predicts an onion shape for the number of modules, and monitors maintainability in terms of deviations from the predicted trend. Myers (1976) and Yin (1979) both approach modularity in terms of modular independence.
9. Testability as a measure of maintainability
   The ease and effectiveness of testing will have an impact upon the maintainability of a product. Testability is measured in the approach of Mohanty

and Adamowicz (1976). The number of tests required is measured by Paige (1980) and the effectiveness of the testing process is measured by Woodward *et al.* (1980).

All these metrics relate to the same fundamental measurable properties, as shown in Table 3.3.

Table 3.3 The metrics' dependence upon seven measurable properties

Measurable property	Associated criteria	No. of metrics	Example of metric
Readability	Usability	2	Gunning (1968)
	Maintainability	3	Gordon (1979)
Error prediction	Correctness	2	Halstead (1977)
Error detection	Correctness	1	Remus and Zilles (1981)
Mean time to failure	Reliability	5	Musa (1975)
Complexity	Reliability	7	McCabe (1976)
	Maintainability	6	McCabe (1976)
Modularity	Maintainability	4	Kentger (1981)
Testability	Maintainability	5	Paige (1980)
Other	Portability	1	Gilb (1977)
	Usability	2	
	Expandability	1	
	Integrity	1	

If we decide to consider only those metrics that depend upon different fundamental properties as 'independent', then only maintainability, reliability and usability may actually be measured in two or more independent ways. Further, we see that each measurable property may be linked to more than one quality criterion (Figure 3.3). In an ideal world, each criterion would be represented by one unique measurable, and the diagram would become a set of single horizontal lines.

The consequence of the complex many-to-many relationships that exist between criteria, measurables and metrics is that the neat theoretical hierarchy which forms the basis of McCall and Boehm's work is a gross simplification, and this reduces the validity of these approaches. There are also problems with the traditional view of metrics, which are discussed below.

3.4 The problem with metrics

The objective measurement of quality through the use of metrics within a hierarchical framework is an attractive one. However, the metrics available from the literature are limited in effectiveness for a whole series of reasons:

CRITERIA

MEASURABLE

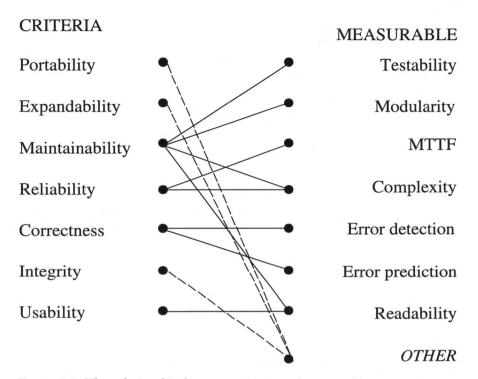

Portability   Testability

Expandability   Modularity

Maintainability   MTTF

Reliability   Complexity

Correctness   Error detection

Integrity   Error prediction

Usability   Readability

                                OTHER

Figure 3.3 The relationship between criteria and measurable properties.

1. They cannot be validated
    As mentioned above, the relationships between the metrics and the criteria that they seek to measure is a complex one. It is difficult to establish the degree of correlation between the metric itself, the measurable upon which it is based, and the criteria which it seeks to measure. As might be imagined, it is harder still to validate the degree of correlation.
2. They are not generally objective
    In an ideal world, measures would be objective, absolute and transferable. In practice, all measures are relative, but the presence of 'fixed points', such as absolute zero and the triple point of water on the temperature scale, allow some scales to be defined as effectively absolute, and hence transferable and objective. In quality, there are no fixed points. Some measures may appear to be transferable and objective, e.g. measures based upon lines of code. However, although the measure is objective, it is hard to show that the correlation between such measures and quality criteria is absolute.
3. Quality is a relative, not an absolute, quantity
    In practice, many aspects of quality can only be judged in relative terms. For example, it is hard to imagine ever establishing an absolute reference point for usability, which can only be measured relative to other experiences. If we accept that quality means meeting user requirements, then there can be no definitive set of user requirements. Even if a system were to meet every requirement laid down by the users at specification, those needs are likely to evolve over time.

4. They depend upon a small set of measurable properties
    One of the most startling facts about the metrics cited by Watts (1987) is the
    small number of fundamental properties used in metric research. There
    appear to be a large number of metrics based upon a variation on a theme.
5. They do not measure the complete set of quality criteria
    Within the set of criteria drawn from McCall's original model, a number of
    criteria are not metricated at all, e.g. efficiency. The research carried out by
    the author suggests that the set of criteria employed is merely a subset of
    those required. Once we look at a broader set of criteria in Chapter 5, then
    the lack of metrics becomes even more alarming.
6. The metrics measure more than one criterion
    The consequence of the complex relationships explored above is that met-
    rics such as McCabe's cyclomatic number are used to measure several cri-
    teria related to program complexity, e.g. maintainability and reliability. It is
    hard to imagine that the correlation between complexity and these two cri-
    teria is the same in each case since the number of failures and the ease of
    putting them right is likely to be related, but not identical.

So far we have assumed that if we can measure the individual quality criteria,
then we can derive a measure of total quality. This is considered in the next section.

3.5 An overall measure of quality

Much of the work in this area has been concerned with simple reduction of a set
of scores to a single 'figure-of-merit'. Five such methods are detailed by Watts
(1987) as part of the MQ approach.

1. Simple scoring
    In this method, each criterion is allocated a score. The overall quality is
    given by the mean of the individual scores.
2. Weighted scoring
    This scheme allows the user to weight each criterion according to how
    important they consider them to be. This approach is compared to simple
    scoring in Table 3.4.
      Each criterion is evaluated to produce a score between 0 and 1. In the
    case of simple scoring the scores are simply added and divided by the num-
    ber of scores to yield a simple arithmetic mean. In the weighted case, each
    score is weighted before summation and the resulting figure reflects the rel-
    ative importance of the different factors.
3. Phased weighting factor method
    This is an extension of weighted scoring. In this method, a weighting is
    assigned to a group of characteristics before each individual weighting is
    considered. If we apply the same weighting as to the previous case, but with
    an additional weighting of 2/3 for those characteristics associated with prod-
    uct operation, compared with 1/3 for those concerned with product revision
    (and an effective zero weighting to those associated with product transition)
    then the overall quality figure becomes 0.65. This approach is illustrated in
    Table 3.5.

Table 3.4 Example of simple and weighted scoring methods

Quality criteria	Metric	Weight	Product
Usability	0.7	0.5	0.35
Security	0.6	0.2	0.12
Efficiency	0.4	0.2	0.08
Correctness	0.8	0.5	0.40
Reliability	0.6	0.4	0.24
Maintainability	0.6	0.4	0.24
Adaptability	0.7	0.1	0.07
Expandability	0.7	0.1	0.07
TOTAL	5.10	2.40	1.57

Simple Score = 5.10/8 = 0.64

Weighted Score = 1.57/2.40 = 0.65

Table 3.5 The phased weighting factor method

Group	Criteria	Metric	Weight	Product	PWF
	Usability	0.7	0.5	0.35	
Product Operation	Security	0.6	0.2	0.12	
	Efficiency	0.4	0.2	0.08	2/3
	Correctness	0.8	0.5	0.40	
	Reliability	0.6	0.4	0.24	
Product Transition	Maintainability	0.6	0.4	0.24	
	Adaptability	0.7	0.1	0.07	1/3
	Expandability	0.7	0.1	0.07	

Product Operation Weighted Mean = 0.660

Product Transition Weighted Mean = 0.633

Overall measure by PWF method = $((2/3) \times 0.660) + ((1/3) \times 0.633) = 0.65$

4. The Kepner–Tregoe method (1981)

   In this method the criteria are divided into 'essential' and 'desirable'. A minimum value is specified for each essential criterion and any software failing to reach these scores is designated unsuitable. 'Suitable' software is then judged by use of the weighting factor method.

5. The Cologne combination method (Schmitz, 1975)
    This method is designed with comparative evaluation in mind. Using the
    chosen criteria, each product is ranked in order. Greater details of this
    approach are given in Watts (1987).

All these schemes are aimed at reducing the quality measure to a single parameter. The final approach retains the multidimensionality of quality, using
polarity profiling.

Polarity profiling

In this scheme, quality is represented by a series of ranges from −3 to +3. The
required quality may be represented and compared to the actual quality achieved.
An example profile is given in Figure 3.4. In the example shown, the software is
lacking in quality in the areas of efficiency and reliability. It is also worth noting
that it is over-engineered in terms of maintainability and adaptability.

It is a common problem amongst software developers that they focus upon
particular aspects of quality. When a user complains of poor quality, they tend
to improve the product further in these areas. Often the product has already
exceeded the users' expectations in these areas, and further improvement does
not improve their overall view of the quality of the product. Thus, effort is wasted. Worse, the users' needs still have not been met in other critical areas, leading to tensions between the developers and users. The use of graphical profiles
can at least highlight the problem. Figure 3.5 shows two different cases of
improved quality.

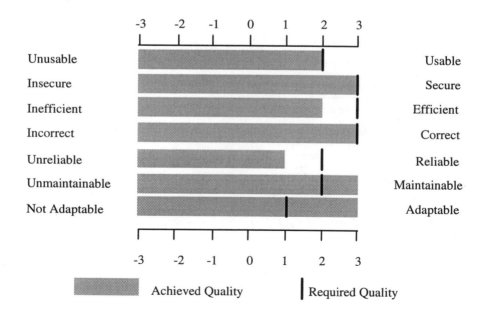

Figure 3.4 An example of polarity profiling.

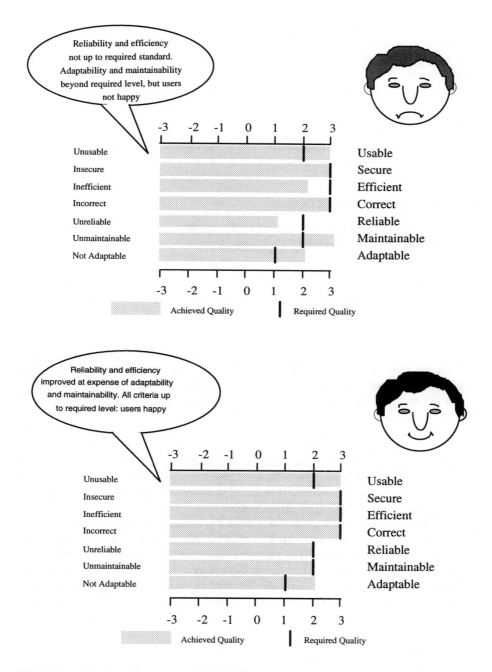

Figure 3.5 Contrasts in improving quality.

Two different outcomes result. In the first case, usability is improved. Unfortunately, reliability and efficiency are still not up to the required standard, and usability was already considered satisfactory. In the second case, improvements in reliability and efficiency are traded for a reduction in adaptability and maintainability, perhaps by 'tweaking' the code. The consequence is that all criteria are now at the required level, resulting in an overall perception of quality and satisfied users.

The use of profiles to represent quality is developed in the next chapter, where we shall continue to consider the problem of measuring quality in the light of more recent developments.

3.6 Questions for discussion

1. Readability scores may be applied to documentation. Consider the two passages from commercial documentation, below.

   (a) Calculate readability scores for the passages.
   (b) What do the scores indicate about the readability of these passages?
   (c) Does this agree with your subjective judgement?

Passage 1

Chapter 9 presented methods for producing tabular, statistical, and graphic output from data files in the ANALYSIS program. For perfectly 'clean' data sets, this would be enough to do a complete analysis. Real-life situations, however, produce 'dirty' data, and often the most time-consuming part of the analysis is the 'cleaning' of the data set.

This chapter describes methods for viewing and editing data in ANALYSIS, sorting records into numeric or alphabetical order, selectively including or excluding records from analysis, defining and assigning values to new variables, grouping or otherwise recoding variables, performing conditional operations (IFs), managing dates and time intervals, and setting a number of options in ANALYSIS that affect results.

These operations are not individually complex, but a given data set may require many such operations before all fields are in satisfactory condition for analysis. It is useful to incorporate the commands for these operations into a program file, so that the program can be run many times as small additions and changes are made. We will therefore describe how to make program files before we discuss the commands useful for data transformation.

Passage 2

The Worksheet for a project is displayed whenever a project folder containing answer sheets is opened.

The Worksheet presents the view of all the answer sheets in your project, the answers to each of the questions on each of the sheets are shown in tabular form, with each answer sheet shown on one line as a row of information divided into columns. Each column contains the answer data relating to the question field whose name appears in a title bar at the head of the column.

The worksheet is a flexible and efficient environment in which to investigate the information you hold and draw meaningful conclusions. It provides the tools to sort the information into order, quickly modify obviously rogue information, select those sheets matching certain conditions, perform a range of numerical analyses and produce cross-tabulations of responses to questions.

Graphical presentations of results can be prepared to be printed directly from PinPoint or for inclusion in another application such as a word processor where a complete report is being prepared. Answer sheets and the results of analysis may also be copied to the clipboard for pasting into other applications for further analysis.

The 'Worksheet control panel' displays information on the sorting and selection criteria which have been applied to a stack of sheets, and contains 'shortcut' buttons by which criteria can be quickly applied or removed. For speed and ease of use, PinPoint's Tool Tidy buttons 'automate' most worksheet operations.

2. Using the following data and the phased weighting factor method, calculate the following:

- product operation weighted mean
- product transition weighted mean
- overall measure by PWF method.

Group	Criteria	Metric	Weight	PWF
Product Operation	Usability	0.7	0.5	
	Security	0.5	0.5	
	Efficiency	0.6	0.2	2/3
	Correctness	0.7	0.5	
	Reliability	0.4	0.4	
Product Transition	Maintainability	0.8	0.4	
	Adaptability	0.7	0.1	1/3
	Expandability	0.7	0.1	

3. Use the following data to produce a polarity profile:

Criteria	Actual quality	Required quality
Usability	0.3	0.7
Security	0.5	0.7
Efficiency	0.3	0.6
Correctness	0.9	0.9
Reliability	0.9	0.9
Maintainability	0.4	0.8
Adaptability	0.4	0.8

Using Perry's model of relationships between software criteria from the previous chapter, discuss the possibilities for user satisfaction in this project.

4. Consider Watts' criteria of a good metric

(a) How critical are the attributes to a usable rather than ideal measure of software quality?
(b) Draw up your own list of attributes for a measure of software quality, rating them as essential or desirable.

5. Software quality is a multidimensional intangible. Consider the measures applied to the economic well-being of a country.

(a) How effective are they as measures?
(b) What lessons may be drawn for the measurement of software quality?

The solutions to questions 1 and 2 are given at the end of the book.

3.7 Further reading

Gilb, T. (1977) *Software Metrics*, Winthrop (out of print).
Watts, R. (1987) *Measuring Software Quality*, NCC/Blackwell.

Chapter 4

Developments in measuring quality

4.1 The work of Gilb

One of the characteristic features of the quality area is the large number of 'gurus' that have emerged, from Deming and Crosby onwards. These individuals have had an inordinate amount of impact upon the field. Often, the words of such people have been adopted as gospel truth written upon tablets of stone. This approach is not always appropriate or helpful. One of the most significant 'gurus' working specifically in the software area over the last 15 years has been Tom Gilb, whose work has, in fact, been extremely useful.

Gilb's work was developed contemporaneously with the models of McCall *et al.* (1977) and Boehm (1978). However, since his first publication in 1977, his work has been substantially developed and improved in the light of experiences. There are two significant strands to the work. The first strand addresses the development process itself (Gilb is an enthusiastic supporter of the evolutionary delivery method). This is considered alongside other development methods in Chapter 5.

Complementary to the evolutionary delivery method is the use of a 'quality template', rather than a rigid hierarchical model. The key feature of the template is that it is designed to be tailored to local requirements. The philosophy behind this is that quality depends principally upon a small set of critical resources, which will vary from one application to another. Within such a view, the role of software engineering is to identify which quality criteria are critical and define the extent to which these must be present. Quality is explicitly built into the product during development, in terms of these critical resources.

Evolutionary development is seen as critical by Gilb (1988) to the satisfaction of these critical criteria. It is an iterative approach aiming to converge towards clear and measurable multidimensional objectives. At each stage, the developer intends to maximize the distance moved towards the ultimate objectives whilst minimizing the resource expended. It is argued that trying to specify a system at the start of a project is a time-consuming and difficult task, which is unlikely to succeed or move the developer nearer their final goal. By developing only part of the system, the developer moves nearer the ultimate goal, gaining an understanding of the needs of the user, finding errors earlier, providing the user with a usable deliverable at an early stage and gaining valuable income from the delivered code.

The process emphasizes the role of the user. This should lead to a product which meets user needs better, allows changes to be made during development, rather than as 'bolt-ons', and gives the users a feeling of ownership of the product.

With such advantages, the reader may be forgiven for asking why everyone is not using such a method.

Gilb himself highlights five problem areas associated with implementation of the method:

1. The simple fact that the method is different.
2. The need for training and re-training and associated costs.
3. The need for effective management.
4. The need to measure progress towards the ultimate goal.
5. Picking up errors earlier may be very frustrating to progress and morale.

Certainly, there is always resistance to change, but the main problem seems to be that the process requires people to think in a different way about solving problems. The process of breaking a project into smaller projects which may be delivered in incremental fashion is alien to many software developers. An analogy may be drawn here with the situation of traditional third-generation programmers moving onto different languages. Languages such as PROLOG and LISP for AI, SmallTalk for object-oriented programming and even fourth-generation languages such as ORACLE and INGRES require different thought processes. Many people are therefore still writing programs in FORTRAN and COBOL. Worse, many people are writing code in these newer languages in the same way that they wrote 3GLs. This may be wholly inappropriate for the new medium.

Many software developers are particularly opposed to the use of evolutionary methods for large-scale projects. However, it is precisely such cases where Gilb argues that the greatest benefits can be achieved. He provides examples from IBM and the System Development Corporation, as well as providing examples of the failure of traditional methods at companies such as Volvo.

Whether or not the need for evolutionary development is accepted, the link between the quality of the development process and the final product is well established. Product quality is measured in terms of a 'quality template'. It models quality in terms of quality attributes, such as usability and resource attributes including time and cost. This division reflects the real-world situation where quality is constrained by the availability of resources. In particular, a small set of resources will be the critical, controlling factors and these are Gilb's critical attributes. Critical resource attributes might be the budget or the time scale for delivery or a staff skills shortage. The quality template is summarized in Figure 4.1.

Attributes

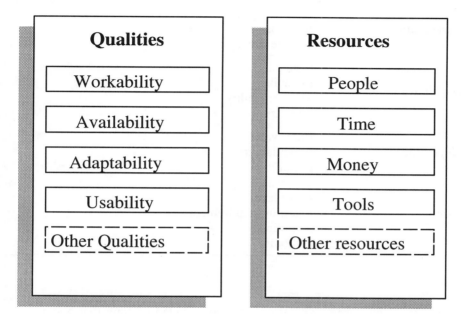

Qualities	Resources
Workability	People
Availability	Time
Adaptability	Money
Usability	Tools
Other Qualities	Other resources

Figure 4.1 Quality template (after Gilb, 1988).

4.1.1 Gilb's quality attributes

Gilb proposes four quality attributes: workability, availability, adaptability and usability, accompanied by the resource attributes of time, money, people and tools.

Workability

Workability is defined as the raw ability of the system to do work, i.e. transaction processing. Just as the quality and resource attributes are subdivided, so each attribute may be further subdivided. Workability may be considered in terms of process capacity, storage capacity and responsiveness, amongst other things.

Gilb defines these terms in the following manner:

- Process capacity is the ability to process transactions within a given unit of time.
- Storage capacity is the ability of the system to store things such as information.
- Responsiveness is a measure of the response to a single event.

Table 4.1 Gilb's attributes and sub-attributes

Attribute	Sub-attribute
Workability	Process capacity Responsiveness Storage capacity
Availability	General Reliability Maintainability Integrity
Adaptability	Improvability Extendability Portability General
Usability	Entry level Learning requirement Handling Likability

Availability

Availability is concerned with the proportion of elapsed time that a system is able to be used. The sub-attributes highlighted here are reliability, maintainability and integrity.

- Reliability
  Reliability is the degree to which the system does what it is supposed to do. Because the purpose of each system is different, and the purpose of different parts of the system is different, the way in which reliability is assessed may also vary.
    Gilb suggests that reliability may be assessed in terms of fidelity, veracity and viability for both logicware (code) and dataware (data files), based upon an analysis by Dickson (1972). The classification is summarized in Table 4.2.
- Maintainability
  Maintainability refers to the process of fault handling. Some of the principal sub-attributes are:

  (a) Problem recognition time is the time required to recognize that a fault exists.
  (b) Administrative delay is the time between recognition of a problem and activity designed to rectify it.
  (c) Tool collection is the time required to gather all relevant information, e.g. program analysis and documentation.
  (d) Problem analysis is the time needed to trace the source of the problem.
  (e) Correction hypothesis time is the time required to come up with a possible solution.

(f) Inspection time is the time taken to evaluate said solution.
(g) Active correction is the time to implement a hypothesized correction.
(h) Testing is the time taken to adequately test cases to validate the change.
(i) Test evaluation is the time needed to evaluate the test results.
(j) Recovery is the time required to recover and restore the system.

Table 4.2 Dickson's classification of reliability criteria (1972)

Logicware	Fidelity	is concerned with the accuracy of the implementation of a specified algorithm
	Veracity	is concerned with the representation of the 'real world' by the specified algorithm
	Viability	is the extent to which an algorithm meets its design specification in terms of performance and requirements placed upon the system
Dataware	Fidelity	is how accurately an idea is represented by the data within an application
	Veracity	is how well the data matches the real world
	Viability	is how well the required data fits the design constraints

- Integrity
  The integrity of a system is a measure of its ability to remain intact whilst under threat. It may be regarded as the ability of in-built security functions to cope with threats. Threats may come from human action (deliberate or otherwise) or machine action, either hardware or software driven. Integrity affects availability. A system with poor integrity is likely to be unavailable for much of the time.

Adaptability

Adaptability may be considered in terms of improvability, extendability and portability:

- Improvability is the time taken to make minor changes to the system where the term 'system' is taken to include items such as documentation.
- Extendability is the ease of adding new functionality to a system.
- Portability is the ease of moving a system from one environment to another.

Usability

Usability may be considered as the ease of use and effectiveness of use of a system. This may be considered in terms of handling ability, entry requirements, learning requirements and likability:

- Entry requirements are the basic human abilities such as intelligence level, language proficiency or culture that are required to operate the system.
- Learning requirements are the resources, particularly time, needed to attain a measurable level of performance with the system.
- Handling ability is a measure of productivity after error time is deducted.
- Likability is a measure of how well people like the system.

The resource attributes

The resource attributes highlighted by Gilb include time, people, money and tools:

- Time resource is of two types: calendar time to delivery and the time taken by the system once developed to carry out a task.
- People resources may be measured in terms of man-years. However, this is a relatively crude 'broad-brush' approach since people resources are often governed by scarce skills. In such cases, the availability of a particular person becomes a critical attribute. If you require a C programmer, all the COBOL programmers in the world will not help you.
- Money resources concern both development and maintenance costs. Since budgets are always a constraint and many authors quote figures as high as 80% for the proportion of software cost spent on maintenance, this area is a favourite target for quality improvement programs.
- Tool resources encompass all physical resources from air-conditioning capacity to debuggers, a much wider range of 'tools' than is conventionally considered. Those tools which impose critical constraints are those which should be carefully considered.

The philosophy underpinning these attributes is that software development does not go in a vacuum and quality cannot be continually improved without regard to cost in its broadest sense. The resource attributes act as constraints upon continual quality improvements (Figure 4.2).

It is often critical constraints which determine the level of quality rather than incompetence. The saying 'do you want it good or do you want it on Friday?' has much relevance to software development. This is explicitly recognized by these resource attributes. It should also be recognized that in any one application, it will be a small subset that will provide the critical constraints rather than all the factors considered here.

Measures for the template

Gilb suggests a range of measures to quantify these attributes. They are not traditional metrics, since they are intended to be locally defined and not necessarily transferable. Taking, as an example, process capacity, it may be measured in terms of units per time, specifically:

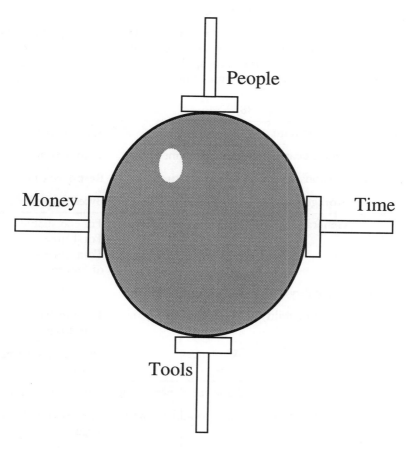

Figure 4.2 Constraints upon quality improvement.

- transactions per second
- records per minute
- bytes per line, or
- bits per node per second.

The measures suggested by Gilb are tabulated in Table 4.3.

Gilb's approach is notable less for the specific attributes than for a number of underlying principles and distinctive features:

- Use of a template rather than a rigid model, with an active encouragement of local tailoring.
- Explicit recognition of constraints upon quality.

- Recognition of critical resources.
- Use of locally-defined measures.
- Close links with the development process.

Gilb's work has strongly influenced subsequent work, notably Kitchenham *et al.* and, not least, this author. However, the work has been criticized because the template is uniquely defined for each application, precluding comparison and making quality measurement very time- and resource-consuming.

Table 4.3 Gilb's measures (1988)

Attribute	Sub-attribute	General measure	Specific example
Workability	Process capacity	Units per time	Transactions/sec
	Responsiveness	Action per time	Response time
	Storage capacity	Units stored	Bytes per record
Availability	General	Probability available	Time available ÷ Total time Total time ÷ Number of failures
	Reliability	Mean time to failure	
	Maintainability	Mean time to repair	Time to fix 90% of test bugs
	Integrity	Wholeness	Degree of software intact
Adaptability	Improvability	Time for minor change	Time to add test set
	Extendability	Time to add a function	Time to add 10% logic
	Portability	Effort for transfer	Percentage of effort for porting
Usability	General	Degree of productivity	Time to reach basic level of ability
	Entry level	Qualification level	Readability
	Learning requirement	Time to learn	Length of training required
	Handling	Net productivity	Tasks per hour
	Likability	Extent of positive attitude	Percentage surveyed

4.2 The COQUAMO project

Some of the most influential work in the UK in recent years has been carried out by Kitchenham and co-workers, resulting in the COQUAMO toolset. Their view of quality is based upon the five views of quality set out by Garvin (1984) and described in detail in the first chapter of this book. Many of the ideas on measurement are based upon the work of Gilb.

Garvin describes quality in terms of five views: transcendent, product-based, user-based, manufacturing-based and value-based. In order to accommodate these differing views Kitchenham (1989b) introduces the concept of a 'quality profile', making a distinction between subjective and objective measures of quality. The quality profile is the view of the overall quality of the system, and is split into the following components:

- Transcendent Properties. These are qualitative factors which are hard to measure, and about which people have different views and definitions, for example, usability.
- Quality Factors. These are characteristics of the system which are made up of measurable factors called quality metrics and quality attributes. The quality factors themselves are either subjective or objective characteristics, for example, reliability and flexibility.
- Merit Indices. These subjectively define functions of the system. They are measured by quality ratings, which are subjective value ratings.

Kitchenham's (1989b) 'quality profile' is shown in Figure 4.3.

The work builds upon the work of Gilb, and shares a common approach including a strong link with the development process. The key weakness in Gilb's work perceived by this group is the requirement for developers to set up their own 'quality template'. Under the auspices of the ALVEY and ESPRIT research programs, the group has worked on a set of tools to aid the assessment and improvement of quality within the software development process.

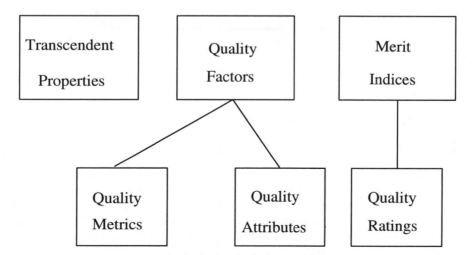

Figure 4.3 Quality profile, after Kitchenham (1989).

The work has led to a constructive quality model known as COQUAMO (COnstructive QUAlity MOdel), named after the earlier COCOMO model (COnstructive COst MOdel) of software economics, due to Boehm. This model forms the basis of tools developed to assist software developers in their objective of supplying a high quality system.

The aim of this model is threefold:

- to predict final product quality
- to monitor progress towards a quality product
- to feed back the results to improve predictions for the next project.

The model uses a similar approach to the earlier COCOMO model (Boehm, 1981) and is delivered as three tools, one to predict quality at the start (COQUAMO-1), one to monitor quality during development (COQUAMO-2) and one to measure the quality of the final product (COQUAMO-3). The measurements are then designed to feed back into the predictive tool (Figure 4.4).

The predictive and measuring tools are said to reflect the user's view of quality; the monitoring tool is said to reflect a manufacturing or developer's view of quality.

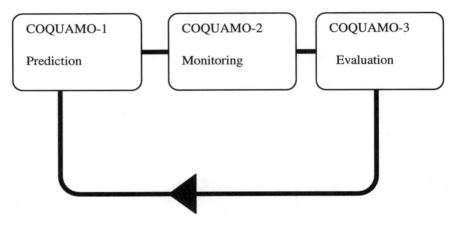

Figure 4.4 The COQUAMO toolset.

4.2.1 The COQUAMO tools

COQUAMO-1: Prediction

The predictive tool makes use of techniques similar to those at the heart of cost estimation models such as COCOMO. The tool requires as input an 'average' quality level for each quality factor considered, derived from other similar projects. This 'average' is then adjusted to cater for the factors that influence quality levels called 'quality drivers' within COQUAMO. COQUAMO makes use of five types of quality drivers:

- Product attributes such as quality requirements, success criticality and difficulty of developing the product in question.
- Process attributes such as process maturity, tool use and method maturity.
- Personnel attributes such as staff experience and motivation.
- Project attributes such as the quality norms and leadership style.
- Organizational attributes such as quality management and physical environment.

COQUAMO-1 can only consider those quality factors which are common to most applications and application-independent in nature. Thus it considers reliability, maintainability, extensibility, usability and reusability as defined below.

- Reliability is defined as the expected time to next failure at the release date.
- Maintainability is defined as the average elapsed time to identify the cause of a fault once reported.
- Extensibility is defined as the average productivity achieved for code changes.
- Usability is defined as the expected time to next non-fault problem report.
- Reusability is defined as the effort used in creating modules (code and design) intended for reuse (a potential cost saving).

The inputs for COQUAMO must initially be estimates, but when fully operational it is envisaged that data from COQUAMO-3 relating to real projects will improve performance.

COQUAMO-2: Monitoring

COQUAMO-2 is based upon a set of guidelines to carry out a number of tasks to assist in the monitoring of quality during a project. The guidelines set out to:

- identify appropriate metrics for each stage of the development process
- indicate methods for setting targets for project-level metrics
- suggest methods of analysis to identify unusual components
- indicate possible causes of unusual components and deviations in performance, and
- indicate possible corrective action.

The automation of COQUAMO-2 is a complex task and at the time of writing is still a matter of research. The manual guidelines have been tested and have proved worthwhile in trials.

COQUAMO-3: Testing

COQUAMO-3 is intended to provide data about the quality of the end product. This is done both to validate the predictions made by COQUAMO-1, and also to provide data for the use of COQUAMO-1 in future projects. The assessment is based upon models for each of the criteria listed above. The technique makes use of a blend of models, some developed internally for the project, e.g. for maintainability and usability, and some derived from other studies, e.g. reliability, based upon work by Brockelhurst *et al.* (1989) and Fergus *et al.* (1988).

The current deliverables from this project show a number of remaining limitations:

- They require a record of past performance, upon which predictions are based. This may not be available or may be inapplicable if working practices are changed to increase productivity, e.g. if CASE tools are introduced.
- They are still dependent upon subjective assessment, although as the tools are used, these assessments are modified in the light of experience.
- They exclude a number of common quality criteria, notably performance and portability. Some common criteria, e.g. usability, that are included are defined in an idiosyncratic way.
- The tools' effectiveness cannot be empirically verified.

The limitations described reflect the problems faced in measuring software quality, and do not preclude the use of these tools to provide helpful results. Where a steady-state software development environment exists, the techniques appear to offer a useful and powerful approach.

4.3 Recent work on metrics

An attempt to put metrics on a more systematic footing has been made by Fenton and Pfleeger (1996). The use of metrics to measure quality criteria is part of an overall scheme including:

- cost and effort estimation
- productivity measurement
- quality control and assurance
- data collection
- quality models
- reliability models
- performance evaluation
- algorithmic complexity
- measures of structure.

The treatment employed is based on the representational theory of measurement, which in turn is based on the use of sets, relations, axioms and functions. In such terms, a measure is not a number in itself, but rather a mapping of the attribute on a numerical scale. This means that the number quoted only has meaning within the context of the scale on which it is defined. A simple example is the length of a program. It could be quoted in bytes or lines of code. The attribute length remains the same, but the number produced by mapping onto each scale will be significantly different.

This use of mapping allows us to distinguish between direct measures such as the measurement of temperature discussed in Chapter 3, and indirect measures such as the trial of strength also mentioned there. An indirect measure is the result of two mappings, whereas the direct measure is the result of only one. Software metrics generally involve two mappings (Figure 4.5).

The detailed scheme is described in Fenton's book, and will not be reproduced here. However, it is useful to consider the framework used by this project to unite the diverse properties listed above. Fenton describes three types of entities whose attributes may be measured: products, processes and resources. The attributes associated with them are classified as 'internal' or 'external'. An internal attribute is one which may be measured without reference to the external environment. Internal measures are the easiest to measure, but external attributes are generally the most useful. The full framework of classification is reproduced in Table 4.4.

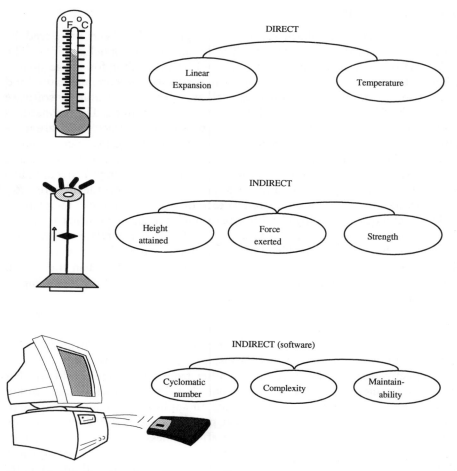

Figure 4.5 Mappings in software quality.

Fenton's treatment represents a reaction against much that has gone before. The framework is a model of thoroughness. The underlying theory of measurement provides rigour which has been lacking in the past. The linking of cost and quality is particularly welcome, since much quality research has been criticized for a lack of appreciation of economic reality. However, its very strengths provide some weaknesses:

- The set theory on which it is based does not make it accessible to all.
- There are places where quality is simply subsumed into cost, e.g. at the detailed design stage where an external quality attribute could relate to user involvement and perception.

Hopefully, when the study is finished, some of the promised tools will actually hide the complexity of the underlying theory from the user and render the work more attractive still.

4.4 Quality profiles

The use of circular graphical techniques in profiles has been pioneered by Kostick as part of the proprietary PAPI technique for personnel profiling. The wider use of such graphs has been suggested by the author for image quality (Gillies, 1990). The graphs are particularly useful for the communication and comparison of multivariate properties such as a personnel profile or software quality. The PAPI technique is used within personnel profiling. The technique is based upon a questionnaire, from which 20 personality characteristics are measured. The characteristics are then gathered into seven groups, namely Work Direction, Leadership, Activity, Social Nature, Work Style, Temperament and Followership. The scores for each of the 20 profiles, in the range 1 to 9 are plotted on a circular graph, using a linear scale, producing a profile (Figure 4.6). These profiles may then be compared to each other or to an 'ideal' template.

This technique is employed within personnel management when trying to match people to a job vacancy or task. The profile does not relate to any overall measure, but rather to the blend of characteristics required for a specific task. As such, it is the shape of the profile that is important rather than the overall area enclosed. The graphs are popular because of their ease of use and comparison, and because of their ability to display multiple data as a single shape.

Suitable graphical techniques should allow the multidimensionality of quality to be retained, whilst providing an overall impression of quality. Kostick's graphs have been suggested as a possible graphical device for displaying IT effectiveness, and by one of the authors for displaying image quality.

IT effectiveness and software quality differ from a personnel profile in that one is not trying to achieve a balance of skills but the best possible value within the constraints of budget and time. In such an application, people are likely to perceive the area enclosed by a particular profile, and perceptually to associate this with an overall measure of quality or effectiveness. Unfortunately, the perceptual measure can be very misleading. There are, however, several factors which make a quantitative link between area enclosed and overall quality more complex than might appear at first sight.

Table 4.4 Fenton's framework of entities and attributes

ENTITIES	ATTRIBUTES	
PRODUCTS	Internal	External
Specifications	size, reuse, modularity, redundancy, syntactic correctness	comprehensibility, maintainability
Designs	size, reuse, modularity, coupling cohesiveness, functionality	quality, complexity, maintainability
Code	size, reuse, modularity, coupling functionality, algorithmic complexity, structuredness	reliability, usability, maintainability
Test data	size, coverage level	quality
PROCESSES		
Constructing spec.	time, effort, number of requirements changes	quality, cost stability
Detailed design	time, effort, number of specification faults found	cost-effectiveness
Testing	time effort, number of bugs found	cost-effectiveness, stability
RESOURCES		
Personnel	age, price	productivity, experience, intelligence
Teams	size, communication, structuredness	productivity, quality
Software	price, size	usability, reliability
Hardware	price, speed, memory size	reliability
Offices	size, temperature, light	comfort, quality

4.4.1 Factors affecting the area in the graph

The factors affecting the area, other than the contributing values of the metrics displayed, are:

- the division of the circle
- the linear scale
- the neighbour effect.

Within the PAPI scheme, the circle is divided into 20 sectors, each corresponding to a measured personality characteristic, and then grouped in seven areas of self-perception. Each factor is allocated an equal sector, making an equivalent contribution to the profile. This equal weighting may not always be appropriate. In the case of software quality, under McCall's GE model (1977), there are 11 characteristics used to describe overall quality and 40 individual measures. Of these, 30 are associated with reliability and maintainability. An equal distribution here would lead to domination by those characteristics which are most easily measured. In practice, this often happens in quality assessment.

For the hierarchical models suggested by McCal *et al.* (1977), Boehm *et al.* (1978) and Watts (1987), each principal characteristic is allocated an equal area within the circle. Within each principal sector, each measure is then allocated an equal share of that sector.

To illustrate the method, consider a simplified view of software quality in terms of four principal characteristics of equal importance: correctness, reliability, maintainability and efficiency. There are also two measures associated with correctness, three with reliability, four with maintainability and one with efficiency, with the resulting distribution being shown in Figure 4.7.

The radial scale

The use of this method permits the plotting of a theoretically infinite number of dimensions around the circle. However, the profile is made up of a series of triangles and the whole area is given by the sum of the areas of these:

$$\text{Area} = \sum_{i=1}^{i=n} \tfrac{1}{2} \cdot x_i \cdot x_i - 1 \sin \tfrac{1}{2} (\Theta_i + \Theta_i + 1) \tag{4.1}$$

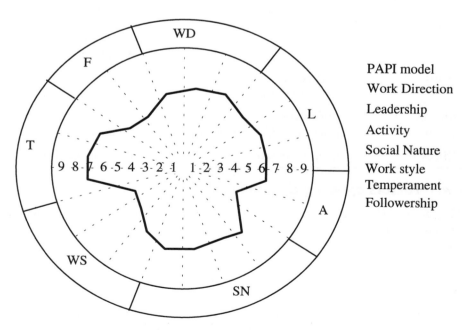

Figure 4.6 Schematic PAPI profile.

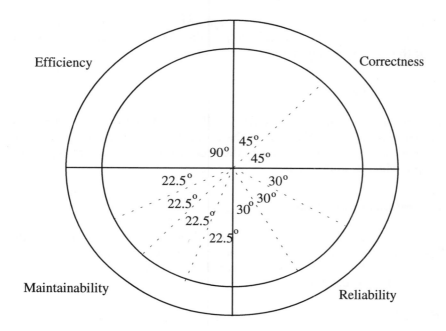

Figure 4.7 Simplified schematic profile.

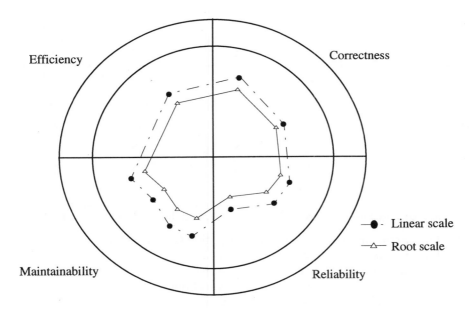

Figure 4.8 Effect of root scale.

This means that, overall, the area contained is proportional to x^2, not x. A better method would, therefore, be to plot the square roots of the values. The effect of this on a schematic plot is shown in Figure 4.8.

The neighbour effect

It may also be seen from equation 4.1 that the area depends not simply on the individual scores, but on the sum of the products of the adjacent scores. This means that the area will be sensitive to the ordering of the characteristics around the graph, which is undesirable.

An illustration of the effects

To illustrate the effects described, two sets of data will be used to calculate actual differences arising from each of the factors mentioned above. The second set is derived from the first. Each value is simply half that in the first set. The test data is shown in Table 4.5.

Table 4.5 Model data sets used to illustrate effects

Criteria	No. of metrics	Metric	Value 1	Value 2
1	4	1	0.8	0.4
		2	0.2	0.1
		3	0.9	0.45
		4	0.2	0.1
2	3	5	0.8	0.4
		6	0.2	0.1
		7	0.8	0.4
3	2	8	0.9	0.45
		9	0.1	0.05
4	1	10	0.6	0.3

Using a spreadsheet, the area enclosed was calculated for a number of cases:

1. Linear scale/measures given equal weighting (as per PAPI).
2. Linear scale/characteristics given equal weighting.
3. Root scale/measures given equal weighting.
4. Root scale/characteristics given equal weighting.
5. Root scale/neighbours arranged to maximize area.
6. Root scale/neighbours arranged to minimize area.

The areas enclosed expressed as a percentage of the whole circle are shown in Table 4.6.

Table 4.6 Effect of different schemes

		% of area of circle	
Case	Description	Data 1	Data 2
1	Linear scale/measures given equal weighting	22.0	5.5
2	Linear scale/characteristics given equal weighting	22.1	5.5
3	Root scale/measures given equal weighting	42.4	21.2
4	Root scale/characteristics given equal weighting	41.2	20.6
5	Root scale/neighbours arranged to maximize area	44.5	22.4
6	Root scale/neighbours arranged to minimize area	25.3	12.6

These examples show that, unless a root scale is used, a halving of scores leads to a quadrupling of the area. They also show that by changing the order of sectors, the area may change by a very significant factor, in this case almost 80%.

Removal of the neighbour effect: a consistent area profile graph

The effect of neighbours is not a severe problem in schemes such as PAPI, where the overall area is not assessed quantitatively and the order of the parameters does not change. However, where the area is intended to give an overall measure of quality, and the parameters themselves may vary, it is essential to make the area independent of the order in which the parameters are plotted. This cannot be achieved whilst the area of each segment depends upon the adjacent values. This means that the current connected polygon must be abandoned. A new scheme is proposed, designed to retain the visual appeal of the current graphs, but within a more rigorous quantitative framework.

Note: The rest of this section is necessarily algebraic and may appear complex to some. These readers may wish to skip to the example at the end of the section.

The circular format is retained with a radial scale. However, the scale runs from the outside into the centre. The profile is plotted from the circumference to the profile points and back between each point. In this fashion, the area depends principally upon the value plotted. A typical profile of this type, based upon the characteristics illustrated in Figure 4.7, is shown in Figure 4.9.

The area of each section may be determined as follows. Consider the profile component shown below.

The area of sector B is given by

Area of Sector B $= r^2 \cdot \Theta_i$ (4.2)

The area of triangle X is given by

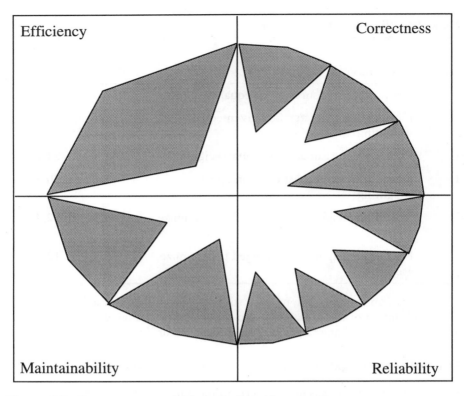

Figure 4.9 Constant area neighbour independent profile.

Area of triangle

So the area of A up to the circumference may be calculated as

$$\text{Area A} = (\text{Area B}) - 2(\text{Area X}) \tag{4.3}$$

$$= \tfrac{1}{2} r^2 \cdot \Theta_i - r \cdot r' \cdot (\sin \Theta_i / 2) \tag{4.4}$$

$$= \tfrac{1}{2} r^2 \cdot \Theta_i - r \cdot (r{-}r_i) \cdot (\sin \Theta_i / 2) \tag{4.5}$$

For small Θ_i, $\Theta_i \sim \sin \Theta_i$ and therefore

$$\text{Area A} = r \cdot x_i \cdot \sin (\Theta_i / 2) \sim r \cdot x_i \cdot (\Theta_i / 2) \tag{4.6}$$

In other words, at small Θi

Area of sector B $\sim$ Area of quadrilateral OPQR

We may correct for this effect by plotting our profile inside a polygon as in Figure 4.9. Now the area of the quadrilateral profile section (OPQR) is given by equation (4.6) for all values of Θ_i. This means that if we define our measures on a scale 0...1, setting r equal to 1, the area contained by the whole profile depends upon the measure and the sine of the angle $\Theta_i/2$.

If the characteristics are represented by differing numbers of measures, then in order to maintain consistent contributions from different characteristics with different numbers of measures, it is necessary to apply a correction factor which corrects for the dependency upon the number of measures, which determines the angle $\Theta_i/2$:

Plotted Value = Measured Value × Correction factor (4.7)

where:

$$\text{Correction factor} = \frac{(\Theta_i/2)}{\sin(\Theta_i/2)} \tag{4.8}$$

and

$$\Theta_i = (\pi/2) \times (1/\text{number of characteristics}) \times (1/\text{number of measures}) \tag{4.9}$$

The Correction factor is then normalized with respect to the maximum correction factor:

Scaled Correction Factor := Correction Factor/Maximum Correction Factor
(4.10)

An example of the effect of this scheme is shown in Tables 4.7 and 4.8. In the example given, the measured values give a mean value of 0.6 for each characteristic. Table 4.7 shows the increasing disparity as the number of measures decreases and the angle Θ_i increases. The same data is then evaluated (Table 4.8) using the correction factor as detailed, and the area contributed by each characteristic is now proportional to the mean of the individual measures.

Plotted in this manner, our profile has the following properties :

(1) The area of the profile depends linearly upon the values (x_j).
(2) The area of the profile is independent of the order of measures.

Table 4.7 Uncorrected values

Criteria	Metrics	M_i	N_i	$\Theta_i/2$	Sin $\Theta_i/2$	Area	Criteria
1	4	1	0.60	0.20	0.20	0.12	0.47
		2	0.50	0.20	0.20	0.10	
		3	0.70	0.20	0.20	0.14	
		4	0.60	0.20	0.20	0.12	
2	3	5	0.60	0.26	0.26	0.16	0.47
		6	0.30	0.26	0.26	0.08	
		7	0.90	0.26	0.26	0.23	
3	2	8	0.40	0.39	0.38	0.15	0.46
		9	0.80	0.39	0.38	0.31	
4	1	10	0.60	0.79	0.71	0.42	0.42

(3) The area of the profile is independent of the number of measures associated with each characteristic, i.e. the area arising from a criterion with one associated measure is the same as the area arising from one with n associated measures, providing the mean value of the measures is equivalent to that of the single measure.

Table 4.8 Corrected values

Criteria	Metrics	M_i	N_i	F_i	$F_i/F_{i\,max}$	Value	Area	Criteria
		1	0.60	1.01	0.91	0.54	0.11	
1	4	2	0.50	1.01	0.91	0.45	0.09	0.42
		3	0.70	1.01	0.91	0.63	0.12	
		4	0.60	1.01	0.91	0.54	0.11	
		5	0.60	1.01	0.91	0.55	0.14	
2	3	6	0.30	1.01	0.91	0.27	0.07	0.42
		7	0.90	1.01	0.91	0.82	0.21	
3	2	8	0.40	1.03	0.92	0.37	0.14	0.42
		9	0.80	1.03	0.92	0.74	0.28	
4	1	10	0.60	1.11	1.00	0.60	0.42	0.42

4.5 Questions for discussion

1. Compare Watts' seven criteria of good metrics with Gilb's measures as applied within his quality template.

   (a) How many criteria do Gilb's measures meet?
   (b) What problems will arise from those that are not met?
   (c) What advantages does Gilb's approach offer?

2. COQUAMO is based upon the earlier COCOMO model. Find out what you can about COCOMO which has been in use for about 15 years. (See Boehm, B. (1981) *Software Engineering Economics*, Prentice-Hall.)
   What problems can you see for a fully implemented COQUAMO model?

3. How helpful do you find the quality profiling schemes outlined in the final section? Discuss the merits of each and compare them to the polarity profiles outlined in an earlier chapter.

4.6 Further reading

Fenton, N. and Pfleeger, S.L. (1996) *Software Metrics: A rigorous and practical approach* (2nd edn), International Thomson Computer Press, London.

Gilb, T. (1988) *Principles of Software Engineering Management*, Addison-Wesley.

Gillies, A.C. and Hart, A.E. (1992) On the use of graphical techniques to describe profiles and quality, *Total Quality Management*, 3 (1).

Kitchenham, B. (1989b) Software quality assurance, *Microprocessors and Micro-computers*, 13, 6, 373–381.

PART 2
THE MANAGEMENT AND IMPROVEMENT OF QUALITY

Chapter 5

The CASE for tools and methods

5.1 The growth of software engineering methods

There are two distinct strands to the development of quality ideas within software development. The first is based upon software engineering, seeking to apply rigorous engineering practice to software development. The alternative is the application of quality management ideas. These are discussed in the next chapter. In practice, the ideas are complementary and may be employed together.

Software engineering is a product of the 1960s. The complexity of software had started to rise as hardware developed. This increase in complexity was unmatched by improvements in software design processes. This in turn resulted in an increased number of errors in the software. The escalating costs required to correct this situation led to solutions being sought to arrest the process. The term 'software crisis' was coined at the time. The software crisis was in fact a crisis in the quality of software.

Software engineering was introduced to try to formalize the development of software, using ideas from other engineering disciplines. The idea that has been pre-eminent ever since is the idea of structuredness. The concept of structuredness is simply about breaking down a large problem which cannot be dealt with easily, into a series of smaller problems which can. The development of systematic procedures to produce structured code, which became known as 'methodologies', was the first widespread attempt to take account of quality issues during software development.

5.1.1 What is a methodology?

The origin of the term 'methodology' is the study of method. However, it has passed into computing jargonese and has come to mean a systematic framework for the development of software. In practice, it is often incorrectly used synonymously with the word 'method'. A methodology may be defined as:

'a framework for the systematic organization of a collection of methods.'
(Lantz, 1989)

Lantz also suggests that a methodology may be characterized by a number of features:

- It can be taught. A methodology involves a collection of methods. They may be ordered as a sequence of steps and the nature and order of each step may be taught.
- It can be scheduled. The time and resources required to complete each stage may be estimated and a project schedule drawn up accordingly.
- It can be measured. This schedule may be used to measure progress of the plan.
- It can be compared. The use of the methodology within a specific project may be compared with its use in another project, or with the use of another methodology.
- It can be modified. Methodologies can be improved in the light of experience. For example, SSADM (Structured Systems Analysis and Design Methodology) is now in its fourth incarnation since its adoption as a UK Government standard in 1981.

Methodologies may be developed for all or part of the software development process. Information System Development (ISD) methodologies such as IEM (Information Engineering Methodology) are concerned with the whole development process. SSADM is only directly applicable to the design and analysis phases of the process.

A methodology for washing up

In order to see how a methodology is applied, consider a methodology for washing up. A 'best practice' approach might be considered in 13 phases, illustrated in Figure 5.1. This provides a rigorous and systematic approach to washing up. Once a clear procedure is in place, then we can put into operation a series of reviews for quality assurance. The process of washing up then becomes a systematic sequential process.

1. Sort washing up into categories
   This process sorts the washing up to be done into categories of increasing dirtiness, glasses, cutlery, crockery, pots and pans used for cooking. This minimizes transfer of dirt and the need for changes of water. An inspection is required to ensure that all dishes are sorted correctly.
2. Clean surfaces
   In order to ensure clean dishes are not placed upon dirty surfaces leading to re-soiling, the surface on which clean dishes are to be placed should be inspected.
3. Rinse dishes
   The soiled dishes should be rinsed to remove excessive dirt. This should be subject to inspection, to ensure that it has been carried out to the required standard.
4. Wash glasses
   The glasses should be washed first, in order to ensure maximum cleanliness. All clean glasses should be inspected to ensure that they are cleaned satisfactorily.

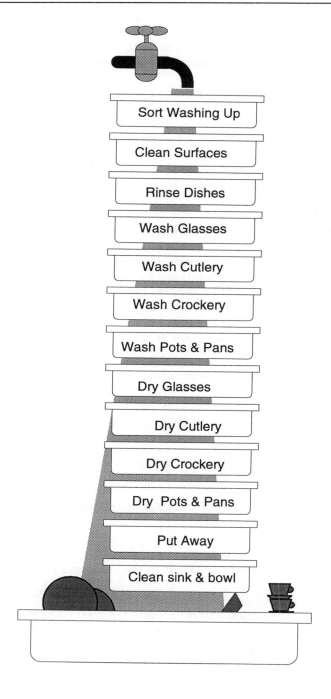

Figure 5.1 A methodology for washing up.

5. Wash cutlery
   The cutlery should be washed next, in order to maximize cleanliness. All clean cutlery should be inspected to ensure that it has been cleaned satisfactorily.
6. Wash crockery
   After the cutlery, the crockery should be washed and inspected for cleanliness.
7. Wash pots and pans
   Finally, the dirtiest items should be washed. After washing they should be inspected.
8. Dry glasses, dry cutlery, dry crockery, dry pots and pans
   The drying should be carried out in the same order. Each phase is followed by an inspection.
9. Put away dishes
   The clean dishes should all be put away and this should be checked.
10. Clean up sink area and bowl
    Finally, the area used, the sink, draining boards and bowl, should be washed down and inspected. A final report on the state in which the area has been left is required to complete the process. Further monitoring is required to check other factors such as:
    - the state of the washing-up water
    - the effectiveness of the detergent used.

A methodology for software development

A report is required if any additional problems are experienced along the way. A good methodology for software development has a number of characteristics:

1. Usability
   It should be easy to use and have good support provided by the vendor, since this is just as important to the long-term usability of the product.
2. Integrity
   A methodology should provide coverage of the whole lifecycle to ensure integrity throughout the process.
3. Adaptability to local needs
   Methodologies are necessarily restrictive if they are to encourage good practice, but they should also be adaptable to the needs of a particular environment.
4. Clarity
   Documentation is a critical and often neglected area. Good documentation can be facilitated by the methodology and partly generated by associated tools. The methodology itself should be jargon-free and produce understandable output.
5. Automation
   Increasingly, methodologies are becoming automated through the use of tools. A good methodology should lend itself to automation.

Different projects have had different needs, leading to a variety of methodologies. Each of these emphasizes different aspects of software development.

Methodologies have also tended to develop as a response to, and as a reaction against, the limitations of existing methodologies. Most software development methodologies are those based upon a sequential waterfall lifecycle.

5.2 Methodologies based upon the waterfall lifecycle

Sommerville (1989) identifies five phases in the waterfall lifecycle: requirements analysis, system and software design, implementation, testing, and operation and maintenance. This view of the waterfall model was illustrated in Figure 1.2.

1. Requirements analysis
    The aims, objectives and limits of the system are established in consultation with the client. They must be defined in a way that is understandable to the client and detailed enough for development staff.
2. System and software design
    The system design is used to allocate tasks to either hardware or software systems. Software design is concerned with transforming the software requirements into a form suitable for representation as a program.
3. Implementation and unit testing
    This section is concerned with coding. It is the stage when the program is actually built.
4. Testing
    Testing occurs in three phases, unit testing, integration testing and acceptance testing. First, each unit is tested to ensure that it functions and conforms to its specification. Following unit testing, the units are combined to form a whole system and the completed system is tested to ensure that it performs according to the overall specification. Finally, the system is shown to the users in order to ensure that it meets their requirements. In practice, this is sometimes done as part of the installation and operation phase. This practice is not recommended, as it is generally too late to act upon users' comments.
5. Operation and maintenance
    The product is installed and used by the client. Maintenance is ongoing, concerned not just with 'bug-fixes' but with improving the product and answering new user requirements as they emerge.

The stereotyped view of such design procedures is of a series of distinct phases, each performed sequentially, each completely documented and 'signed off' as agreed with the client at the end of each phase. The practical consequence of this is that once the requirements analysis determines the specification, it is cast in stone and nothing may depart from it. Unfortunately, most problems do not permit a complete and accurate specification at the start of the project. As the project progresses, the problem will become better understood and changes to the specification may be beneficial. Rigid adherence to the original specification is likely to ensure high technical quality, e.g. maintainability and reliability, at the risk of not matching the client's needs.

In practice, a degree of iteration is often employed, the later stages shedding light on the shortcomings of the initial requirements analysis. Clearly, there is a need to ensure that consistency is maintained in such instances and tools may prove helpful in achieving this. In many projects, the degree of iteration is limited by the need to meet a deadline for that particular project phase, rather than by the reaching of a particular standard of product quality.

We shall consider two specific methodologies of this type: Structured Systems And Design Methodology (SSADM) and Information Engineering Methodology (IEM).

SSADM is an example of an analysis and design methodology, that does not cover the whole lifecycle. IEM is a comprehensive methodology that forms the basis of the Texas Instruments CASE tool Information Engineering Facility (IEF).

5.2.1 SSADM

SSADM has been the mandatory methodology for UK Government projects for approximately ten years. It incorporates the ideas of structured analysis within a systematic framework for system analysis and design. The aim of SSADM is to ensure that user requirements are reflected in the design for the system. It is a design methodology rather than a complete system development methodology. There are three underlying principles of SSADM to ensure that the aim of fully representing user requirements is met.

- **Principle 1: User involvement**
  User involvement is an essential part of the SSADM procedure. At each stage of the methodology, documentation is produced to ensure that the specification and the design match the users' actual requirements. By providing feedback to users, differences between the specification and users' needs can be identified and corrected as early as possible.

- **Principle 2: Quality assurance**
  The feedback to users is part of an overall quality assurance review which is held at the end of each stage of the methodology. Each review requires the relevant documentation to be checked by users, developers and external auditing staff. The documentation is assessed for completeness, consistency and applicability. Once satisfied, users 'sign off' each stage of the work.

- **Principle 3: Separation of logical and physical design**
  Within SSADM, the design is separated into logical and physical design. The logical design is considered first, allowing problems to be addressed without consideration of the constraints and additional complexity provided by the hardware and software environments. The separation aids identification of errors, particularly by users who do not have to consider aspects of the technology with which they are unfamiliar.

The significance of SSADM amongst its peers arises from a number of factors:

- UK Government endorsement and adoption as a *de facto* standard.
- The maturity of the methodology.
- Arising from the above, there is much experience available about its use.
- It has been adapted and improved in the light of experience.
- It provides three distinct and complementary views of the design.
- It allows for a degree of flexibility.

Many of the techniques found in SSADM are found in other methodologies which trace their origins back to the work of the pioneers of structured methods such as Yourdon (1989), DeMarco (1979) and Jackson (1983).

The design stages of a typical sequential software development process are illustrated in Figure 5.2, together with the stages of the SSADM methodology that supports them. The stages of the SSADM method are summarized in Figure 5.3:

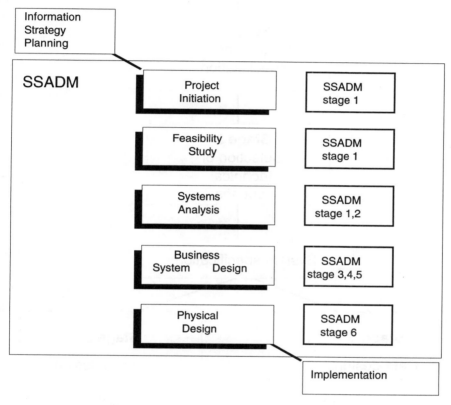

Figure 5.2 SSADM mapped onto a typical development process.

- Stage 1: Analysis of current system
  The starting point for systems analysis is the performance, operation and problems associated with the current system, where such a system exists. The aim of this stage of SSADM is:

  (a) to allow the analysts to learn the terminology and functionality of the users' environment
  (b) to provide for investigation of current data
  (c) to introduce users to the techniques used within SSADM
  (d) to define limits for the project.

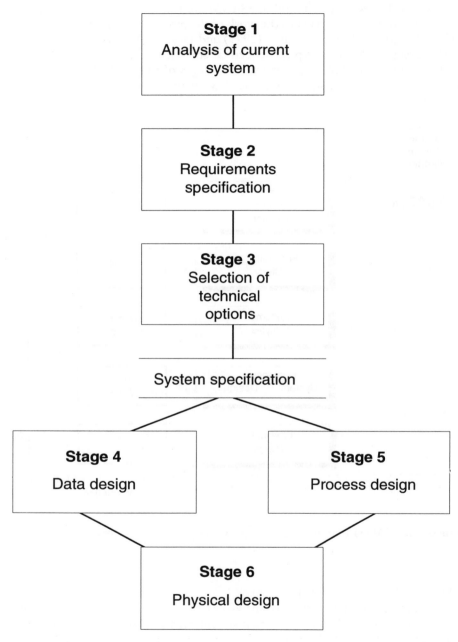

Figure 5.3 The stages of SSADM.

It is generally assumed within the SSADM approach that whilst functionality may change significantly when a new system is introduced, the underlying data is relatively constant. There may be circumstances where this is not appropriate. For example, the data needs for a poll tax system for UK local authorities were very different from the data needed to administer the old rates.

- Stage 2: Requirements specification
  This stage is concerned with drawing up the user requirements. However, in order to move the system away from the constraints of the old system, a number of steps are followed. The current system is re-drawn in terms of a logical view, that is a description of what it does with no reference to how this is achieved. This emphasizes current functionality and points to omissions and required enhancements. This approach is again built upon the idea that users can identify what they don't want more readily than what they do.
  The next step is consideration of the Business System options, involving a re-organization of the system to meet the new business objectives. Once a business system option is selected, the job of drawing up a detailed specification is begun and this is the final product of the requirements analysis stage. Before release, the specification is subject to extensive checks.

- Stage 3: Selection of technical options
  Once the detailed requirements specification is drawn up, enough information is available to make decisions about the hardware required for implementation. The developers cost out each option together with an outline of the benefits. These form the basis for the users to make the final choice of hardware.

- Stage 4: (Logical) data design
  The aim of this stage is to expand the data design from the requirements specification to the level of detail required at implementation. Within this stage, the data is cross-checked by relational analysis to ensure that all the required data is present. The data design must also be checked against the logical process design developed in Stage 5, to ensure consistency between the logical process and the data designs.

- Stage 5: (Logical) process design
  This stage is complementary to Stage 4, expanding the process design conceived within Stage 2 to provide all the detail necessary to build the system. Once such a design has been established, it must be cross-checked with the data design to ensure consistency.

- Stage 6: Physical design
  The role of this stage is both synthesis and conversion. The two logical designs must be synthesized into a single design, which is then converted to a physical design that will run on the target hardware environment.
  The initial physical design will require 'fine tuning', particularly to ensure that performance requirements are met. Although this represents the final stage of SSADM, much of the documentation produced at this stage will prove valuable in converting the final physical design into a working system during implementation.

Techniques used within SSADM

SSADM makes use of a number of techniques, both diagrammatic and non-diagrammatic, summarized in Table 5.1.

Table 5.1 Techniques within SSADM

Diagrammatic techniques	Non-diagrammatic techniques
Data flow diagrams	Relational data analysis
Logical data structures	First-cut rules
Entity life histories	Physical design control
Logical dialogue outlines	Project estimation
	QA reviews

Data flow diagrams (DFDs)

Data flow diagrams are used for representing information flows within a system. The notation used within SSADM is based upon the notation of DeMarco (1979), although there are some minor differences.

Logical data structures (LDSs)

Logical data structures represent the information that should be held within the system. The approach adopted is based upon entity modelling found in other techniques. The data model is developed through a series of progressively more detailed data structures (Figure 5.4).

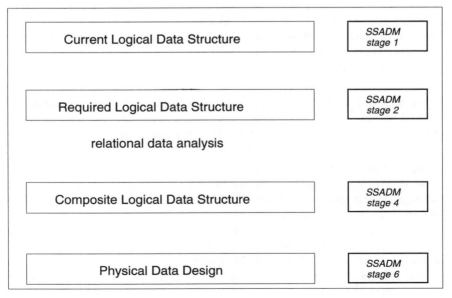

Figure 5.4 Logical data structures.

Entity life histories (ELHs)

The entity life histories represent the change of data with time, using a notation based upon work by Jackson (1983). This is based upon a matrix of entities and events, describing the data changes in terms of the entities contained within the LDS.

Logical dialogue outlines

These are produced at the requirements analysis stage of SSADM and are designed to facilitate user interface design by recording every occasion on which data flows across the human–computer boundary (Figure 5.5).

Relational data analysis (RDA)

RDA is incorporated into the logical data design stage of SSADM. It is concerned with normalization of the data within the application and complements logical data structuring carried out during the requirements analysis stage. The process eliminates duplicated data items by a stepwise procedure.

'First-cut' rules and physical design control

The process of establishing a practical and implementable physical design from the logical design is made up of two phases. In the first, simple rules are applied to achieve a 'first-cut' physical design. After this, the physical design is fine-tuned to ensure that the performance targets are met.

Figure 5.5 Logical dialogue outlines.

Project estimation

Project estimation is used to estimate time-scales for the whole project. As the design proceeds, so more information is available and the estimate may be refined.

QA reviews

Quality assurance reviews are held at the end of each stage of the methodology. Each review requires the relevant documentation to be checked by users, developers and external auditing staff. It is assessed for completeness, consistency and applicability.

An alternative analysis and design methodology is the classic structured analysis methodology due to DeMarco (1979) and Yourdon (1989). This makes use of three principal techniques which form the basis of much modern structured analysis: data flow diagrams, mini-specifications and structure charts.

1. Data flow diagrams
   A data flow is an individual item of data. This is considered to be transmitted from one process to another. Data starts from a data source and ends at a data sink. An example of a source or sink is a human being or a machine component. A process may require data from an external file or database. This is represented as two horizontal lines. In practice, data flow diagrams are multilevel and lend themselves to computerization, since graphical software can aid both design and understanding. Each level gives a more detailed representation than the one above. The elements in a data flow diagram and an example of a multi-level data flow diagram are given in Figure 5.6.

2. Mini-specifications
   Associated with each process node at the bottom of a data flow diagram is a task which may be described by a mini-specification, more commonly known as a mini-spec. Mini-specs describe their task in terms of algorithms which may be represented in a number of ways, e.g. pseudo-code, flowcharts, computer design language, decision trees or a decision table. These mini-specifications are designed to be translated into code subroutines, either automatically by the CASE tool or manually by the programmer. A mini-spec will typically include a process name and number, an input data list, an output data list and the body of the algorithm whose purpose is to transform the input data into the output data.

3. Structure charts
   Structure charts are designed to turn the requirements specification into a design specification. A structure chart represents the design specification in terms of modules and the data paths between them (Figure 5.7).

   Each module should be simple and self-contained. The programmer seeks to minimize coupling between modules and maximize cohesion, i.e. the degree to which a module contains all the code required to carry out its function.

The structured analysis methodology and its descendants such as SSADM have been around for a number of years now and have evolved in a number of

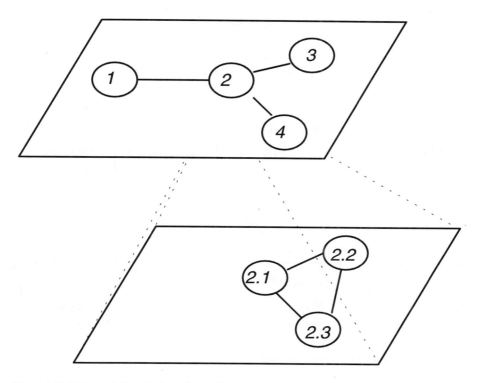

Figure 5.6 A multilevel data flow diagram.

areas. Initially, little attention was paid to user interfaces, yet they are one of the principal influences on user satisfaction. In theory, interfaces should vary enormously according to the level of expertise of the user. In practice, they are often designed like a ready-to-wear suit of clothes: they don't fit anyone very well, but neither do they mismatch people totally. In practice, there is little methodological basis for interface design beyond certain basic ground rules. However, the interface design is now a recognized stage within the structured analysis process. Interface prototyping tools are generally tailored drawing packages, allowing the user of the tool to create interfaces rapidly. More recent methodologies often attempt to cover the whole of the development process, including planning and implementation. An example of this type is the 'information engineering' methodology (IEM).

5.2.2 Information engineering methodology

IEM proposes a framework approach to software development. Like structured analysis, it is top-down in approach, but it defines its data and relationships from the business policy of the organization rather than from data flows.

Thus the top levels of the design process are concerned with business planning and strategy rather than computer systems. In this way, it is hoped that the

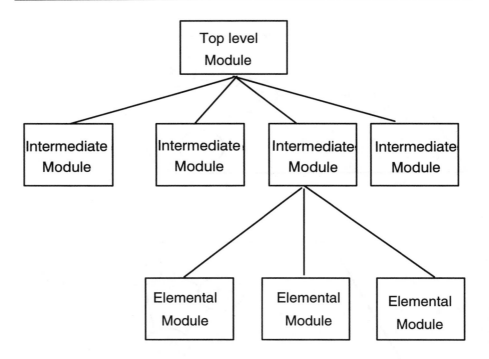

Figure 5.7 Example structure chart.

systems resulting will serve better the business needs of the organization ensuring that the solutions are not only technically accurate, but effective in a commercial sense.

The IEM methodology divides the software development process into seven phases, shown in Figure 5.8. These phases are:

1. *Information Strategy Planning* (ISP). ISP is concerned with a high-level analysis of business IT needs. The end result is an Information Strategy Plan which forms the basis for the next phase.
2. *Business Area Analysis* (BAA). BAA takes a particular segment of the business and analyses it in greater detail. The result of this stage is a Business Area Description, which is used in the Business System Design.
3. *Business System Design* (BSD). BSD produces a detailed target-independent description of the application system required to support the specific area of business described in the BSD. This description is known as the Business System Specification.
4. *Technical Design* (TD). TD considers the specific requirements of the operating environment and tailors the specification according to those needs, resulting in the Technical System Specification.
5. *Construction* is the phase during which the executable code is created.
6. *Transition* and *Production* are concerned with integrating and operating the constructed application within the organization.

IEM was first proposed by Martin and Finkelstein (1981). It offers a range of advantages:

- it links systems development to business needs
- it covers the whole lifecycle, and
- it facilitates the use of a CASE tool.

However, it is complex to use and requires a wholesale change in practice by software developers. Its chief advantage comes when it is used in conjunction with a CASE tool, but this brings further complexity and expense as we shall see in the next section.

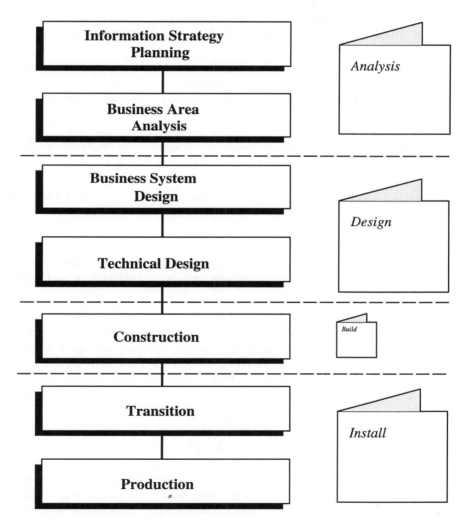

Figure 5.8 Information Engineering Methodology (IEM).

5.3 CASE tools

CASE (computer-aided software engineering) tools are computer-based tools to assist in the software engineering process. In practice, any CASE tool is made up of a set of tools or 'toolkit'. CASE, at the time of writing, is being heavily promoted as a solution to the quality problems experienced by software developers. The claimed advantages for CASE tools include:

- Productivity
  Good system developers are scarce and the aim of these tools is to maximize productivity.

- Consistency
  The tools provide a central data encyclopaedia to which all developers must refer. It enables several developers working separately to maintain consistency in terms of variables, data, syntax and so on. In large software projects, this alone can justify the use of tools.

- Methodology automation
  Many tools are associated with an underlying methodology, and they ensure that the developer sticks to the methodology. This improves consistency, but restricts creativity.

- Encourages good practice
  Provided that the underlying methodology is sound, the tools ensure that good practice such as structured programming is carried out.

- Documentation
  This is a notoriously undervalued area of system development. Tools can provide varying degrees of automation to assist in the process of document production.

- Maintenance
  The principal driving force behind the introduction of CASE tools has been the cost of maintenance. Tools can help improve initial quality and make changes cheaper to implement.

The toolsets within a CASE tool are bound to a central data encyclopaedia which maintains consistency across different component tools. It is this consistency which gives CASE tools much of their value, especially in large projects.

CASE tools are divided into three types. The classification is based upon the part of the development cycle supported by the tool concerned. The relationship between the different types of tools and the development lifecycle is shown in Figure 5.9.

1. Front end or upper CASE tools
    These tools are concerned with the design phases of the lifecycle. Their purpose is to assist in requirements analysis and design. They may be tied to a specific methodology or may allow the use of the user's own methodology. An example of this type of tool is the Excelerator product, described below. These tools are associated with analysis and design methodologies such as SAM or SSADM.

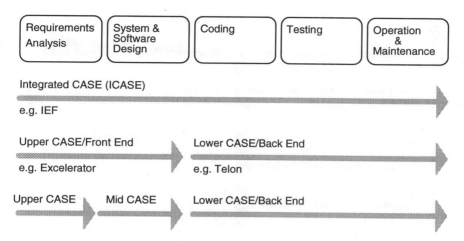

Figure 5.9 Types of CASE tools (schematic).

2. Back-end or lower CASE tools
    These tools are concerned with the implementation stages of the lifecycle, typically coding, testing and documentation. They aim to increase the reliability, adaptability and productivity of the delivered code. 4GLs may be considered as back-end CASE tools, as may products such as Telon.
3. Integrated CASE tools
    Integrated CASE (ICASE) tools aim to support the whole development cycle and are linked to specific methodologies. They are often complex and expensive, but offer the developer the greatest integrity of all approaches through the use of a single data encyclopaedia throughout the lifecycle. ICASE tools are closely linked with the comprehensive development methodologies such as IEM. CASE tools based upon IEM include IEF (information engineering facility) and IEW (information engineering workbench).

5.3.1 The Excelerator CASE tool

A popular example of a CASE tool based upon the structured analysis methodology is the front end tool Excelerator, from the Index Technology Corporation.

The product is based around a set of diagramming tools (Figure 5.10) supporting five levels of representation of the design. It integrates the Yourdon/DeMarco Structured Analysis Methodology with data modelling and structured design methodologies. The top level of the multilevel data flow diagram is known as the context data flow diagram and provides an overview of the whole system. The remaining techniques provide more detailed information as the levels are descended.

In addition to the diagramming tools, Excelerator offers a number of facilities to assist the designer. A screens and reports facility allows the designer to set up mock-ups of inputs and outputs for interface prototyping. Outline COBOL code may be generated automatically using a separate product. Whilst this is not implementable COBOL, it provides a good outline from which programmers can work.

Increasing level of abstraction

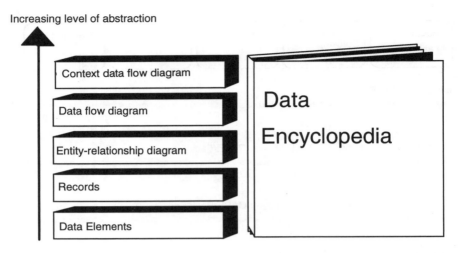

Figure 5.10 The Excelerator CASE tool (schematic).

5.3.2 The information engineering facility (IEF)

The IEM is supported by the IEF CASE tool, supplied by Texas Instruments. Each of the first five stages from the IEM is supported by a toolset within IEF, as shown in Table 5.2.

Table 5.2 IEF supports and automates the IEM

Phase of IEM	IEF toolset	Tools provided within IEF
Information Strategy Planning	Planning and Analysis	Indented list editor Matrix processor Entity relationship diagram editor Process hierarchy diagram editor Process dependency diagram editor Process action diagram editor
Business Area Analysis	Analysis	Entity relationship diagram editor Process hierarchy diagram editor Process dependency diagram editor Process action diagram editor
Business System Design	Design	Dialog flow diagrams Screen design Procedure action
Technical Design	Design	Largely automated
Construction	Construction	Automatic code generation facilities
Transition		
Production		

The use of a central data encyclopaedia ensures consistency between phases. IEF is an ICASE tool supporting the whole lifecycle and with many automated facilities.

The information engineering methodology makes extensive use of entity-relationship (E-R) models for information modelling, which attempts to model both data structures and their interrelationships. E-R models are attractive because of their simplicity. They contain only two elements: entities and the relationships between them. Entities are the objects or data structures under description. They may be specific real objects such as people or machinery, or abstract concepts such as services. The relationships between them are classified into a number of types, according to the number of entities involved. Commonly, one-to-one, one-to-many and many-to-many relationships are defined, but these are complicated by the possibility that a relationship to zero is also possible in some cases.

Consider the following example, part of the data structure for a computerized database of customer records for a telephone company. Each customer lives at a single address. We shall not consider the possibility that the telephone company might have two customers in the same household. This means that 'customer' and 'house no.' are entities within our data model and have a one-to-one relationship. A street is made up of many houses. Therefore, 'street' is an entity and is linked by a one-to-many relationship to house.

Similarly, a town is made up of many streets. Thus, 'town' is an entity and is linked by a one-to-many relationship to street.

Each customer is assumed to have at least a telephone number to be entered on the database. They may have more than one telephone line, e.g. separate lines for domestic and business purposes. Each line, therefore, has a purpose associated with it in a one-to-one relationship. Similarly, each customer may or may not have at least one fax machine. Thus the relationship between customer and fax number is one to 'zero-or-many'.

The model described is shown in Figure 5.11, together with a summary of the notation used for E-R diagrams within the IEF CASE tool. E-R models are particularly helpful in designing database systems. For example, the end result produced by the IEF tool is COBOL code together with DB2 calls to an associated database. The choice of delivery vehicle for IEF is influenced by the envisaged market for the tool: large commercial organizations, whose principal interest is in information processing.

IEF offers many advantages, notably its close links with business planning and the integrity of the integrated approach. The chief disadvantages of this tool are its size and complexity. In practice, many organizations use only those parts of the methodology and the associated tool that they find helpful, which limits the effectiveness of the tool as a whole. A side effect of the complexity of such tools is high cost.

The use of tools in this way faces a number of problems. Apart from the heavy financial investment required, the principal problem is the lack of standards across different manufacturers. This is seen in two different ways:

1. Notation
    Even where the diagrams are representing the same model view of the problem the notation may not be identical. Consider as an example the entity-

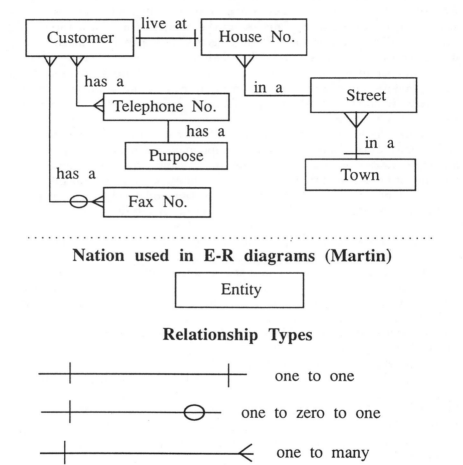

Example E-R diagram for a data record
for a telephone database

Nation used in E-R diagrams (Martin)

Relationship Types

one to one

one to zero to one

one to many

zero or many to many

Figure 5.11 Simplified E-R model.

relationship diagram. Two systems are commonly found, Chen notation and
Martin notation. We have used Martin's notation, as found in the IEF tool,
but Chen's notation is also common.
2. Incompatibility between output
   More serious is the lack of standards to allow transfer of output from one
   manufacturer's tool to another. This means that the absolute integrity of a

CASE tool only lasts as long as we remain within the same tool. For commercial reasons, CASE tools attempt to tie down the developer to one tool. In practice this means that we are most likely to be able to make use of CASE tools at the early high-level stages of design.

5.4 The contribution of methods and tools to quality

The contribution of software engineering methods and tools to quality will be considered in terms of two questions:

- How does software engineering impact upon quality?
- How widely have rigorous software engineering practices been adopted?

5.4.1 How does software engineering impact upon quality?

Software engineering was developed to address the problem of handling complexity through a structured approach. In this way, it was hoped to reduce costs through increased productivity during initial development by reducing errors. It was also intended to reduce ongoing maintenance costs through making software more reliable.

The introduction of software engineering has clearly increased the quality of software in terms of technical parameters such as reliability and maintainability when measured in a narrow technical way. It has also improved its quality in terms of 'conformance to specification'. Thus, in terms of Garvin's views of quality, quality has been improved from the manufacturing view.

However, the underlying problem which software engineering was set up to address was the cost of software maintenance. In spite of 25 years of software engineering, there is still grave concern about the cost of software maintenance, and the percentage of development budgets devoted to maintenance rather than new systems development. In the UK alone, the Centre for Software Maintenance estimates that maintenance costs over £1 billion a year. Estimates for the USA are as high as $30 billion annually.

Reasons for this maintenance effort may be classified under three headings:

- Error correction ('bug fixing'). Software engineering should reduce this type of maintenance effort, as detailed above.
- Failure to meet users' initial needs. Software engineering can actively reduce quality under this view (Garvin's user-based view) through freezing the requirements at a stage when the problem may not be clearly understood.
- Failure to cope with evolving needs. Structured code should be easier to adapt to meet evolving needs. However, it tends to encourage a view that a system, once developed, is a finished product and changes may be difficult to accommodate.

For the above reasons, software engineering tends to be more highly regarded by developers than users of systems since it favours a manufacturing-based view of quality, or conformance to specification.

CASE tools should further enhance the effectiveness of software engineering methods. As we shall see in the next section, this is not always the case. Some of the alternative approaches described below have developed because software engineering fails to address fundamental quality issues from a user-based viewpoint.

5.4.2 How widely have rigorous software engineering practices been adopted?

In spite of the comparatively long history of software engineering methods, they can only have an impact on the quality of systems if they are universally adopted. Many of the claims for the benefits, particularly those arising from automation through the use of CASE tools are due to enthusiasts or suppliers with a vested interest in taking an optimistic view.

One of the best pictures of the current state of software engineering practice has been built up by the Commercial Software Engineering Group at the University of Sunderland. A number of surveys of the uptake of methods and tools in the UK have been undertaken by staff (Stobart, Thompson and Smith, 1991; Davis *et al.*, 1993). The surveys were undertaken by sending a postal questionnaire to 500 organizations involved in the development of commercial software. A 25% response rate was achieved.

In 1991, the survey found that for the front end of the lifecycle, i.e. analysis and design, 62% were using a structured method. SSADM was by far the most popular, being used by 37% of the total sample. For the back end of the cycle, 69% of respondents were using a structured sequential approach based upon the waterfall model.

The results are summarized in Table 5.3.

Table 5.3 Extent of software engineering practice in UK (after Stobart *et al*, 1991)

Methods adopted	Percentage of respondents
Front end	
SSADM	37
Yourdon	8
Other	18
Total using SE method	62
No method adopted	38
Back end	
Waterfall-based method	69
Prototyping	21
None	10

The survey then went on to see how many organizations had automated their method using CASE tools. A total of 18% of respondents were currently using CASE, as shown in Table 5.4. However, follow-up enquiries revealed that non-respondents had not replied because they did not use CASE. There appeared to be a relatively low (18%) usage of CASE among those people who replied to the survey. The enquiries amongst non-responders suggested that the actual uptake was considerably lower since most people who did not reply did so because they were not using CASE.

Table 5.4 Uptake of CASE amongst respondents

Response	Percentage
Currently using CASE	18
Currently evaluating CASE	26
Considered but dismissed	13
Willing to purchase	6
Not evaluating	26
Not sure	11

The survey also revealed a degree of scepticism about the benefits of CASE, as shown in Table 5.5.

Table 5.5 Reasons for rejecting CASE

Reason for rejecting CASE	Percentage
Cost of currently available tools	31
No management backing for CASE technology	16
Current approaches appear to be satisfactory	13
Lack of belief in the claimed productivity benefits	8
Lack of supported methods	8
Poor quality of tools	7
Staff refusal	1
Lack of belief in the claimed quality benefits	1
Other	15

The survey highlighted some cultural differences between users of CASE tools who may be regarded as enthusiasts for software engineering and non-users. The users of CASE saw the solutions to problems more in terms of technical factors rather than human and management issues, which were emphasized by non-users (Figure 5.12).

In terms of views of quality, this means emphasizing a manufacturing view of quality (conformance to specification) rather than a user-based view (fitness for purpose).

This emphasis and a perceived neglect of the user-based view has led to the use of a number of alternative approaches which generally seek to improve quality from the perspective of the user-based view and improve fitness for purpose.

5.5 Alternative approaches to software development

5.5.1 Prototyping

It is often observed by exasperated programmers that clients are better able to say what they don't want than define what they do. Presenting the client with a possible solution focuses their attention to detailed considerations vital to the acceptability of the product.

A methodology based upon the waterfall lifecycle can lead to a correct solution to the wrong problem if the specification is drawn up before the problem is completely understood. In prototyping methodologies, the development process defines the specification as the project progresses. The user is provided with pro-

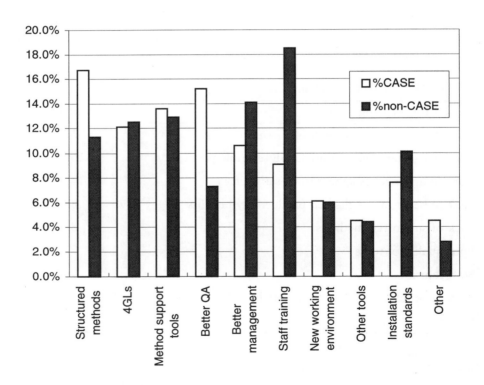

Figure 5.12 Differences in perceived solutions between CASE users and non-CASE users.

totype systems to allow them to say 'That's not what I meant' before the specification is finalized. A typical prototyping approach is illustrated in Figure 5.13.

The advantages claimed for prototyping methodologies are:

- increased user involvement leading to greater user satisfaction
- a reduction in the number of errors in the specification
- an improvement in communication.

One of the biggest problems with prototyping methodologies is the issue of 'adequacy', or, in simple terms, 'When do we stop?' However, the biggest criticism is that the resulting code is badly structured leading to future maintainability problems.

User satisfaction will be short-lived if the product is found to be unreliable in use and difficult to maintain. One solution is the 'throw away' prototype. In this case, prototyping is used to enhance the requirements analysis stage of a conventional sequential development method. However, the prototype is never used and the outcome from the process is an improved set of requirements

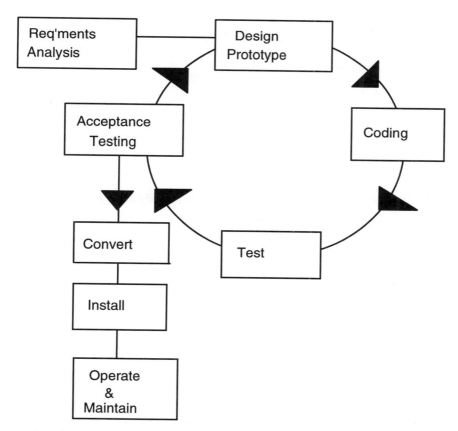

Figure 5.13 A typical prototyping methodology.

implemented in the normal way. Ill-structured problems in particular can benefit from this approach. The following mini case study illustrates this approach.

Organization of Combat (OFC): Dunkelberger (1989)

Organization of Combat (OFC) was a battlefield expert system developed for the United States Department of Defense. The system advises battlefield commanders on how to deploy artillery support for their battalions of foot soldiers. As such it was required to be implemented in Ada and developed in accordance with STD 2167A, which specifies an extremely rigid process for software development. The final system was required to run on a 4.77 MHz 8088-based ruggedized PC.

In order to capture the user requirements, an expert systems development environment was used to develop a prototype. The prototype was developed in an ART environment on a Symbolics workstation to prove the feasibility of the project.

From this prototype, a set of user requirements was drawn up and used to develop a second prototype. This was written in the 'C' language and implemented on a desktop PC AT machine. This prototype was refined until the customers were happy with it.

Finally, from this prototype a new set of requirements was drawn up in accordance with STD 2167A, and from this the final system was built in Ada.

The system as delivered met all the initial requirements including a fast response time on very limited hardware.

The chief disadvantage of this approach is the cost involved in discarding one or even two prototypes. However, these costs must be weighed against ongoing development costs arising either from ill-structured code if full-blown prototyping is used, or not meeting users' needs if a sequential method is used.

5.5.2 Evolutionary delivery

Gilb (1988) argues that it is simply not possible to identify user needs at the start of a project as required by a conventional software engineering approach:

'If only we had the intellectual capacity and the necessary knowledge to do these things accurately. In reality, we have to admit that we cannot tackle such tasks adequately for any but trivially small projects.'

In support of this claim he has identified case studies where the adoption of such a traditional approach led to major problems in the proposed solution. He cites instances where the critical attributes of the system are obscured, rather than highlighted by the requirements analysis. For example, he cites the case of a corporate information system which failed because the critical attribute of required processing power could not be met. Unfortunately, this was not discovered until late in the project and the consequence was a large and expensive failure. An evolutionary approach, together with an emphasis on elicitation of the critical attributes, should have found this much earlier.

The evolutionary approach suggested by Gilb sees the requirements specification as a constantly evolving entity which seeks to approach the actual requirements but never gets there. This is illustrated graphically in Figure 5.14. Even if

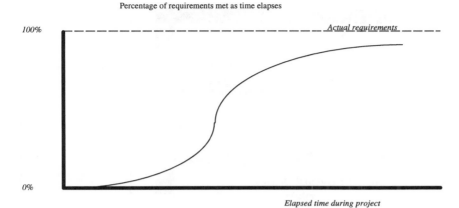

Figure 5.14 Requirements evolve over time.

the original requirements were met, by the time they are met they will have changed.

The evolutionary approach to system design proposed by Gilb and others such as Mills (1980) is unashamedly based upon prototyping. Prototyping is not generally well received by the software engineering community. This may seem odd when software engineering is compared to other engineering disciplines, where prototyping is a widely used technique. An executive from the Ford Motor Company compared the production of information systems to cars: every car component is prototyped before production and yet his software engineers were reluctant to prototype any information systems. The argument that if it is designed properly it will work is simply not borne out by experience.

The evolutionary approach to software design as described by Gilb is summarized in Figure 5.15. The code is implemented in a series of 'mini-projects' which may be managed in the same way as any other software project. Since they are likely to be smaller in scale than a full-blown traditional software project, there may be advantages through the reduction in complexity.

The following benefits are claimed for its use:

- user requirements are easier to establish
- users feel more involved and are more highly motivated
- critical attributes are identified earlier
- problems within the development team are exposed earlier
- early delivery of a tangible piece of code can gain credibility
- it tests the models at the heart of the design against the real world before completion
- it emphasizes the importance of user documentation, which cannot be provided as an afterthought.

However, a number of objections have been raised to this type of approach. The first may be seen as resistance to change. There is a substantial investment

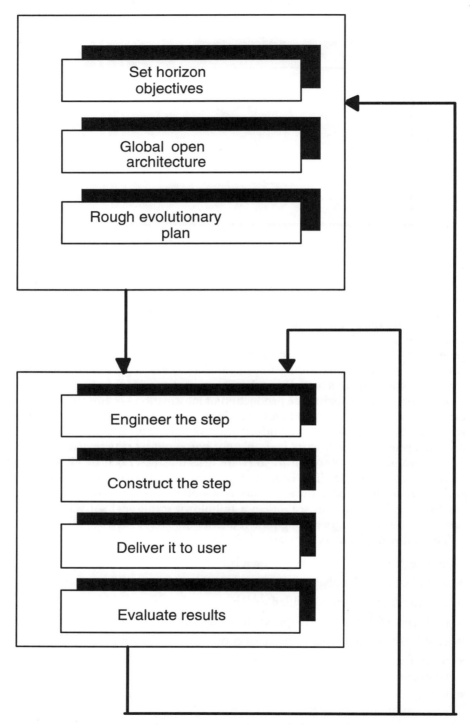

Figure 5.15 Evolutionary software development, after Gilb (1988).

in the existing sequential approach. Any change will require a further investment in re-training. It may take a long time to change old ways and attitudes.

Many development staff will not see the need for the change, since by the technical parameters that they use to judge software, their programs do not appear to fail. They may also feel threatened by user involvement, which may be seen as telling them how to do their job.

Perhaps because of their insecurity and resistance concerning change, system developers raise a number of practical objections. They make comments like:

'The problem can't be divided'
'Evolutionary development takes longer'
'Management won't like it'
'Designers don't know how to do it'

There is evidence that these objections can be readily overcome where there is a will to do so. However, this will only be achieved with the co-operation of staff. Thus, the best hope for this type of approach is as part of a total quality program which seeks to promote a complete cultural change within an organization to orient it towards quality. The remaining chapters are all concerned with approaches to improve quality, not simply through better development methods, but through cultural change.

However, before we consider these we shall consider the impact on quality of the growing popularity of object-oriented methods.

5.5.3 Object-oriented design and implementation

Object-oriented methods are not new, although they have recently become more popular. This may be attributed to at least two factors. The first is the availability of C++ and the growth of object-oriented databases, which meant that object-oriented designs may be implemented in languages and tools that are industry standards. Tools like IEF, described in section 5.3, are being expanded to cope with object-oriented techniques.

The second factor is the demand for applications which require or benefit from object-oriented techniques, including multimedia systems, geographical information systems and expert database systems.

The combination of available tools and demand for applications has led to a rapid growth in the use of these techniques.

From a technical point of view, the use of object-oriented design methods offer the following advantages (Somerville, 1989):

- Objects are independent entities which may readily be changed because all state and representation information is held within the object itself. No access and hence no deliberate or accidental use of this information by other objects is possible. Thus changes can be made without reference to other system objects.

- Objects may be distributed and may execute either sequentially or in parallel. Decisions on parallelism need not be taken at an early stage of the design process.

The advantage to the developer is that system design is more flexible and easier to modify. Reusability should be greatly enhanced. The advantage to the user is that systems should be more easily adapted to changing business needs. Thus quality should apparently increase under both the manufacturing-based view and the user-based view.

However, there are some problems in using these techniques. The object-oriented paradigm is different from conventional techniques based on functional decomposition. This may require a change in paradigm and working practices for existing developers, which could meet with resistance.

Some problems do not lend themselves to an object-oriented approach, and this may lead to unnatural data constructs.

Finally, it may be difficult to operate object-oriented systems alongside existing systems. The re-engineering of old systems as new object-oriented systems has been offered as a solution (e.g. Ayre *et al.*, 1995). However, this has so far proved to be extremely difficult and expensive.

5.6 Standards based on the software engineering lifecycle

There are some software quality standards which are based upon a model which emphasizes the lifecycle approach.

A good example of a standard of this type is the American Department of Defense (DoD) standard DoD 2167A, laid down for all mission-critical systems. The model of a lifecycle contained within the standard encompasses both software and hardware development.

The standard prescribes a structured top-down approach to system design and development. The software development procedure is based upon the standard waterfall lifecycle model. Emphasis is placed upon the requirements analysis phase and design specification phases of the project. However, a well-documented structured methodology is required throughout the whole procedure. A specific requirement is that each of the requirements is traceable throughout the system:

> 'Traceability of requirements to design: The contractor shall develop traceability matrices to show the allocation of requirements from the system specification to the Computer Software Configuration Item, Top Level Computer Software Components, Lower Level Computer Software Components and Units and from the Unit level back to the system specification. The traceability matrices should be documented in the Software Requirements Specification, Software Top Level Design Document and the Software Detailed Design Document.'
>
> (DoD 2167A, Clause 4.2.8)

As may be seen from the sample clause quoted above, standards of this type can become very complex. The standard acquires a jargon all of its own, which must be waded through to extract the requirements.

Documents of compliance are required by the DoD, and therefore all the system requirements documents must be written to facilitate this process. At each review point, documentation is required to demonstrate compliance. Unlike the ISO standards, the documents must be written in a particular format to satisfy the requirements of the standard.

DoD STD 2167A has acquired a somewhat tarnished image amongst some practitioners. This is due to a number of factors:

- It has been described as bureaucratic, with an excessive amount of documentation required. Figure 5.16 illustrates the documents required to support a procedure complying with the standard.
- It has proved difficult to implement in a number of cases. As a result, relaxations of the standard have been allowed, reducing its effectiveness as a standard. A standard with exceptions is no longer a standard.

In spite of these objections, whilst defence remains a major customer for IT systems, and the US DoD in particular, the importance of this standard will remain. Some assistance is available through the use of CASE tools sourced from the USA, which produce documents in a form acceptable for STD 2167A procedures.

This highly prescriptive approach is carried through to all aspects of system development. For example, the US DoD and UK MoD have specified that all systems should be developed in Ada and run on approved hardware. This can cause headaches for system developers.

Many people would argue that this procedure was unnecessarily cumbersome and long-winded. However, the example of OFC given above demonstrates that the product is of high quality, excelling in two important areas:

1. Run-time efficiency. The product was required to have a response time of less than one second to be fit for the purpose. The initial version had a response time of three or four seconds. The final version, running on much slower hardware, reduced this by a factor of ten.
2. Maintainability. The final product is easily maintained through its well-structured and well-documented design. AI prototypes are notoriously difficult to maintain.

The final version also shows high quality in the areas of usability and interoperability.

Whether the procedure is overkill or not, it is difficult to deny the high quality of the final product. Whether any non-military customer would have been prepared to foot the bill for three implementations is another matter. Military projects often have more flexible budgets, and this can alter one's perspective of quality and how it may be achieved.

5.7 Questions for discussion

1. Consider the washing-up methodology in section 5.1:
   (a) What advantages does it offer?
   (b) Does it improve the end result?
   (c) Why doesn't everyone wash up this way?
   (d) What analogies can you see with methodologies for software development?

2. There are three underlying principles of SSADM stated in the text.
   (a) How are they reflected in the method themselves?
   (b) How far do you think they are realizable in practice?

3. Stobart *et al.*'s (1991) study reveals the following data:

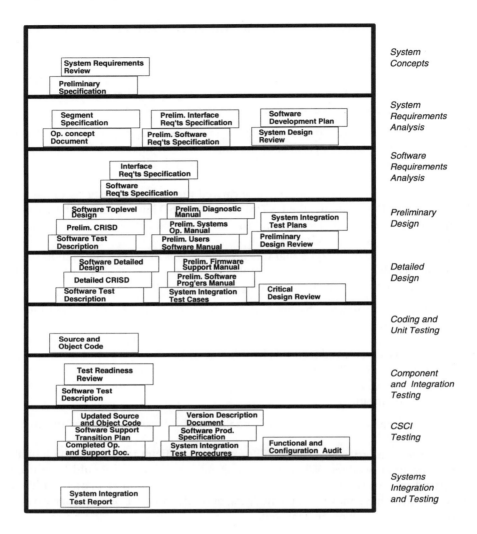

Figure 5.16 Documentation required for STD 2167A.

	CASE tool users	Non-CASE tool users
SSADM	28.6%	38.7%
Yourdon	23.6%	4.0%

SSADM and Yourdon are the commonest analysis and design methods used.

(a) What does the data tell you about the way that the methods are used?

(b) A Fisher exact chi-squared test reveals a p-value of 0.025. Does this confirm your view?

(c) What does this say about the importance of the ease of automation as a factor in the widespread use of SSADM as a method in the UK?

(d) What is the principal factor in the widespread use of SSADM in the UK?

(e) Does this suggest anything about developers' belief in its effectiveness?

4. One business manager commented to the author that they would not dream of producing a mechanical component without prototyping it first, neither would they dream of incorporating prototypes into final production.

(a) Is software different?

(b) Is throwing away a prototype likely to prove cost-effective?

(c) Do you agree with Gilb's statement quoted in the text that it is simply not possible to define user requirements at the start of a project?

5.8 Further reading

Ayre, J., McFall, D., Hughes, J. and Delobel, C. (1995) A method for re-engineering existing relational database applications for the satisfaction of multimedia based requirements, *Conference Proceedings at the 6th International Hong Kong Computer Society Database Workshop*, 3–4 March.

Davis, C., Gillies, A.C., Smith, P. and Thompson, J.B. (1993) Current quality assurance practice amongst software developers in the UK, *Software Quality Journal*, 2 (3), 145–61.

DeMarco, T. (1979) *Structured Analysis and System Specification*, Yourdon Press, Englewood Cliffs.

Fisher, A.S. (1988) *CASE: Tools for Software Development*, Wiley, New York.

Gilb, T. (1988) *Principles of Software Engineering Management*, Addison-Wesley, Wokingham.

Gillies, A.C. and Smith, P. (1994) *Managing Software Engineering*, Chapman & Hall, London.

Jackson, M.A. (1983) *System Development*, Prentice-Hall, New Jersey.

James Martin Associates (1988) *An Intorduction to Information Engineering*, Texas Instruments.

Lantz, K.E. (1989) *The Prototyping Methodology*, Prentice-Hall, New Jersey.

Martin, J. and Finklestein, C. (1981) *Information Engineering*, Savant Research Studies, Carnforth.

Mills, H.D. (1980) *IBM Systems Journal* 4.

Sommerville, I. (1989) *Software Engineering*, 3rd edn, Addison-Wesley, Wokingham.

Stobart, S.C., Thompson, J.B. and Smith, P. (1991) The use, problems, benefits and future directions of CASE in the UK, *Information and Software Technology*, 33 (9), 629–36.

Yourdon, E.N. (1989) *Modern Systems Analysis*, Prentice-Hall, New York.

Chapter 6

Quality management systems

6.1 A historical perspective

The area of quality management is dominated by the ideas of a few key individuals who have become known as 'gurus'. The most important of these 'gurus' are Deming, Juran and Crosby.

The man generally credited with inventing 'quality management' is Dr Edward Deming. Following the Second World War, he offered his ideas on quality to US Government and industrial leaders. The ideas were not well received at the time: an error which has ensured immortality for Dr Deming in the light of subsequent events. Deming was posted to Japan to help with the census there. He contacted JUSE (the Union of Japanese Scientists and Engineers) about his ideas. The rest, as they say, is history. Together with the ideas of Juran on fitness for purpose, the ideas of Deming formed the basis for Japanese economic recovery and subsequent Japanese domination of the world market.

Once the proof of Deming's and Juran's ideas was seen in the successful recovery of Japanese manufacturing industry, their ideas were rapidly accepted, particularly back home in the United States, where they were joined as quality 'gurus' by Phil Crosby, the man famous for 'zero defects' and his book, *Quality is Free*. This dominance by a few personalities and, particularly, the often uncritical acceptance of their ideas has not been universally well received.

There is a backlash currently being witnessed in some quarters. Total quality management (TQM) has become passé in many circles, to be replaced by new acronyms such as CQI (continuous quality improvement) and business process re-engineering (BPR). Enthusiasts will argue that these are radically new developments. However, there is an inevitable scepticism amongst those who have seen other fashions come and go. Many articles on the subject reinforce the view that the 'gurus' are treated with uncritical respect. Their expertise is often presented in terms of a set of pithy sayings.

Consider, for example, the following. One author quotes Deming:

'Management's overall aim should be to create a system, in which everybody may take joy in his work.'

This particular author continues:

'Who but Deming would have thought or dared to raise such a far-reaching outlandish unrealistic concept as "joy in work"?'

This kind of uncritical adulation is not well received by many striving to bring engineering precision to software development. At the same time, as we shall see later in the chapter, there is clearly a need to improve quality management in the software area. It is, therefore, important to look beyond superficialities to see what quality management ideas can be usefully applied to software.

However one regards the prominence of the quality 'gurus', the history of the subject of quality management is largely the development of the ideas of the three principal figures: Deming, Juran and Crosby. They each have different emphases and offer varying, if complementary, approaches to quality management (Figure 6.1).

Dr Edward Deming's background was in statistics. His definition of quality was:

'A predictable degree of uniformity and dependability at low cost and suited to the market.'

(Deming, 1986)

He was a strong advocate of statistical quality control and employee participation in decision making. He argued that it is insufficient for employees to do their best, that they must know what to do. For this reason he was opposed to the sorts of poster campaigns promoting quality found in many organizations, arguing they were misdirected and can cause frustration and resentment. He suggested 14 points for management, shown in Table 6.1, which should be used both internally and by suppliers.

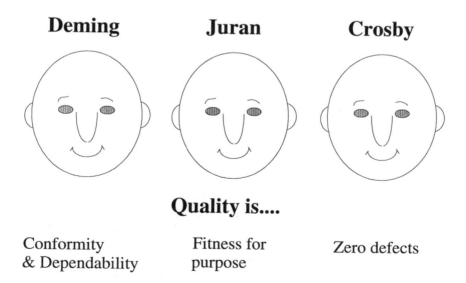

Figure 6.1 A comparison of the emphases of Deming, Juran and Crosby.

Table 6.1 Deming's 14 points for management

1.	Constancy of purpose
2.	A new philosophy
3.	Cease dependence on inspection
4.	End lowest tender contracts
5.	Improve every process
6.	Institute training on the job
7.	Institute leadership
8.	Drive out fear
9.	Break down barriers
10.	Eliminate exhortations
11.	Eliminate targets
12.	Permit pride of workmanship
13.	Encourage education
14.	Create top management structures

Deming was a believer in single sourcing of supplies, arguing that the benefits of a strong co-operative relationship with suppliers more than outweighs the short-term cost gains from competitive tendering. He advocated complete co-operation with suppliers, including the use of statistical process control (SPC) techniques, described below, to ensure the quality of incoming supplies.

J. M. Juran rose to fame with Deming in post-war Japan. He is credited with coining the phrase 'fitness for purpose', and is therefore particularly influential when we come to consider the use of quality management ideas in software development. He has argued strongly that definitions of quality based upon 'conformance to specification' are inadequate. His approach was not dissimilar to that of Deming, and where it differed it is often complementary. This is not always true when we compare the ideas of Juran with those of Crosby. For example, Deming and Juran both argue against poster campaigns exhorting staff to achieve perfection. They both favour the use of SPC techniques, although Juran counselled against a 'tool-based approach'. However, Juran rejected both the main thrusts of Crosby's approach, 'zero defects' and 'conformance to specification'. He argued further that the law of diminishing returns applies to quality control and that 'quality is NOT free'. Juran has produced ten steps to quality improvement (Table 6.2).

Juran's approach was very much people-oriented. Thus, it placed a strong emphasis upon teamwork and a project-based approach.

The third principal guru is Crosby. His approach, as has already been suggested, diverges from that of the other two gurus, especially Juran. He is best known for originating the concept of 'zero defects' and for the provocative title

Table 6.2 Juran's ten points for quality improvement

1. Build awareness of need and opportunity for improvement

2. Set goals for improvement

3. Organize to reach the goals

4. Provide training

5. Carry out projects to solve problems

6. Report progress

7. Give recognition

8. Communicate results

9. Keep score

10. Maintain momentum by making annual improvement part of the regular process of the company

of one of his books, *Quality is Free* (Crosby, 1979). His approach may be summarized as prevention, rather than the traditional inspection and testing procedures. He equates prevention with perfection and this is often the prevalent view expressed today, particularly in the manufacturing arena, where Crosby's ideas seem most appropriate. He suggests a three-point 'quality vaccine', intended to prevent non-conformance, the *'bête noire'* of the Crosby approach. The vaccine consists of determination, education and implementation. He proposes four 'absolutes' of quality:

- Definition: conformance to requirements.
- System: prevention.
- Performance standard: zero defects.
- Measurement: the price of non-conformance.

He too offers 14 steps to improvement, targeted at management (Table 6.3).

At this point, the author must declare his hand and confess a greater discomfort with the ideas of Crosby than the other two experts, for the following reasons:

- The approach is process-, not people-, oriented.
- It emphasizes conformance to specification and elsewhere in this book it has been argued that this can be problematical when applied to software.
- It is difficult to accept that there are absolutes in quality: if there are, then they are likely to be more subtle than the four pillars of Crosby's case.

At the same time, the emphasis upon continual improvement is a very positive contribution.

The three approaches are compared in Table 6.4.

Table 6.3 Crosby's 14 steps to quality improvement

1. Make it clear that management is committed to quality.

2. Form quality improvement teams with each department represented.

3. Determine where current and potential problems lie.

4. Evaluate the cost of quality and explain its use as a tool.

5. Raise the quality awareness and concern of all employees.

6. Take actions to correct problems identified.

7. Establish a committee for the 'zero defects' programme.

8. Train supervisors to actively carry out their role in quality improvement.

9. Hold a 'zero defects day' for all employees to highlight the changes.

10. Encourage individuals to establish improvement goals.

11. Encourage communication with management about obstacles to improvement.

12. Recognize and appreciate participants.

13. Establish quality councils to aid communication.

14. Do it all over again to show it never ends.

6.2 Terms

The field of quality management has spawned its own nomenclature, and it is necessary to define three principal terms, often identified by their abbreviations, QMS, TQM and QIP.

6.2.1 QMS: Quality management system

The International Standards Organization (ISO) defines a quality management system as:

> 'The organisational structure, responsibilities, procedures, processes and resources for implementing quality management.'
>
> ISO8042 (ISO, 1986)

The QMS provides a structure to ensure that the process is carried out in a formal and systematic way. Within software development, the adoption of a structured methodology may often provide the basis for a QMS. However, the QMS goes further than a methodology in ensuring that responsibility is clearly established for the prescribed procedures and processes. If the methodology is intended to lay down which procedures should be carried out, the QMS should ensure that the procedures are actually carried out to the required standard.

Table 6.4 Comparison of principal ideas (after Oakland, 1989)

	Crosby	Deming	Juran
Definition	Conformance to requirements	Predictable degree of uniformity and dependability at low cost	Fitness for purpose
Senior management responsibility	Responsible for quality	Responsible for 94% of problems	Responsible for >80% of problems
Performance standard	Zero defects	Many scales: use SPC	Avoid campaigns to exhort perfection
General approach	Prevention	Reduce variability: continuous improvement	Emphasis on management of human aspects
Structure	14 steps	14 points	10 steps
SPC	Rejects statistically acceptable level of quality	SPC must be used	Recommends SPC, but cautions against tool-based approach
Basis for improvement	A process, not a programme	Continuous: eliminate goals	Project-based approach: set goals
Teamwork	Quality improvement teams: quality councils	Employee participation in decisions	Team/quality circle approach
Costs of quality	Quality is free!	No optimum, continuous improvement	Optimum, quality is NOT free
Purchasing	Supplier is extension of business	Use SPC through strong co-operation	Complex problems, use formal surveys
Vendor rating	Yes	No	Yes, but work with suppliers
Single sourcing of supply		Yes	No

At best, it provides a disciplined and systematic framework. At worst, it can become a bureaucratic nightmare. Some people experiencing this scenario have dismissed the QMS as a system for 'the better documentation of errors'. This misses out on a vital part of any QMS, the requirement for continual improvement to correct the errors documented. Thus, an essential part of any QMS is a feedback loop, possibly first suggested by Shewhart, but made famous by Deming as the 'plan–do–check–act' wheel (Figure 6.2).

A comprehensive QMS should include quality assurance and quality improvement functions. Many focus upon the quality assurance function at the expense of the quality improvement element.

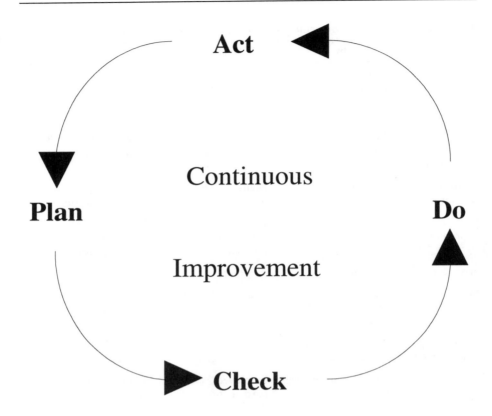

Figure 6.2 Plan–check–do–act cycle, after Shewhart and Deming.

6.2.2 TQM: *Total quality management*

TQM is described by Oakland (1989) as

> 'A method for ridding people's lives of wasted effort by involving every-body in the process of improving the effectiveness of work, so that results are achieved in less time.'

Kanji (1990) describes it thus:

> 'Quality is to satisfy customers' requirements continually.
> Total quality is to achieve quality at low cost.
> Total quality management is to obtain total quality by involving everyone's daily commitment.'

TQM is often misunderstood, perhaps because of the publicity that Crosby's 'zero defects' idea has attracted. In the mind of the author, total quality management refers to the involvement of all people and all processes within the quality management exercise. It does not imply, promise or guarantee perfection.

6.2.3 QIP: Quality improvement programme

This term, which appears to have originated with Crosby, refers to programmes designed to improve quality. Such a programme will be based on the introduction or refinement of a QMS. The strength of this term is its emphasis on improvement rather than monitoring the current state of affairs. The disadvantage is that quality improvement may be seen as a specific short-term programme, rather than an ongoing continual process.

6.3 Elements of a QMS

We shall focus on the requirements of a QMS. The ISO definition of a QMS lists five components:

- organizational structure
- responsibilities
- procedures
- processes
- resources.

The organizational structure must seek to assign responsibility for quality. Most wisdom on TQM stresses the importance of senior management commitment; quality must have a clear line of responsibility running right up to the top to an individual who is ultimately responsible for quality. However, the chair of responsibility must also be a line of two-way communication. Each employee must contribute 'total' quality. This means that:

- first-level supervision is vital to educate, encourage and supervise the 'workers' about quality;
- many ideas for quality improvement will come from the workers themselves and supervisors should encourage and facilitate this process.

The establishment of a 'quality culture' is so important that it is discussed separately (section 6.4). The procedures required by a QMS are summarized in Table 6.5. In order to improve quality, it is necessary to be able to measure and analyse current performance. The tools to achieve this are an essential part of the TQM approach, whichever brand (Deming, Juran or Crosby) you choose to follow.

6.3.1 Statistical process control

In order to monitor a process, it is necessary to define the inputs and outputs of the process. The nature of the process is the operation of transforming the inputs not the outputs. The scope of the process must be clearly defined to prevent ambiguity.

Statistical process control (SPC) methods allow us to calculate levels of nonconformity and also provide a strategy for the reduction of variability. Many SPC techniques are very simple. Ishikawa (1985) has suggested seven basic tools for the collection and analysis of quality data (see Table 6.6).

Table 6.5 Procedures in a QMS

Procedure	Purpose
Contract review	To establish order entry procedures to ensure the requirements are clearly established in writing and can be met.
Design control	To control and verify design of products or services.
Document control	To control production of all documentation to ensure use of one consistent up-to-date version of each document.
Purchasing	To ensure that all products and services purchased meet the organization's requirements.
Customer supplies	To ensure that all products and services supplied by the customer meet the organization's requirements.
Traceability	To identify and trace materials from raw material to finished product.
Process control	To ensure sufficient instructions for any process required.
Checking, inspecting, measuring and testing	To verify incoming products, 'in process', finished product and test equipment.
Non-conforming product or services	To document and segregate any non-conforming product or service.
Corrective action	To provide corrective action to prevent non-conformity.
Protection of quality	To prevent quality being eroded by incorrect handling, labelling or packing.
Training	To identify, carry out and document necessary training.
Statistical process control	To use SPC techniques to gather and analyse information on the state of control and capability.
Quality system audit	To ensure the QMS is being carried out according to documented procedures.

Process flow charting is a diagramming technique to illustrate the inputs and flow of a process. This technique is described in detail in Chapter 5 of Oakland (1989). An example is shown in Figure 6.3.

Tally charts are used in conjunction with histograms to collect and display data. Tally chart forms should be clear and easy to use.

Pareto analysis is designed to show what percentage of faults may be attributed to each cause. An example is shown in Figure 6.4.

Cause-and-effect analysis is represented by an Ishikawa or fishbone diagram which maps the inputs affecting a quality problem (Figure 6.5). Scatter diagrams

Table 6.6 SPC techniques

SPC technique	Purpose
Process flow charting	To show what is done
Tally charts	To show how often it is done
Histograms	To show overall variations
Pareto analysis	To highlight big problems
Cause-and-effect (Ishikawa) diagrams	To indicate causes
Scatter diagrams	To highlight relationships
Control charts	To show which variations to control

can highlight positive and negative correlation between parameters (Figure 6.6). Control charts are used to monitor how a parameter, e.g. the number of defectors, varies over time through the process.

Other more sophisticated techniques such as regression analysis may be employed but the additional effort required is rarely repaid in terms of a better understanding of the data.

One particular group of methods popular in TQM within manufacturing are the Taguchi methods, named after their Japanese originator. Taguchi methods are based around statistically planned experiments. Some of Taguchi's methods have been criticized recently in work by Box and Jones (1990). However, Taguchi methods remain popular within manufacturing organizations, where they form a vital part of TQM.

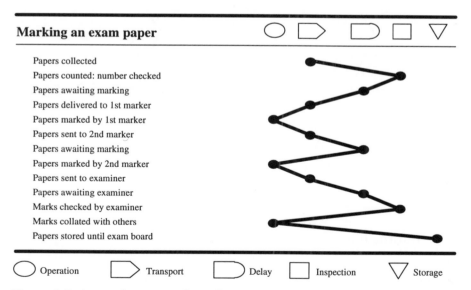

Figure 6.3 A sample process flow diagram.

Students failing to hand in assignments

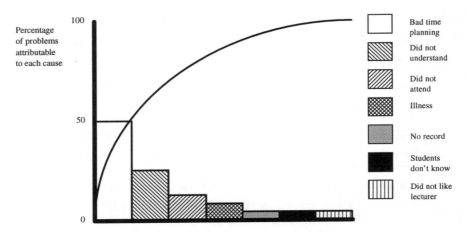

Figure 6.4 Sample Pareto analysis graph.

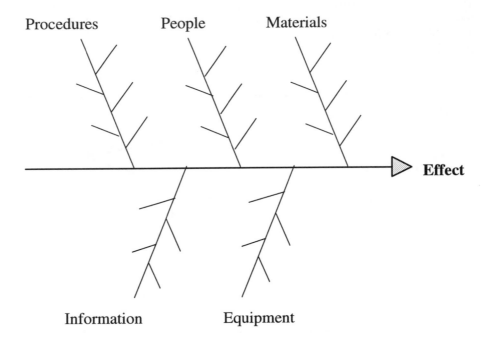

Figure 6.5 Cause-and-effect diagrams (after Ishikawa, 1985).

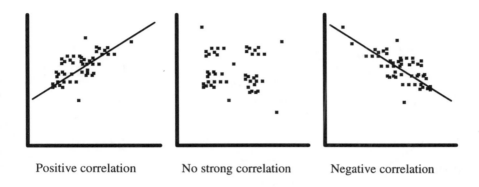

Positive correlation   No strong correlation   Negative correlation

Figure 6.6 Correlations may be seen on scatter diagrams.

Like many TQM ideas, SPC methods were first developed in the manufacturing area. They require some adaptation to other areas if they are to be put to good use. A discussion of some of the issues arising from the use of SPC techniques in 'non-product' applications is given by Bissell (1990).

Mini case study: Software quality control at Hitachi
Japanese quality control in the manufacturing arena has led the world. It is therefore worth considering how the Japanese view quality within software and the software development process. Yasuda (1989) gives an account of software quality assurance procedures within Hitachi Ltd. He argues that Japanese companies such as Hitachi have views and procedures that are a 'unique combination of Western software engineering expertise and Japanese quality control'.

Yasuda states that quality means the degree of user satisfaction. In order to achieve user satisfaction, it is necessary to have a high-quality product that conforms to a standard either national, in-house, or as defined by the customer within the specification. This is referred to as program quality. However, it is also necessary for the design specification to match the user requirements. This is known as design quality. Program requirements are expressed in terms of internal specifications, whilst user needs are expressed within the external specification, together forming the whole software specification. This view is summarized in Figure 6.7.

The Japanese established the first 'software factory' in 1969. The 'production' of software emphasizes the need for quality to be built-in throughout the development process, from inception to 'shipment'. They place a great emphasis upon continuity within the software development environment. Hitachi software developers treat the production of software like the production of soap powder, electronic hardware or any other product.

Within the factory process, quality is achieved by quality control. Quality control, in Japanese terms, is defined as

'A systematic method of economically providing products or services that meet the user's requirements.'

JIS (Japanese Industrial Standards)

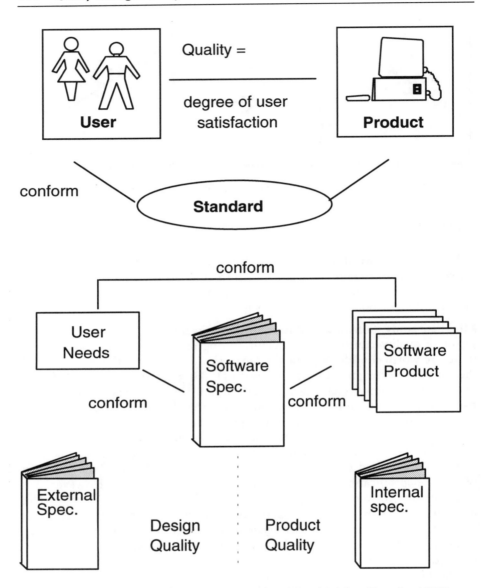

Figure 6.7 Software quality assurance within Hitachi (after Yasuda, 1989).

Quality control in Japan emphasizes the following aspects:

- Quality must be the highest priority, since this brings long-term benefits.
- All personnel must be involved.
- Quality control must be oriented towards the consumer.

Quality control is applied in practice in a number of ways arising from the factory production approach to software. Within this approach, the design and implementation functions are kept separate, with a further distinct process control function. As a separate entity, the inspection department has the right to reject any products not of the required standard. However, quality is not seen as the inspection department. Rather, all workers are perceived to contribute to software quality control and are encouraged to raise and discuss problems that arise. The software factory approach to quality control is illustrated in Figure 6.8.

The Hitachi process of quality assurance is built around three key stages:

1. Design review and document inspection.
2. Intermediate quality audit.
3. Product and system inspection.

1. Design review and documentation inspection

    Boehm (1981) has pointed out that the cost of removing errors from software rises dramatically as the development proceeds. This early review of the design is intended to eliminate as many errors as possible at as early a stage as possible, and therefore to minimize cost. Yasuda lists a number of features required for an effective design review including specified dates for the review, a comprehensive design review checklist, a record of previous errors, adequate preparation and thorough investigation of the review findings.

    Documents are viewed as products of the software development process alongside the code itself. Documents may be considered as internal or external. An example of external documentation would be the manuals for distribution to the users. The quality of documentation is closely linked with the quality of the software and particularly user satisfaction with the final product. However, during the software production process, they can be used both to pre-empt errors in the software, e.g. by spotting discrepancies between the specification and the user requirements, and to act as a check on completion of specific tasks within the software production process.

2. Intermediate quality audit

    The aim of this audit is threefold:

    (a) To forecast submerged errors, allowing an estimate of the number of errors to be detected.
    (b) To compare target and actual numbers of errors.
    (c) To analyse and investigate errors.

    The audit makes use of the computer to apply statistical methods for error prediction based upon a technique known as a quality probe. If the number of errors found or predicted exceeds the target set then the product is rejected. Further targets are set for the reduction of errors during the audit. If the errors cannot be eliminated at the required rate then the software is again rejected.

3. Product and system inspection

    This is the final inspection stage before delivery. The procedures employed are similar to those employed during the intermediate quality audit. Again use is made of computerized statistical methods.

    The first check is made to ensure that the product meets its specification both in terms of its internal specification and its external specification. This is the product inspection stage. If the product is successful in this aim, then it is passed for system inspection. This tests whether the software will meet the user's requirements within an identical environment to the user's own.

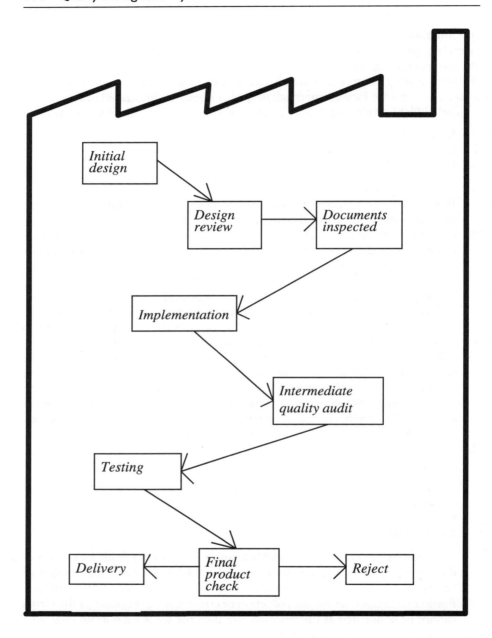

Figure 6.8 The 'software factory' approach to building in quality.

It is essential that system inspection and testing is carried out with applications and conditions as close to the user's actual environment as possible.

Simulation tools are employed together with constructed data sets in order to achieve this aim.

The Hitachi view of quality assurance is typically thorough. However, there is a discrepancy between its avowed aims and its procedures. The factory approach developed from manufacturing is targeted towards producing 'zero defect' software. The procedure is intended to ensure that the software will be error-free not just under development conditions but also within the user's own environment. This is all highly desirable, but it is still not enough to satisfy Yasuda's stated aims for software quality. Matching user needs is about more than making sure that the system performs correctly under real conditions. It is concerned with making sure that the system addresses the right question as well as ensuring that the system provides a good answer. This issue will be addressed when we consider the growth of Kaizen techniques in Japan in section 6.8.

6.4 The key to quality management: a human quality culture

There are two important parts to a QMS. There are the tools and procedures, discussed above, and then there are the people. The procedures, tools and techniques are only there to enable the people to achieve a quality result.

Staff acceptance is therefore vital. This will not happen by itself. The management of change is critical to the success of the process. The danger is that the introduction of a QMS by management will be seen as the imposition of new working practices. The system can only work if staff perceive the benefits to themselves. These include the potential for:

- greater job satisfaction
- less time spent on pointless activity
- greater pride in work
- more group participation
- more staff input into the way they do their job.

However, Oakland points out that staff will not be well motivated towards a quality programme in the absence of top management commitment and action, organizational quality climate and a team approach to quality problems. It is particularly important that communication is a two-way process. For staff to be motivated, they must feel 'involved' and that their contribution and ideas will make a difference.

One of the principal means of getting staff involved is through the use of quality circles (Figure 6.9). A quality circle is a group of workers who are asked, not told, to join. They will generally have a trained leader, who might be their foreman or line manager. There should be an overall supervisor to co-ordinate the whole quality circle programme throughout an organization. Finally, management must be committed to the programme. Whilst they retain the right and obligation to manage, they must not reject recommendations without good reason or they will strangle the idea at birth.

Quality circles are generally made up of between three and 15 people. Larger than this and the group becomes fragmented, with some members opting out. The author strongly recommends a group size in single figures to obtain maximum benefit. They are better if held at a site away from the work area. Optimum frequency of meeting appears to vary from one to three weeks, depending upon the problems under consideration.

The circle should decide for itself which problem to consider, although management usually retains the right of a polite veto. The circle may call in outside experts in the role of consultants, but the decision-making and problem-solving roles must remain within the circle. Quality circles will not simply happen. Training is a vital ingredient in the success of a quality circle. The leader needs to be trained in encouraging people to contribute, in structuring a discussion and ensuring that the group is not dominated by one or two characters. The team members need training in basic quality techniques so that they know how problems may be solved.

An alternative, but complementary, approach to organizing for quality is the quality improvement team (QIT), an idea apparently originating with Crosby, to tackle a specific problem. It brings together a blend of knowledge, skills and experience in a multidisciplinary approach. The optimum size of a QIT is typically five to ten people. The life of a QIT is likely to be limited, as they come into being to address a specific problem. It is important to create a stimulating environment for discussion and to encourage people to think creatively. It is likely that obvious solutions have already been tried and discarded before the QIT comes into being. It is therefore probable that a genuine solution will arise from a piece of 'lateral thinking'. Each member has been invited to join the team because of their expertise. What appears to be a fanciful thought may in fact be the start of a solution.

In a recent discussion on problem-solving strategies, in which the author was involved, it was pointed out that many tricky problems were difficult to solve because to reach the solution or goal state, it was necessary to take a first step in what was apparently the wrong direction. This can make team leadership very tricky. The division between 'lateral thinking' and irrelevance can be difficult to spot. It can also prove difficult to build up a team identity when its existence is ephemeral and success will inevitably lead to the group disbanding.

As with other techniques, QITs are offered as another tool. On their own, they will not cause a revolution but they can make a useful contribution to an overall programme. They should be seen as complementary to quality circles rather than conflicting (Table 6.7).

Table 6.7 A comparative summary of quality circles and quality improvement teams

Property	Quality improvement team	Quality circle
Purpose	To bring together specific expertise to solve a particular problem	To allow workers the chance to contribute ideas to solve problems occurring
Membership	Five to ten experts from a range of disciplines	Up to 15 'front-line' workers
Led by	Person most concerned with task success	Foreman/line manager
Lifetime	Limited	Ongoing
Training needs	Need to work as group	Basic quality methods

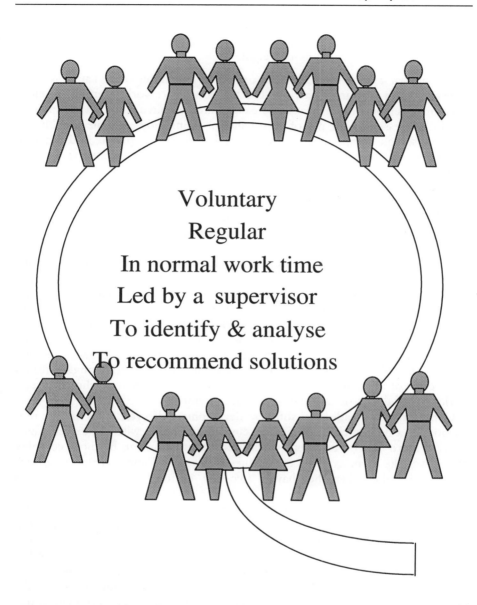

Voluntary
Regular
In normal work time
Led by a supervisor
To identify & analyse
To recommend solutions

Figure 6.9 A schematic of a quality circle.

Juran is a strong advocate of team working practices as a way of motivating people towards quality. The advantages cited by Oakland (1989) for team working include:

- A greater variety of problems may be tackled.
- A greater variety of skills, knowledge and expertise is available.
- The approach is more satisfying and builds team morale.

- Cross-departmental problems can be dealt with more easily.
- Recommendations carry more weight.

The author agrees with all these comments but notes some cautions from observing team working in action. The teams need to work internally in close proximity. Personality clashes can be exaggerated within a confined group. This may be addressed by the use of personality profiling. Some people say this can help to assemble compatible groups, others disagree. Some people find adapting to the new way of working very difficult and may be more isolated as a consequence. Tensions can arise between different groups because of different priorities. Once again, the staff need to be convinced of the benefits, and changes must be introduced by co-operation rather than imposition. The pros and cons of team working are illustrated in Figure 6.10.

One of the biggest problems that can arise in any organization whether team-based or not, is a lack of appreciation of the interdependence of each contribution. For example, if an organization is organized into business analysis and software implementation groups, then it is often useful for the groups to consult each other; for instance, the business group needs to know that any contracts obtained are feasible to be implemented. This leads to the concept of 'internal' and external customers. Since Juran's work on fitness for purpose, quality has been recognized as meeting customer needs, which refers to the needs of the external customer who is footing the bill. However, there is a growing perception of the value of the concept of the 'internal' customer, sometimes referred to in terms of a 'quality chain'. An internal customer is anyone who receives a service or product from another group or individual.

Consider a very traditional software development lifecycle. This may be represented as a quality chain of internal customers, ending with the external customer (Figure 6.11). However, sometimes the situation can be more complex still. If we take as an example the business analysis and implementation groups mentioned earlier, then they have a two-way 'customer/supplier' relationship (Figure 6.12).

In managing any situation, a large factor in the success is not connected with the procedures employed, but with the day-to-day running of the organization. It has been one of the criticisms of TQM that it focuses upon procedures and although procedures can help and facilitate, they can also obstruct and hinder. What they cannot do is to guarantee success. This must ultimately depend upon the performance of the people concerned, who may or may not choose to take advantage of the help provided by systems or procedures. The problem in trying to analyse the factors at work is that they are often difficult to generalize and strongly influenced by personalities and specific environments. We shall, therefore, consider the environment first and then take two stereotypical personality types which form the extremes of a spectrum.

6.4.1 Top down or bottom up?

A tension exists in any organization where a quality culture is being established. The tension exists between a force acting from the top down and a force

Staff morale

time

Staff morale should increase

Individuals may find it hard to fit in

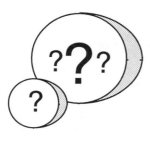

The size and scope of problems
to be tackled should increase

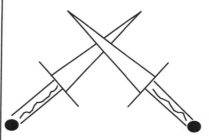

Different objectives may lead to
conflict between teams

The recommendations of a group
carry more weight than those from
an individual

Personality clashes may be
exacerbated within a team

Figure 6.10 The pros and cons of team working.

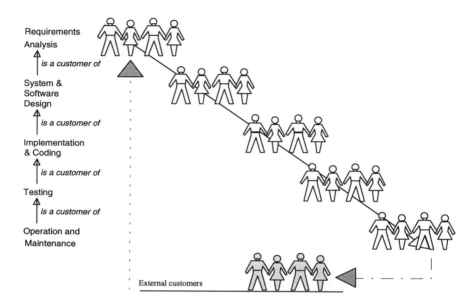

Figure 6.11 Software development as a quality chain.

coming up from the bottom. The top-down force is the 'desire to manage'. Management is absolutely necessary; it is not possible to achieve quality by committee. Without firm management, there will be no policy, no strategy, no consistency in decision-making, and chaos will ensue.

However, there is a clear need to feed ideas up the organization. A quality culture will actually increase the flow of ideas from the work force. Strong management can verge on autocracy. What one person might regard as a well-organized stable environment may in fact be stagnant rather than stable. People with ideas

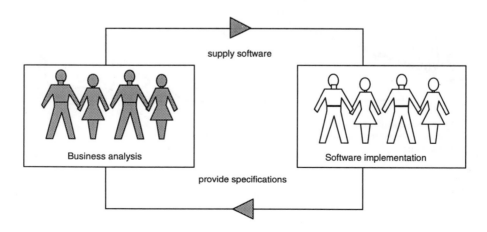

Figure 6.12 Customer/supplier relationships should be two-way.

which conflict with those of management can be seen as trouble makers. A perception that the last person to have an idea was sacked for it will not encourage others to come forward. There are no clear rules on this. Ask a well-regarded manager the principles he or she uses and you may well be quoted a set of ideas and statements. Ask how he or she does the job and you will probably hear phrases such as 'by experience' or 'one instinctively knows'. Intuition ultimately plays a large part in managing people. This is unhelpful when trying to identify best practice. It is even less helpful when a badly regarded manager says the same thing!

A balance between structure, direction and policy on the one hand and innovation, lateral thinking and creativity on the other is required. Views of quality which emphasize conformance in components can too easily lead to an emphasis on conformance when dealing with staff. There is a time for doing things 'by the book' and a time for not. One of the best definitions of an expert is someone who knows when the rule book can be safely discounted.

6.4.2 Managing people: the first stereotype

The first stereotypical character we shall consider is the cynic. They have been there, seen it, done it and heard it all before. They appear to have been at Deming's inaugural lecture in Japan and they know that it won't work. This sort of person can be very destructive in many situations. However, they can also offer much:

● They are usually experienced staff with a wealth of experiential knowledge which could be usefully exploited.

● The role of devil's advocate can be an extremely useful one, particularly in the situation where outside consultants have been employed.

● They are likely to become strong advocates of good practice if they can be convinced. How often have you heard, 'Well, of course, I always thought ...' shortly after a U-turn of amazing proportions?

One strategy is to try to carve out a role for such a person which exploits their strengths of experience and scepticism whilst trying to insulate many other younger impressionable staff from their negative attitude. Many such people will thrive on being given such a role.

6.4.3 The second stereotype: the enthusiast

Enthusiasm is a valuable commodity but it can cause as many headaches as it solves. Enthusiasm tends to be short-lived. People who become enthusiastic tend to get bored and move onto the next idea that comes along. Enthusiasm can also lead people to be uncritical and not to see potential pitfalls until it is too late. It might seem an attractive proposition to put our enthusiast and cynic together, as the best of both would be almost ideal. However, such a combination is likely to be destructive before it ever bears fruit. Rather than put the two together it is often more useful to allow their influences on a group of people to balance each other out. If this can be achieved without bringing the two bodies together in an explosive combination, then the net effect may be beneficial.

The role of the enthusiast should be to feed other people with ideas and enthusiasm. The group being fed will filter out the more zany ideas at the start. However, they will hopefully adopt and develop some of the ideas at least. These embryonic ideas may then be exposed to the sceptical gaze of our cynic, under which more will wither and perish. The ideas remaining are likely to be both useful and sustaining. It is rare though very valuable to find a creative enthusiast with the potential to develop their ideas.

Fortunately, perhaps, most people fall between our two stereotypical images. However, the balance between nurturing creativity and maintaining structure can be tricky. Ensuring that everyone has a role to play in a work force aiming at quality is a challenge and reinforces the views of all three gurus, that ultimately the buck stops with senior management.

6.5 Quality in software: the current situation

Many software developers appear to be quite content with the current state of the quality of software. They are resistant to new ideas, which are seen as a threat to their integrity and professionalism. They argue that quality management techniques are 'just another big idea' (Figure 6.13). Further, they argue that current practice based upon software engineering principles should be quite adequate and that new ideas are unlikely to help.

Figure 6.13 Quality management ... just this year's big idea?

It is therefore worth considering the state of quality practice in the UK and to compare two surveys from 1988 and 1993, carried out by Price Waterhouse (Price Waterhouse/DTI) and the University of Sunderland (Davis *et al.*) respectively.

In the 1988 Price Waterhouse survey, companies were asked, 'Do you carry out the following activities?' The responses were classified into one of three groups:

(1) Yes: fully, with external monitoring.
(2) Yes: normally, but with no monitoring.
(3) No: not at all.

The results of the survey are shown in Figures 6.14 and 6.15.

The results are grouped under the following headings: quality assurance, quality management, quality control and testing. The procedures identified under quality control and testing were planning, team meetings, design reviews, test documentation, error logging, change control, configuration management, document control, and system and acceptance testing.

The quality assurance function was not fully implemented and monitored in any of the firms surveyed. Over half had no QMS written, and since none had a QA function, we may assume that those who had written their own QMS were not monitoring its effectiveness.

Good documentation is often cited as a necessity for good software development practice and yet this is not reflected in practice. Test documents were rarely fully monitored, and controls on changes and documentation were lacking in a number of cases. One of the biggest gripes of customers of IT is that suppliers assume that they know what's best for users. The results given here for testing activity suggest that old attitudes of 'give the customer what's good for them' rather than 'what they want' are still prevalent. Although all the firms surveyed carried out full system testing, less than half carried out thorough acceptance testing. In other words, companies tested to see if the system worked but not to see if it met user requirements adequately.

The more recent study undertaken by Davis *et al.* (1993) does not suggest that matters have improved dramatically. From a postal questionnaire survey of 500 companies, a sample of 151 respondents was obtained (20% response rate). Eighty-nine respondents (59%) stated that they did use a quality assurance procedure, and 62 (41%) stated that they did not. The results are shown in Figure 6.16.

The 89 respondents that used a quality assurance procedure were further broken down into whether their quality management systems were subject to external scrutiny by a first, second or third party. Some respondents indicated multiple levels of certification. They are classified in Figure 6.17 according to the most rigorous level employed.

The results do not suggest grounds for complacency and challenge the assumption that software engineering ensures that basic engineering principles are adhered to within software development. The results show that without a systematic framework, quality management becomes inconsistent. The lack of a QA function suggests that it is not only necessary to implement a QMS, but to monitor its performance effectively. This reinforces the need for external standards for QMSs.

Survey of Existing Quality Management (1)
Quality Assurance & Testing

Data: Price-Waterhouse (1988)

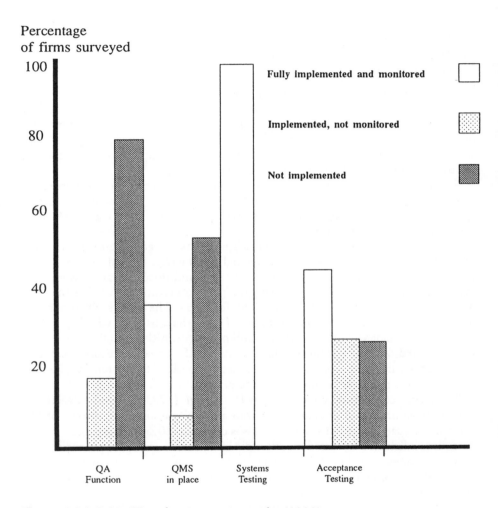

Figure 6.14 Price Waterhouse survey results (1988).

The two surveys taken together suggest that little progress has been made between 1988 and 1993, in spite of a number of UK Government initiatives to promote quality assurance within software.

Overall, two problems emerge. The first is that although procedures and techniques exist to ensure that software meets the quality requirement to conform to its specification, the implementation and monitoring of those procedures is patchy at best. The second problem is even more serious and this concerns the

Survey of Existing Quality Management (2)
Quality Control activities

Data: Price-Waterhouse (1988)

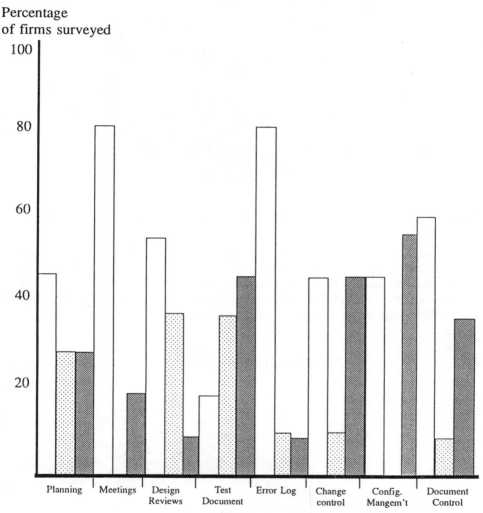

Figure 6.15 Price Waterhouse survey results (1988).

quality requirement of 'fitness for purpose'. Users of IT are claiming that software developers are still ignoring their views and there is little evidence to refute the charge. We shall consider this further in the next section.

6.6 The problem of user requirements

There always seems to be a crisis in software. People have talked about a market for this year's solution to the problem. However, it is possible to identify a

Respondents with QA function

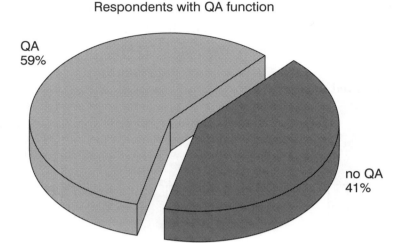

Figure 6.16 Percentage of respondents with a quality assurance procedure.

time when the complexity of software began to outstrip the design methods available and errors began to rise unacceptably. This would appear to be a turning point in the history of software development and the result was the rise of software engineering detailed in the previous chapter. The crisis arose because the problem became unacceptable to the customer.

Accreditation of QA function

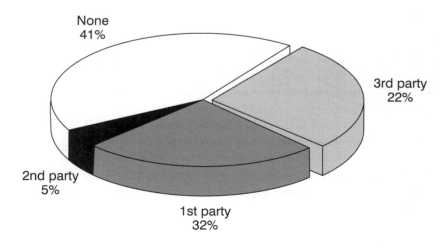

Figure 6.17 Extent of external accreditation of quality assurance procedures.

It is arguable that a similar crisis point has now been reached. Customers are once again saying that a problem has reached unacceptable proportions and are becoming reluctant to sign more cheques. The problem this time is not so much that the system doesn't work, but rather that it doesn't do the required job. In other words, in Juran's terminology, it is not fit for the intended purpose.

Large IT customers have invested heavily in the technology and are starting to ask questions about a return on their investment. The days of vast savings through replacing manual repetitive tasks are gone and the return on investment is now projected in terms of 'competitive edge' and other more nebulous concepts. The customer has become more discerning and more sceptical and wants a better quality product. This new software crisis may be compared with the original crisis in the 1960s (Table 6.8).

Table 6.8 Software crises from the 1960s to the 1990s

	Software in the 1960s	Software in the 1990s
The problem	Complexity outstrips design technology	User requirements outstrip delivered quality
The solution	Structured methods leading to tools and methodologies	Quality management? Business analysis tools? Rapid prototyping?

Many solutions have been proposed, but it is too early to say at present which of the present proposed solutions, if any, will prove helpful in solving the current 'crisis'.

The first difficulty in trying to analyse the problem is that it is perceived differently by the user and developer camps. Reasons given by the developers include:

- users don't know what they want
- users can't express what they need
- what users want is not feasible
- requirements change too fast to be met.

The user camp, on the other hand, sees things differently. They point to the money spent on IT, the claims of the salesmen, and the adverse attitude of many developers. It seems self-evident to the author that the first requirement is actually to try to get agreement on the definition of the problem and to break down adversarial attitudes. The author's own work through LOQUM (Gillies, 1992, 1993) tackles the problem of adversarial attitudes and goes some way in trying to find common ground.

Developers of tools and methods have tried to provide graphical representations to provide a common language, e.g. entity-relationship diagrams, data flow diagrams, process hierarchy diagrams. To judge their success, take an entity-relationship diagram to a real IT novice and ask them what's going on. The author's experience is that such techniques have a limited role to play in aiding communication, although it is certainly easier to train a novice to understand these diagrams than it is to train them to understand C source code or even high-level pseudo-code.

Rapid prototyping has also been suggested and used with some success, as detailed in Gilb (1988) and mentioned earlier. The problem with rapid prototyping is when to stop. Once the user sees that things can be altered, there is always the temptation to tweak one more thing and the person who calls a halt at any stage is seen as an ogre.

In practice, it may be argued that all the available techniques have been shown not to be generally applicable or effective. In the end, any process-based technique will founder on the twin rocks of a lack of understanding of the problem by all parties and the often rapid rate of change in the requirements. In other words, it is necessary not only to provide tools for the job, but also to increase motivation to achieve the goal. An analogy might be that an Englishman and a Frenchman, neither of whom speaks the other's language, are more likely to reach an understanding than two equipped with a dictionary who are not motivated to use them. One would expect the ones who want to communicate to achieve their goal through a combination of drawing, sign language and other media.

Quality management correctly employed offers the best hope for improving software quality because it addresses attitudes as well as processes. If a QMS is restricted to processes and does not address staff attitudes, then it will not achieve its stated goal.

6.7 A QMS for software

Many of the principles of quality management can be usefully applied to software development, provided the particular features of software quality problems are borne in mind. The problems of software are not unique. User requirements are often highlighted as the worst problem area. Juran highlighted this area in manufacturing 40 years ago. The kitchen company case study in Chapter 9 indicates that problems can still arise in discerning user requirements even in apparently simple contexts. Software developers also claim to have particular problems arising from complexity. Certainly, complexity requires careful management in all contexts, but software cannot claim a monopoly here. Thus the quality problems of software development represent a particular blend of problems, rather than something completely different. Any proposed QMS should reflect this.

It is suggested that there are four principal aspects to a QMS for software development:

1. Development procedures. This includes the use of design and development methodologies and tools, testing and associated staff training.
2. Quality control. This includes many activities for the monitoring of quality during development, e.g. planning, progress meetings, user sign-off, configuration management, change control, documentation control, design reviews, code walk-throughs, error reporting, system testing and acceptance testing.
3. Quality improvement. This includes all activities aimed at establishing a human quality culture amongst the staff, such as quality improvement teams, quality circles and so on.
4. Quality assurance. Where a quality system is in place, QA becomes the monitoring of the system itself to ensure that it is being carried out correctly.

Many people have argued that these processes are already in place in many organizations. The aim of a QMS is to ensure that they are carried out systematically and comprehensively. The DTI 1988 survey reinforces the need for this systematization process.

The benefits of such a quality scheme, cited by Price Waterhouse (1988) in their DTI report, are considered under five headings: cost, timeliness, reliability, functionality and maintainability.

1.   Cost
     Standardization itself may reduce costs through uniformity and better project planning. This should lead to better monitoring and the fixing of errors earlier in development: Boehm (1981) has shown costs are lower at the start of the project. If the system is working correctly, the effort required in QA and testing should be reduced. These costs must be balanced against cost of implementation and certification.

2.   Timeliness
     In principle, a quality system should reduce the number of overruns in terms of time and budget. Better records should also enable better future estimates of time taken to complete a project. However, in practice, many overruns cannot be foreseen, and the Price Waterhouse survey did not detect a significant reduction in overruns where a quality system was in place.

3.   Reliability
     A quality system should reduce the number of faults delivered to users through a combination of better project control, development and testing.

4.   Functionality
     In the DTI/Price Waterhouse (1988) survey, the most commonly reported fault was that it did not meet their requirements, i.e., it failed in terms of fitness for purpose. The use of a certified quality system ensures that design reviews and acceptance testing are in place. It remains to be seen whether such processes are sufficient to ensure a high degree of fitness for purpose.

5.   Maintainability
     A quality system addresses this issue in two ways:

     ● by reducing the need for change
     ● by facilitating such change as is necessary.

A quality system is designed to effectively move maintenance to earlier in the lifecycle. This will lead to a reduction in both time and effort.

All these benefits must be shown to happen in practice. Once quantified in financial terms, the benefits must be weighed against the cost, which may be considered in two stages. First, there is the cost of introducing a quality management system. Once established, there are specific costs associated with certification.

In 1988, the cost of introducing a QMS to a typical supplier was estimated at £230,000 a year. In addition, set-up costs were estimated at £120,000. This estimate, broken down in Table 6.9, is for a company with 50–100 employees and a turnover of £3million.

The quality management scheme that follows is considered under the four headings mentioned at the start of this section: development procedures, quality control, quality improvement and quality assurance.

Table 6.9 The cost of implementing a QMS (see text for details)

Item	Initial costs	Annual costs
Setup		
Quality manual	£90,000	
Training	£30,000	
Subtotal	£120,000	
Maintenance of above		£18,000
Operating		
QA		£60,000
QC		£150,000
Total costs	£120,000	£228,000
Percentage of turnover		8% of £3 million turnover

6.7.1 Development procedures

The development procedures phase is concerned with the selection of tools and methods to support the development of the software. The choices made here will influence the rest of the project, as the methodology plays a dominant role in software development, forming the foundation on which the QMS is built.

The first consideration must be any contractual obligation. Many UK Government contracts will specify SSADM as the analysis and design methodology. The US Department of Defense specifies that all mission-critical software must be developed using the procedures contained within STD 2167A (see next chapter for details). In such a situation, the choice of methodology is already made. If options are available, then the factors to consider include previous experience, the nature of the problem and the customer's own experience. Experience is important as any methodology takes time to learn and, particularly, time to exploit to its maximum advantage. A good reason, therefore, is needed for a change in methodology.

Once a methodology is selected, then a decision must be made on the degree of support provided by automated tools. Once again, there is a learning time before tools can be fully exploited.

Deciding upon the decision methods and tools to be employed is critically affected by experience. Once the decision is made, it is vital that sufficient expertise is available in all areas to make effective use of the tools and methods and to ensure a satisfactory result. Two factors affect the availability of expertise. The first is distribution. The company may possess enough expertise globally but find that it is concentrated in a few areas, leaving weak links in the chain. It is important to ensure that the experts and their knowledge are evenly distributed.

The second is the overall level of expertise. It is likely that there will still be gaps in expertise even after optimum distribution. These must be plugged by the provision of adequate training. However, a raw recruit coming off a training course with his or her head full of theoretical knowledge about a methodology is not an 'expert', but merely an informed novice, and needs to be reckoned as such.

The final step in this phase is to ensure that the decisions made regarding methodology do not conflict with other parts of the quality plan, i.e. QC, QIP and QA. In particular, it is necessary to ensure that the phases of the methodology facilitate the requirements of the quality control plan in terms of reviews and documents. This in turn should ensure that all the resources required by the QA function are also available.

6.7.2 Quality control

The following quality control procedures are based upon a plan suggested by Taylor (1989). The full plan is given in the book cited at the end of the chapter. It also highlights the differences between quality management for software development and other areas such as manufacturing, service industry, and so on. The procedures are defined under the headings of 'general' (Table 6.10) and 'requirements' (Table 6.11).

Table 6.10 General procedures for software quality control system (after Taylor, 1989)

General procedures	Explanation
Scope	This defines the requirements of the company for software design and development work within the project.
Application	Sets out when the procedure is to be applied.
Definitions	Sets out definitions used within the project.
Referenced documents	Details all documents referenced in the main plan.

6.7.3 Quality improvement

Much of what has gone before has been concerned with eliminating errors from the development process. As should be clear by now, the author believes that Juran's 'fitness for purpose' view is just as important. It has also been argued that the processes themselves will only work well within a 'quality culture'. This phase is concerned with trying to establish a quality culture.

The author suggests four activities which can make a positive contribution to the quality culture: training in quality methods, quality circles, quality improvement teams and LOQUM. Their respective roles are shown in Table 6.12.

The use of quality circles and improvement teams has been discussed earlier. The role of training is, however, vital to the success of the whole exercise. Training should be tailored according to the level of organization. A sample quality training program is suggested in Table 6.13.

The timescales suggested reflect the reality that staff time is limited and expensive. The further up the organization you go, the more expensive and more limited it becomes. The line managers are seen as the linchpins of the whole scheme and therefore are allocated the most training time.

A number of features should be noted about this scheme:

- Everyone from MD to apprentice gets some training.
- Each group has different needs and aspirations and this is reflected in the programme.

Table 6.11 Requirement procedures for software quality control system
(after Taylor, 1989)

Requirement procedures	Explanation
Review of operational requirements	An operational requirements specification is prepared. This will cover size, scope, multifunctionality, operational functions, implementation details, modularity and the tools, techniques and methods used.
Design and development planning	A phased project management plan is prepared to cover the work and resources required. A quality control plan will also be developed. Plans will be drawn up for the acquisition of all resources, together with methods to identify, record and correct non-conformances.
Organization	The management structure for the project will be identified and recorded. Responsibility will be clearly identified for all aspects of quality control and quality assurance. A representative will be appointed to resolve quality matters to the satisfaction of the customer.
Training	Training will be provided for all new personnel working on the project in the matters of software development and quality assurance techniques. It will be ensured that all personnel have the required academic expertise and level of knowledge to fulfil their role.
Quality programme	A quality programme will be prepared and documented. The programme document will include graphical descriptions of the work to be carried out, testing plans, documentation of the occurrences of non-conformance together with corrective action and definitions of the points at which each component can undergo formal qualification testing.
Management visibility and control	Methods and tools will be employed which positively encourage quality, particularly a formal ISD development methodology.
Design and development reviews	Reviews will be planned at the end of each development phase. The review should be carried out by independent staff, and open to scrutiny by the customer or an external body. Review documentation will include objectives, personnel functions, scope, provision for analysis and recommendations and procedures for verification of corrective actions.

Table 6.11 Continued

Requirement procedures	Explanation
Documentation	Documentation shall include the OR specification, planning and design documentation, the coded program and QA documentation giving the results of the QA processes.
Support tools, techniques and methods	The tools and methods used should be identified, documented and validated.
Non-conformity, prevention and corrective action	Non-conformities should be eliminated as far as possible through the use of reviews and, where necessary, re-reviews at each stage.
Configuration control	Procedures should be drawn up to identify modules or programs, keep master versions secure, provide validated copies, obtain approval for modifications, ensure modifications are integrated, software media is properly marked, handled, and that non-conforming software is kept rigorously separated.
Subcontractor control	Procedures should be set up to ensure the quality of all subcontractor procedures, tools, methods and products and to delineate responsibility for the above.
Customer-supplied items control	Procedures should be set up to ensure the acceptance, storage and maintenance of all items supplied by the customer.
Change control management	Procedures for the control of change should be prepared, established, implemented and maintained.
Testing and formal qualification	Testability of the requirements should be established. Reviews of criteria, test procedures and documentation should be established. Any tools or data used in testing must be identified and verified.
Preparation for software delivery	Procedures must be established for the delivery of the software, and conformance to the original requirements established.
Software embedding and hardware integration	Compatibility of software and hardware must be established.
Access, accommodation and assistance	Facilities should be provided to allow the customer to check that all requirements have been discharged.

- At the top end, the emphasis is on strategic and financial considerations.
- Motivation is vital, especially at the operational level.

Table 6.12 Activities designed to help establish a quality culture

Activity	Intended role in establishing a quality culture
Quality training	Provide all levels of organization with appropriate knowledge with respect to quality.
Quality circles	To provide a forum to discuss problems. To build up a team approach and group culture.
Quality improvement teams	To bring together specific expertise to tackle particular problems.
LOQUM	To provide a framework to boost communication between users and developers.

Table 6.13 Training needs for a quality culture

Level	Duration	Topics to be covered	Emphasis
Board level	0.5 days	Cost of bad quality Strategic element Need for leadership Effect upon competitive edge Summary of methods Benefits	Financial and strategic
Senior managers	1 day	Cost of bad quality Strategic element Need for leadership Effect upon competitive edge Description of methods Impact upon staff Benefits	Financial Impact upon management and staff
Line managers	2 days	Cost of bad quality Description of methods Managing for quality Managing change Motivating staff Benefits	How to do your job How to manage others within a quality culture
Workers	1 day	Examples of bad quality Discussion of problems Quality methods New culture Team working Benefits to you	How quality will help you Reassurance Motivation

Techniques such as LOQUM (Gillies, 1992, 1993) have been found by the author to be extremely beneficial in providing a framework to allow communication between users and developers. Whilst it will not help define user needs directly, it helps establish the basic criteria which the users will apply. It also helps the users understand some of the constraints under which the system developers are operating. As such it promotes trust and understanding and is highly recommended as part of a programme to establish a quality culture, especially where users and developers are found in the same organization.

6.7.4 Quality assurance

Quality assurance is not a phase of the quality plan, it is an ongoing process to ensure that the plan is being carried out according to the procedures laid down. It should also have a role in monitoring the effectiveness of procedures intended to establish a quality culture.

The role of quality assurance is to ensure that the quality of the procedures and processes results in a product that fully meets the users' requirements. As such it is suggested that the QA function be carried out by an independent group of people whose function is solely to monitor the implementation of the quality plan, under the first three headings. The group will require as far as possible a cross-section of both management and technical expertise. It should also include representatives of different levels of the company.

6.8 Quality assurance or quality improvement?

The historical origins of quality management in the work of Deming, Juran and others clearly demonstrate the crucial role of quality improvement. It is not enough to monitor current levels of quality or to inspect your product and eliminate those failing to meet a specification.

The process improvement cycle is crucial to any quality initiative, since it is from reducing waste and improving quality that most economic benefit is derived. One manifestation of quality improvement is the Japanese concept of Kaizen. In some ways, Kaizen is just another successor to TQM in those circles where TQM is now considered passé, but it has something to offer because of its emphasis upon improvement as well as inspection.

6.8.1 Kaizen

Quality assurance is defined by the JIS as

> 'A manufacturer's systematic activities intended to ensure that quality fully meets consumer needs.'
>
> JIS (Japanese Industrial Standards)

This may be compared with the US IEEE/ANSI definition which emphasizes conformity to specification and replaces 'full satisfaction' with 'adequate confidence':

'A planned and systematic pattern of all activities to provide adequate confidence that the item or product conforms to established technical requirements.'

(IEEE/ANSI)

This customer-centred view as opposed to a process-centred view is at the heart of Kaizen. To many engineers (software or otherwise), Kaizen may seem more like a mystic religion than an approach to quality. Huda and Preston (1992) describe it thus:

'Kaizen is a holistic approach to problem solving and its difference lies in being people-centred rather than system-centred. It recognizes the overriding importance of the human element and gives a new perspective to problem solving by minimizing conflict and of eliminating blame, so that people work together instead of individually towards goals.'

Imai (1986) represented Kaizen as an overarching umbrella (Figure 6.18). Because Kaizen is a philosophy rather than a particular set of methods, it is difficult to compare it with other approaches. Indeed, many of the techniques used are common to other approaches. What marks Kaizen out is its emphasis on small group co-operative working and the emphasis upon worker suggestions, which may be seen in the following mini case study from Fujitsu in Japan, reported by Itakura and Takei (1994).

Mini case study: Kaizen at Fujitsu
Small group activity began at Fujitsu in 1966. It was part of a company-wide quality improvement campaign led by the company president. The campaign became known as the High Reliability Campaign.

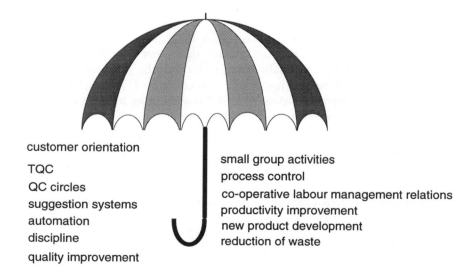

customer orientation

TQC

QC circles

suggestion systems

automation

discipline

quality improvement

small group activities

process control

co-operative labour management relations

productivity improvement

new product development

reduction of waste

Figure 6.18 The Kaizen umbrella (after Imai, 1986).

By 1992, the campaign encompassed over 40,000 employees in 4,596 small groups, with an average group size of 8.2. The average number of suggestions per person across the whole company is 4.5. However, in systems development, the figure is a much lower 0.2.

Each group has the following aims:

- to improve reliability of company products
- to make job processes more accurate, quicker, more effective and safer, and
- to develop, improve and standardize technology and processes that assist in the first two aims.

Each group goes through six stages:

1. Theme setup.
2. Evaluation scale setup.
3. Study of present values.
4. Improvement target setup.
5. Group meetings and daily efforts to achieve targets.
6. Suggestions for achieving the goal.

Suggestions are reported to the management.

A group of six software engineers met to improve management within their area, responsible for developing a production system within an ironworks. The group first met in February 1993, when the project had reached the system design stage.

The group was faced with a number of problems at their first meeting:

- The system must be completed within a short time scale, by October 1993.
- Close co-operation would be needed with machine-tool manufacturers, none of whom Fujitsu had worked with in the past.
- The customer does not understand the needs of system development.
- Only the leader is experienced.

The first meeting set out three goals:

1. Break down the units of management to provide greater control.
2. Cut down management workload through design of tools.
3. Standardize procedures to allow knowledge transfer to other projects.

Six meetings were held in total during the period. At the second meeting, the activity plan was drawn up:

Theme	Breakdown of management procedures to improve accuracy
Members	6
Period	February 1993 to November 1993
Evaluation scale	Reduce management work time for the project Current value 250 hrs/month
Target	Reduce value to 150 hrs/month

At the third meeting, a tool was established in Lotus 1-2-3 to record progress information and simplify report generation.

At the fourth meeting the tools was reviewed and problems highlighted in the review eliminated.

At the fifth meeting, a report was prepared for the in-house conference.

At the sixth meeting, some further enhancements were added to the tool.

The final reduction in management workload of 30% was achieved, short of the 40% target set, but a substantial improvement (Figure 6.19).

Further details of this case study may be found in Itakura and Takei (1994).

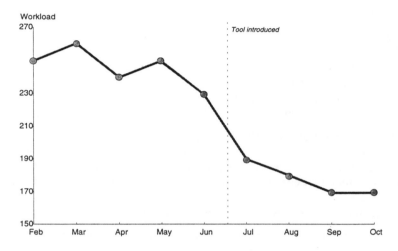

Figure 6.19 Reduction in management workload achieved through the use of Kaizen (after Itakura and Takei, 1994).

6.9 Questions for discussion

1. Compare the approaches of Deming, Juran and Crosby.

    (a) How do they reflect Garvin's views of quality?
    (b) How well do they apply to software development?
    (c) What techniques are common?
    (d) How do they compare with Kaizen?

2. The QKZ2 metric for software quality (Moeller and Paulish, 1993) is defined as:

    Number of defects counted at quality control per thousand lines of code
    Considering the data given below:

    (a) Calculate the scores for QKZ2 for each module.
    (b) Calculate the mean and standard deviation for the metric.
    (c) Plot a frequency distribution for the scores for the bands <3, 3 to 6, 6 to 9, 9 to 12, 12 or over.
    (d) Calculate the correlation between middle size and QKZ2. Can you glean any information about the occurrence of errors?

Module	'000 lines of code per module	No. of errors	QKZ2
1	20	134	
2	23	138	
3	22	122	
4	24	234	
5	30	295	
6	35	323	
7	17	130	
8	23	209	
9	32	292	
10	34	248	
11	21	207	
12	12	104	
13	15	142	
14	32	271	
15	21	160	
16	23	205	
17	12	100	
18	18	172	
19	6	34	
20	21	159	
		Mean	
		Standard deviation	
		Correlation	

The solution to this question is given at the end of the book.

3. The text suggests that there is a new software crisis.

   (a) How far have we solved the issues from the original software crisis?
   (b) What evidence can you find for and against the existence of a new software crisis?
   (c) There is little difference between the 1988 and 1993 surveys of quality procedures. Why do you think this is so?

6.10 Further reading

Crosby, P.B. (1986) *Quality is Free*, McGraw-Hill.
Deming, W.E. (1986) *Out of the Crisis*, MIT Center for Advanced Engineering Study, Cambridge, Mass.
Juran, J.M. (1979) *Quality Control Handbook*, 3rd edn, McGraw-Hill.
Oakland, J. (1989) *Total Quality Management*, Heinemann.
Taylor, J.R. (1989) *Quality Control Systems*, McGraw-Hill.

Chapter 7

The ISO9000 series of quality management standards

7.1 The purpose of standards

Standards are generally defined in terms of a model of best practice, against which all others may be compared. Thus the role of standards is not to build the proverbial better mousetrap, but to ensure conformance to a standard (Figure 7.1).

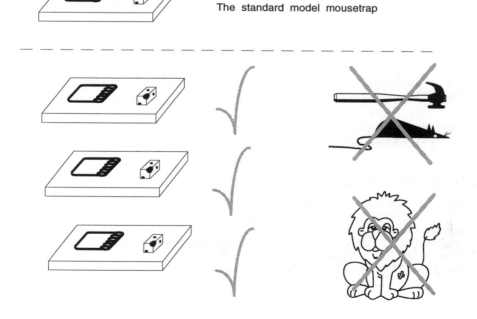

The standard model mousetrap

Conformance   Non-Conformance

Figure 7.1 Standards for mousetraps.

This is true of the standards available for software quality management. The standard establishes the model, in this case of a quality management system, to be employed and then the accreditation body, e.g. BSI QA in the UK for the ISO9000 series, is called in to ensure that the implementation meets the required standard and indeed continues to meet the required standard over time.

In practice, three levels of accreditation are encountered, summarized in Table 7.1.

Table 7.1 Types of accreditation

Accreditation type	Description
First party	Internal monitoring only
Second party	External monitoring by a customer
Third party	External monitoring by an independent standards body

It is obviously more effective to have the quality management system accredited externally. The advantage of third party accreditation over second party accreditation is that the supplier only has to satisfy one accreditor. Clearly, to have to justify one's quality practices to six different customers is undesirable, in terms of cost and time expended. In the past, certain key customers have assumed almost third party status. For example, the defence industries in many countries, e.g. the UK MoD and the US DoD, are such key customers of software houses that their second party accreditation is accepted by many as a *de facto* standard.

It is vital that all parties understand that a standard neither improves quality directly, nor ensures perfection. It should, however, ensure that the correct procedures are in place and being carried out. The standard provides a model, and the accreditation procedure the incentive to ensure that things are done correctly. The accreditation process provides a number of potential benefits to the supplier:

- It provides external validation to see whether the investment made in the QMS is being effective.
- It gives the supplier and their quality system external credibility.
- It allows the supplier to sell to those customers who insist on accreditation as a condition of tender.
- It qualifies the supplier to be included in buyers' guides compiled by the accreditation bodies and circulated to potential customers.

The cost of accrediting a satisfactory QMS to one of the ISO9000 series standards is small in relation to the cost of setting up the QMS in the first place. The figures for a typical supplier, in 1988, were estimated at £10,500 initially, with a further annual cost of £4,500 (Table 7.2). In order to examine the question of standards further, we shall consider the ISO9000 series of standards more fully in the next section.

Table 7.2 The cost of accrediting a QMS to ISO9001 (source: Price Waterhouse, 1988)

Item	Initial costs	Annual costs
Preparation		
Staff time	£2,000	
Assessment		
Staff time	£4,000	
Fees	£4,500	
Operating		
Staff time		£2,000
Fees		£2,500
Total costs	£10,500	£4,500

7.2 The ISO9000 series: a generic quality management standard

The ISO9000 series of standards are the international standards defined for quality management systems. The series dates from 1979, when BS 5750 was introduced in the UK. In 1987, the corresponding ISO, BS and EN standards were harmonized to produce three identical series of standards. In this text, we shall use the ISO numbers for consistency.

Some minor modifications were introduced in 1994. The corresponding European and British standards are given in Table 7.3, which also lists the function of each standard.

Table 7.3 The ISO9000 series of quality management standards

ISO	EN	BS	Description
ISO9000	EN29000	BS 5750 pt0	A guide to selecting the appropriate standard for a quality management system.
ISO9001	EN29001	BS 5750 pt1	The specification of a QMS for design, development, production, installation and service.
ISO9002	EN29002	BS 5750 pt2	The specification of a QMS for production and installation.
ISO9003	EN29003	BS 5750 pt3	The specification for a QMS for final inspection and testing.
ISO9004	EN29004	BS 5750 pt4	Guidance in setting up a QMS to meet the ISO9001/2/3 standards.

The three main standards are ISO9001, 9002 and 9003. ISO9001 is intended for applications where there is a significant design element. Since most software applications require significant design input, ISO9001 is generally the standard applied within software development. ISO9002 is intended for many manufacturing situations where the product is produced to a predefined specification, and ISO9003 for easy applications where the quality can be determined by a simple final inspection and testing procedure. ISO9000 provides guidance on which standard to adopt and ISO9004 assistance on how to establish a QMS which meets the requirements of the ISO9000 series.

In their report on Software Standards commissioned by the DTI for the UK Government, Logica (1988) made the following recommendations regarding the adoption of ISO9001:

- Standards for software should be harmonized, using BS 5880 as a basis.
- In the medium term, ISO9001 should be tailored to take account of the specific needs of software.
- An authoritative guide to the application of ISO9001 to software is required.
- Associated methods and tools should be brought into line with ISO9001.
- Increased confidence in certification is required.
- ISO9001 should be promoted throughout the UK.

However, the author's own consultation with IT professionals suggests that the widespread adoption of the standard faces a number of problems. Suppliers are sceptical about the benefits in a number of ways.

ISO9001 is perceived, erroneously, as a manufacturing standard. Suppliers do not think a manufacturing standard is appropriate to IT. They do not believe that accreditation to the standard will bring sufficient competitive advantage.

They don't think their customers will have heard of it and even when they have heard of it, customers may be sceptical about the benefits, especially if they are asked to pay a higher price for better quality.

This is discussed further at the end of the chapter when quantitative evidence of the take-up rate of ISO9000 standards in the UK is explored.

In the UK currently, the situation is being driven by those suppliers whose customers are insisting on accreditation as a prerequisite for bidding for contracts. For many years, the MoD has operated its own AQAP accreditation scheme, which it is now hoped can be harmonized with the ISO standards. The MoD and other government agencies are asking for accreditation of all suppliers, and this is forcing many suppliers to pursue accreditation.

7.2.1 The contents of the standard

In this section, we shall deal with the requirements of the ISO9001 standard. The ISO9002 and ISO9003 standards may be thought of as subsets of the ISO9001 standard, and in any case most software applications will require the full range of ISO9001 activities.

The standard is based around a model specification for a quality management system. This underlying model is based around two fundamental principles:

- Right first time.
- Fitness for purpose.

The standard is intended to be realistic and implementable and, therefore, sets no prescriptive quality performance targets, referring instead to standards agreed as part of the contract with the customer and acceptable to them. The standard focuses upon ensuring that procedures are carried out in a systematic way and that the results are documented, again in a systematic manner.

The main requirements are dealt with in Clause 4 of the standard under 20 subclauses: the headings of each subclause in Clause 4 are summarized in Table 7.4. Those clauses also found in ISO9002 and ISO9003 are marked with a tick in the right-hand columns. It should be noted that in ISO9003, some of the clauses are simplified.

Table 7.4 Comparison of the requirements of the three principal standards

Clause	ISO9001	ISO9002	ISO9003
4.1	Management responsibility	✓	✓
4.2	Quality system	✓	✓
4.3	Contract review	✓	
4.4	Design control		
4.5	Document control	✓	✓
4.6	Purchasing	✓	
4.7	Purchaser supplied product	✓	
4.8	Product identification and traceability	✓	✓
4.9	Process control	✓	
4.10	Inspection and testing	✓	✓
4.11	Inspection, measuring and testing equipment	✓	✓
4.12	Inspection and test status	✓	✓
4.13	Control of non-conforming product	✓	✓
4.14	Corrective action	✓	
4.15	Handling, storage, packaging and delivery	✓	✓
4.16	Quality records	✓	✓
4.17	Internal quality audits	✓	
4.18	Training	✓	✓
4.19	Servicing		
4.20	Statistical techniques	✓	✓

The function of each section is detailed below.

Clause 4.1: Management responsibility

The model recognizes the importance of management responsibility for quality throughout the organization. Whilst it is impossible for senior management to oversee everything personally, the standard explicitly provides for a management representative who is directly responsible for quality and is accountable to senior management.

This clause also sets out the basic principles for establishing the quality system within the organization and sets out many of its functions, which are then described in greater detail in later sections.

Clause 4.2: Quality system

The model requires the organization to set up a quality system. The system should be documented and a quality plan and manual prepared. The scope of the plan is determined by the activities undertaken and consequently the standard (ISO9001/2/3) employed. The focus of the plan should be to ensure that activities are carried out in a systematic way and documented.

Clause 4.3: Contract review

Contract review specifies that each customer order should be regarded as a contract. Order entry procedures should be developed and documented. The aim of these procedures is to:

- Ensure that customer requirements are clearly defined in writing.
- Highlight differences between the order and the original quotation, so that they may be agreed.
- Ensure that the requirements can be met.

The aim of this clause is to ensure that both the supplier and customer understand the specified requirements of each order and to document this agreed specification to prevent misunderstandings and conflict at a later date.

Clause 4.4: Design control

Design control procedures are required to control and verify design activities, to take the results from market research through to practical designs. The key activities covered are:

- Planning for research and development.
- Assignment of activities to qualified staff.
- Identify interfaces between relevant groups.
- Preparation of a design brief.

- Production of technical data.
- Verification that the output from the design phase meets the input requirements.
- Identification and documentation of all changes and modifications.

The aim of this section is to ensure that the design phase is carried out effectively and to ensure that the output from the design phase accurately reflects the input requirements. The importance of this process in a software context cannot be underestimated.

Clause 4.5: Document control

Three levels of documentation are recognized by the standard:

Level 1: planning and policy documents.
Level 2: procedures.
Level 3: detailed instructions.

The top level documents the quality plan and sets out policy on key quality issues. Each level adds more detail to the documentation. Where possible, existing documentation should be incorporated. The aim should be to provide systematic documentation, rather than simply to provide more documents. It is important that each level of documentation is consistent with the one above it, providing greater detail as each level is descended.

It is a common complaint that the standard requires a prohibitive amount of documentation to be produced. Supporters of the standard argue that systematizing of documentation can actually lead to a reduction in volume due to the removal of obsolete and surplus documents. It is more likely that some reduction will be achieved, which will offset greater volumes in other areas.

Good existing documentation should be incorporated into any new system and this is facilitated by the standard not specifying a particular format, but merely specifying that documents be fit for their intended purpose.

Clause 4.6: Purchasing

The purchasing system is designed to ensure that all purchased products and services conform to the requirements and standards of the organization. The emphasis should be placed on verifying the supplier's own quality management procedures. Where a supplier has also obtained external accreditation for their quality management systems, checks may be considerably simplified. As with all procedures, they should be documented.

Clause 4.7: Purchaser-supplied product

All services and products supplied by the customer must be checked for suitability, in the same way as supplies purchased from any other supplier. In order to ensure this, procedures should be put in place and documented, so that these services and products may be traced through all processes and storage.

Clause 4.8: Product identification and traceability

To ensure effective process control and to correct any non-conformance, it is necessary to establish procedures to identify and trace materials from input to output. This also enables quality problems to be traced to root causes. It may be that the problem can be traced back to supplied materials, in which case the problem may lie outside the quality system altogether.

Clause 4.9: Process control

Process control requires a detailed knowledge of the process itself. This must be documented, often in graphical form, as a process flow chart or similar. Procedures for setting up or calibration must also be recorded. Documented instructions should be available to staff to ensure that they have the capability to carry out the task as specified.

It is staggering how often organizations do not understand their own processes properly. The discipline of documenting the actual process precisely and unambiguously for accreditation purposes can be very educational.

Clause 4.10: Inspection and testing

Inspection and testing are required to ensure conformance in three stages:

- Incoming materials or services.
- In process.
- Finished product and/or service.

All incoming supplies must be checked in some way. The method will vary according to the status of the supplier's quality management procedures, from full examination to checking evidence supplied with the goods.

Monitoring 'in process' is required to ensure that all is going according to plan. At the end of the process, any final inspection tests documented in the quality plan must be carried out. Evidence of conformity to quality standards, together with details of any supporting 'in-process' monitoring may be included. In an effective system, however, the final inspection and test should not have to be as extensive as it otherwise would be. In addition, it should not reveal many problems, since they should have been eliminated by this stage.

Clause 4.11: Inspection, measuring and testing equipment

Any equipment used for measuring and testing must be calibrated and maintained. Procedures to ensure that calibration and maintenance activities are properly implemented should be documented, identifying the measurements required and the precision associated with each. Records must be kept of all activity.

Checking and calibration activities should become part of regular maintenance. Management should ensure that checks are carried out at the prescribed intervals and efficient records kept.

Clause 4.12: Inspection and testing status

All material and services may be classified in one of three categories:

- Awaiting inspection or test.
- Passed inspection.
- Failed inspection.

This status should be clearly identifiable at any stage. It is important that material awaiting inspection is not mistakenly allowed to miss inspection at any stage, as non-conformance may go undetected.

Clause 4.13: Control of non-conforming product

The standard defines non-conforming product as all products or services falling outside tolerance limits agreed in advance with the customer. Once again it is not prescriptive about performance levels. All non-conforming products or services should be clearly identified, documented and, if possible, physically separated from the conforming product. Procedures should be established to handle non-conforming products by reworking, disposal, re-grading or other acceptable documented courses of action.

There are circumstances where the standard permits the sale of non-conforming product provided that the customer is clearly aware of the circumstances and is generally offered a concession. Representatives of accreditation bodies suggest that this an area where organizations often become lax after a while, relaxing procedures and allowing non-conforming product through.

Clause 4.14: Corrective action

Corrective action is the key to continual improvement. Such action should be implemented via a systematic programme which provides guidance and defines the duties of all parties. Records should be kept of any action taken so that future audits can investigate its effectiveness.

Clause 4.15: Handling, storage, packaging and delivery

Handling and associated activities must be designed to protect the quality built into the product. Subcontractors employed for transportation should be subject to the same documented procedures as internal employees. The scope of this clause is determined by the contract with the customer. The clause covers all activities which are the contractual obligation of the supplier.

Clause 4.16: Quality records

Quality records are vital to ensure that quality activities have actually been carried out. They form the basis for quality audits, both internal and external. They do not have to conform to a prescribed format, but must be fit for their intended purpose. As many will exist before the accredited system is implemented, the aim is to systematize and assimilate existing practice wherever possible, to reduce wasted effort in reproducing previous work in this area.

Clause 4.17: Internal quality audits

The quality system should be 'policed' from within the organization and not dependent upon external inspection. Procedures should be established to set up regular internal audits as part of normal management procedure. The role of internal audits should be to identify problems early in order to minimize their impact and cost.

Clause 4.18: Training

Training activities should be implemented and documented. In particular, written procedures are required:

- To establish training needs.
- To carry out training activity.
- To record the training requirements and completed activities for each member of staff.

It is a requirement of the standard that, at all stages, the staff required to carry out a particular function have the skills, knowledge and tools necessary to do a proper job. Training refers not just to formal courses but to informal knowledge-sharing as well.

Clause 4.19: Service

Where servicing procedures are required, they should be documented and verified. The procedures should ensure that servicing is actually carried out and that sufficient resources are available. It is necessary to set up good interfaces with the customer if this function is to be carried out effectively. The same monitoring procedures as are applied to internal processes should be carried out within the servicing function.

Clause 4.20: Statistical techniques

Statistical techniques are required to be used where appropriate. The standard does not specify particular techniques or methods but does specify that once again they should be appropriate for the intended purpose. Their use may be necessary in order to satisfy other requirements, notably process control, detailed in Clause 4.9.

7.2.2 Seeking accreditation

Organizations seeking an accreditation should first implement a quality system, in accordance with the requirements of the standard. This may require outside help, such as quality expertise provided by consultants. However, the most important requirement is gaining acceptance for the system internally at this stage. Once the system is accepted by the staff and has been operating for a few months to iron out inevitable teething troubles, then it is often advisable to have a pre-inspection quality audit carried out by a third party. This will highlight problems and if carried out effectively should ensure that the real inspection goes smoothly. Once this inspection has been carried out successfully, the accreditation body should be contacted and the accreditation process proper started. They will require pre-inspection examination of the relevant documentation. They will then visit the organization to ensure that the system meets the required standard.

Once satisfied, a certificate of accreditation may be issued. This may be withdrawn at any time if the system is not properly maintained. Surprise inspection visits may be made twice a year after certification to ensure continuing conformance.

7.2.3 An assessment of the ISO9001 standard

ISO9001 can be an extremely powerful incentive to organizations to get their quality procedures right. Further, accreditation is powerful external evidence of this fact. However, it still does not provide a complete solution. Apart from the problems experienced in getting the IT community to accept the validity and appropriateness of the standard, there are a number of genuine limitations. Because of its generic nature, the standard is not prescriptive, e.g. it does not specify any particular tools or methods at any stage. Further, it does not require any specific levels of performance, merely that an appropriate level of performance is achieved consistently. Superficially, this may appear to be open to abuse. In practice, any accreditation body worth its salt should ensure that the performance levels set in the quality plan do conform to 'good practice'.

However, the author's biggest concern about the model of a quality system which forms the heart of ISO9001 is its emphasis on quality control procedures. There is very little in the standard about establishing a human quality culture. It may be argued that such a culture is implicit within the model, and that it is necessary to meet the other requirements. However, the human element is too important to be left as an implicit requirement: its omission leaves the standard open to the accusation made by some that it is simply a record-keeping system. Without the establishment of a quality culture and a formal requirement for procedures to facilitate the process, the vital process of continuous improvement which takes quality management beyond the recording of errors and performance may be omitted.

7.3 ISO9000-3: notes for guidance on the application of ISO9001 to software development

One of the biggest barriers to acceptance of ISO9001 amongst IT practitioners is its generic nature and its origins as a manufacturing standard. Although

ISO9001 has been applied in many service and tertiary businesses, many IT people still feel it is inappropriate and difficult to apply. The response to this from the standards bodies is to issue 'notes for guidance' on the application of ISO9001 to software development. It should be stressed that these do not supersede the standard, but rather amplify its contents with the aim of explaining how the standard should be applied in a software context. These notes, published in 1991, are known as ISO9000-3.

7.3.1 ISO9000-3

The ISO9000-3 notes for guidance (1991) should not be confused with either ISO9003, the standard relating to quality management by final inspection, or ISO9004, which provides general guidance on how to implement a QMS conforming to ISO900n.

ISO9000-3 has a target audience of the IT community. It is intended as a complete document in its own right, and its structure therefore differs from ISO9001. The structure of ISO9000-3 is as follows:

Introductory material
The first three clauses of the standard are concerned with defining the scope of the standard, references to other standards and definition of seven terms as used in ISO9000-3.

Section 4: Quality system – framework
This part contains four subsections: management responsibility, quality system, internal quality audit and corrective action.

Section 5: Quality system – lifecycle activities
This section contains nine sections, dealing with activities related to one or more parts of the lifecycle. Many of the corresponding sections in ISO9001 seem unsubstantial in comparison when applied to software.

Section 6: Quality system – supporting activities
This section contains nine items which cover the remaining activities. Some, such as configuration management, are mentioned only briefly in ISO9001. New activities covered include configuration management, measurement, rules, practices and conventions, and tools and techniques. Most of the content makes explicit the implicit requirements of ISO9001.

ISO9000-3 headings are summarized in Table 7.5, which gives all the principal section headings and lists the corresponding clauses in ISO9001, classifying the degree of guidance provided as none, minor, significant or major.

The key areas of guidance provided by ISO9000-3 are requirements definition, lifecycle definition, configuration management and measurements. Software is considered to be different from other applications because:

- it is considered as an intellectual object
- the development process has its own characteristics and importance
- replication always gives an exact copy
- software does not wear
- once a fault is fixed it will not reoccur.

Table 7.5 The ISO9000-3 notes for guidance on the application of ISO9001 to software development

Section heading	Sub-section	Subsection title	Related ISO9001 clauses	Addition to ISO9001
4. Quality system – framework	4.1	Management responsibility	4.1	Significant
	4.2	Quality system	4.2	Significant
	4.3	Internal quality audits	4.17	Minor
	4.4	Corrective action	4.14	Minor
5. Quality system-lifecycle activities	5.1	Contract reviews	4.3	Significant
	5.2	Purchaser's requirements specification	4.3a, 4.4	Significant
	5.3	Development planning	4.4.2	Significant
	5.4	Quality planning	4.2	Significant
	5.5	Design and implementation	4.4, 4.9	Significant
	5.6	Testing and validation	4.10, 4.13	Significant
	5.7	Acceptance	4.10, 4.13	Significant
	5.8	Replication, delivery and installation	4.15	Significant
	5.9	Maintenance	4.19	Major
6. Quality system – supporting activities	6.1	Configuration management	4.4, 4.8, 4.5	Major
	6.2	Document control	4.5	Significant
	6.3	Quality records	4.16	None
	6.4	Measurements	4.20	Major
	6.5	Rules, practices and conventions	4.9, 4.11	Significant
	6.6	Tools and techniques	4.9, 4.11	Significant
	6.7	Purchasing	4.6	Minor
	6.8	Included software product	4.7	Significant
	6.9	Training	4.18	Minor

However, in spite of these differences, it is stressed by ISO that these 'notes for guidance' are not a new or different standard. Quality systems are still assessed against ISO9001. They are conceived as an aid to users of ISO9001 seeking to apply it in a software environment. They are not intended to add to the requirements of ISO9001. Their scope is defined as providing guidance:

> 'where a contract between two parties requires the demonstration of a supplier's capability to develop, supply and maintain software products.'
>
> (ISO, 1991)

Quality management in the IT field is 'still very immature' (TickIT, 1991). With some national variation, this statement appears to apply to the rest of Europe. However, with the advent of the Single European Market (SEM) in 1992, there is growing pressure for accreditation to recognized international standards. In recognition of this trend, the UK Government has launched the TickIT initiative to boost awareness of certification issues and to increase levels of accreditation amongst IT firms in the UK. This programme is designed to promote the EN29001 standard together with the ISO9000-3 notes for guidance for software development.

It is easy to measure the effectiveness of such programmes in terms of the number of firms achieving accreditation. It is less easy to quantify the overall effect upon software quality.

7.4   The impact of ISO9000 and TickIT

A survey of the uptake and awareness of TickIT and ISO9000 standards in general was carried out in late 1991. As such it represents a snapshot of practice at that time which falls between the initial publicity for TickIT and the more recent (1993) DTI campaign.

The purpose of the survey was to seek to answer a number of questions:

- How far has the UK IT industry adopted quality assurance (QA) procedures?

- How many companies using QA procedures have received third-party certification?

- What is the impact of business size and type on the adoption of accredited quality assurance procedures?

- Why do developers seek certification? Or if not why not?

7.4.1   Survey design

In an attempt to maximize the usefulness of the results from the survey, the questionnaire design was based on survey design methods by Brigham (1975), Fowler (1988), Oppenheim (1966) and Sinclair (1975), together with practical experience gained in previous surveys at the University of Sunderland.

It was decided that a postal survey would be most effective because it would enable access to a widely dispersed sample and it would also be relatively low in cost and require minimal manpower. A response rate of between 20% and 30% was anticipated. Five hundred questionnaires were sent out and a response rate of 151 (30.2%) achieved.

In order to maximize response, the questionnaire was designed to be attractive and quick to answer; closed questions were used wherever possible, in a form that could be answered by simply ticking a box. It was, however, impossible to gain sufficient detail with the exclusive use of closed questions. Therefore, some open-ended questions needed to be asked. A balance was required between making the questionnaire compact and easy to answer and extracting a greater level of detail requiring more effort from the respondent, and therefore increasing the likelihood of non-response.

A pilot questionnaire was sent to 12 project managers in industry for their appraisal. They all replied and some very valuable structural amendments were made as a result.

7.4.2 Questionnaire format

The questionnaire was in five sections:

Section A: Private and confidential information

It was intended that this section would provide the background to the information received. Within this section the respondents were asked to indicate their primary business function, the number of people employed by the organization, the number of people employed on software development and the computing services provided.

Section B: System development

The aim of this section was to ascertain whether organizations used formal methods and techniques to develop their software and how large their projects were. Development was split into three sections: Project Control, System Specification/Design and Program Specification/Design.

Section C: Quality assurance

This section was to be completed by respondents with a quality assurance procedure in place. Respondents were asked to distinguish between Third, Second or First Party certification of their quality systems, as defined by the DTI (TickIT, 1991). Those with a Third Party Quality Standard were then asked to give more details, such as: which standard was applied and for how long, the reason for applying a third party quality standard and if the organization felt that an improvement in the process of software development had been observed.

Section D: Use of quality procedures not externally accredited

Reasons for not seeking third party certification QA standard were addressed in this section. Respondents were asked if they thought their business would benefit from applying a third party QA standard, why they had not implemented an external standard and whether they intended to in the foreseeable future.

Section E: Additional information

Additional space was allowed for respondents to clarify or enlarge on any part of the questionnaire.

7.4.3 Findings

In the previous chapter, the findings in relation to the introduction of quality assurance procedures were discussed: 89 respondents (58.9%) stated that they did use a quality assurance procedure, and 62 (41.1%) stated that they did not (Figure 6.16).

The 89 respondents that used a quality assurance procedure were further broken down into whether their quality management systems were assessed by a first, second or third party (Figure 6.17).

In this section we are interested in third party assessed quality systems, conforming to ISO9000. The respondents are classified as either having no recognizable quality assurance procedure (Non- QA), a quality management system assessed to first or second party assessment (QA Procedure), or third party assessment (third party).

Respondents came from a wide range of business types; 20 business types were initially identified. These were grouped as eight broad business sectors. Figure 7.2 shows the distribution of certification type in each sector. Third party accreditation was most common in specialist organizations.

7.4.4 Impact of organization size upon uptake of third party accreditation

Respondents were asked to indicate the size of their organization/branch by the number of staff employed. Figure 7.3 shows the uptake of certification classified according to four size bands, measured in terms of the number of employees: 1–100, 101–500, 510–2,000, 2,000+.

Respondents were also asked to indicate the number of staff employed on software development in their own organization. To simplify the task for respondents, the numbers of staff were split into eight categories as shown in Figure 7.4.

7.4.5 Historical development of third party accreditation

The respondents that had third party assessment were asked to list the current standards applied to their software development. The responses are illustrated

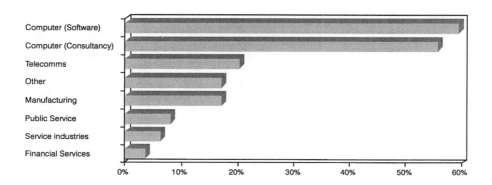

Figure 7.2 Percentage of respondents with third party accreditation by sector.

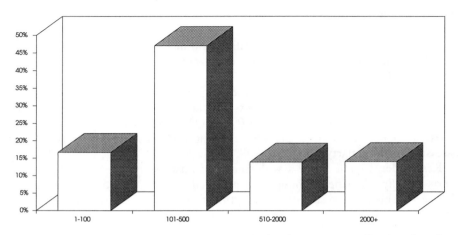

Figure 7.3 Percentage of respondents with third party accreditation by size, measured as total number of employees.

in Figure 7.5. The length of time that the company had been accredited was then considered, and Figure 7.6 shows the results.

When asked if the organization had applied a QA standard before the one which they currently used, 14 replied that they had and 19 that they had not. Of the 14 that had, 11 used their own QA standard, and the rest, second party standard. (N.B. The significance of the MoD as a software customer has led some people to regard the AQAP standards as 'third party'. They are counted here as second party.)

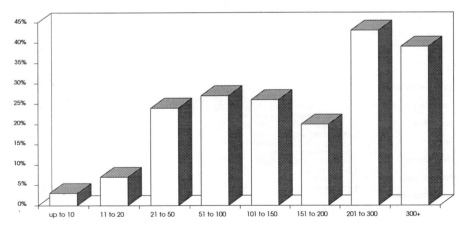

Figure 7.4 Percentage of respondents with third party accreditation by size, measured as total number of employees engaged in software development.

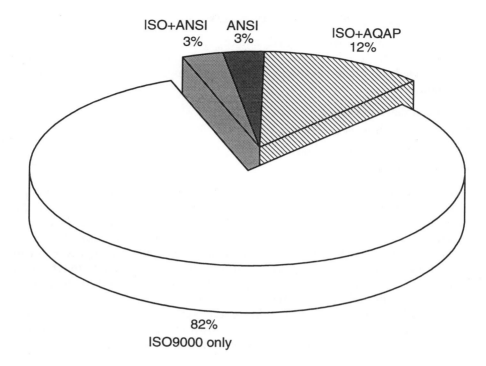

Figure 7.5 Type of third party standard currently in use.

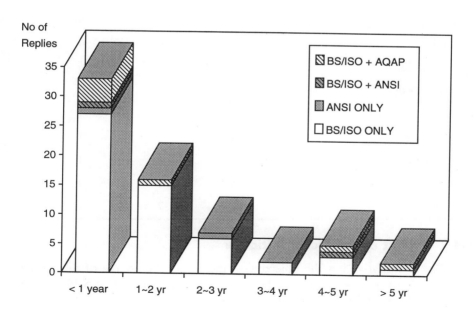

Figure 7.6 Length of time having accreditation.

7.4.6 Benefits from third party assessment

A list of possible reasons were given and the respondents were asked to indicate whether they felt the influence of each was low, medium or high. The reason that received the highest response rate was 'To improve reliability'. Almost as common were:

- commercial success
- earlier detection of errors
- to produce a system of known quality
- to receive certification.

Respondents were asked to indicate the percentage of improvement (if any) in the software development process and the quality of the product since the introduction of a third party quality standard. For ease of completion the answer was divided into grades of percentage increase, or 'too soon to estimate'.

Most respondents felt that it was too soon to estimate any improvement in the software development process (55%) or in the product quality (61%). This is, however, not surprising considering that 48% of the respondents with third party assessment had been assessed for less than a year.

Respondents were asked to indicate the extent of adjustment that was required in certain areas. The results are shown in Table 7.6, which expresses the responses as percentages of the responses relating to each actvity.

Table 7.6 The degree of change required for each activity

	None	Low	Medium	High
Planning	2	7	9	9
Analysis	7	10	6	4
System design	6	10	5	6
Program design	5	13	6	3
Code generation	7	17	3	1
Prototyping	10	11	5	1
Maintenance	8	9	6	4
Project control	2	5	11	9
Testing	4	7	7	8

7.4.7 Impact of the TickIT initiative

The TickIT initiative has the objective of increasing the uptake of third party certification of quality practice within software development to EN29000/3 in the UK and the rest of Europe (TickIT, 1991).

Respondents were asked about their awareness and attitude towards the initiative. They were asked whether they were aware of the TickIT initiative

(Table 7.7) and further whether they would be seeking TickIT certification in the near future (Table 7.8).

Table 7.7 Awareness of TickIT initiative

	Aware of TickIT	Unaware
Accredited	70% (23)	30% (10)
Not accredited	23% (28)	77% (90)
Total	33% (51)	67% (100)

Table 7.8 Respondents seeking TickIT certification in the near future

	Third party assessed	Not third party assessed
Yes	13 (39%)	26 (22%)
Perhaps	6 (18%)	31 (26%)
No	6 (18%)	41 (35%)
Don't know	8 (24%)	20 (17%)

7.4.8 Views of those not currently third party accredited

Respondents who were not third party assessed were asked if they felt their business could benefit if they did receive external certification. Thirty-four (29%) respondents said 'Yes' and 47 (40%) gave 'Perhaps' as their response.

Twenty-nine of the 34 respondents who felt that their business could benefit from being third party assessed gave reasons for their response. These are shown in Table 7.9. Although some organizations may feel that their business would benefit from an external standard, other criteria prevent them proceeding.

Table 7.9 Reasons given for 'Yes' responses

Reason	Replies
Were in the process of preparing for BS 5750	13
Needed to concentrate on own QA procedure first	2
Did not have the time to implement	4
Had to postpone work on quality due to other priorities	2
Could see the benefits of having a formal QA standard as keeping in line with Engineering Standards	1
Sees external QA standard as a means of decreasing maintenance costs and maintaining profitability	3
Commercial pressure	4

Forty-seven respondents stated that 'perhaps' their business could benefit from third party assessment. Out of the 47, 34 gave a reason for that response and these are recorded in Table 7.10. Of these, 11 stated that they felt their own standard was more relevant, and nine respondents were not sure that an external standard would be appropriate. This gave a total of 20 (59%) respondents who were not sure about the appropriateness of an external standard.

Twenty-four respondents did not feel that their business could benefit from an external standard. Sixteen respondents gave reasons and these are shown in Table 7.11. Again, it is evident that some respondents find their own QA more appropriate.

Eight respondents, out of 13, gave reasons why they 'did not know' if their business could benefit from an external standard. These are shown in Table 7.12.

Table 7.10 Reasons for a 'Perhaps' response

Reason	Replies
Own standard more relevant	11
Not sure that external standards are appropriate	9
Considering future of QA at present	5
Time or cost prohibitive	4
Commercial pressure	4
Need more understanding about QA standards	1

Table 7.11 Reasons given for 'No' responses

Reasons	Replies
Finds own QA more appropriate	10
Projects too small to justify external QA	3
Time prohibitive	2
Cost prohibitive	1

Table 7.12 Reasons given for 'Don't know' responses

Reasons	Replies
Own QA more appropriate	3
External QA has not been considered before	2
Does not understand what external standard means	1
Thinks QA lowers productivity	1
Small projects with tight time scale	1

7.4.9 Reasons for not having external accreditation

Respondents without an external standard were asked why they had not applied to have their software development processes third party assessed. For ease, the respondents were offered eight reasons. The reasons were classified as having Low, Medium or High influence.

The findings are summarized in Table 7.13.

Table 7.13 Influence of factors on resistance to third party certification

Factor	Level of influence		
	Low	Medium	High
Cost	13	24	26
Lack of management support	13	16	21
Time involved to implement	5	32	30
No productivity benefit	14	16	20
Current methods satisfactory	13	29	34
No clear guidance for standardization	16	17	15
Lack of confidence in third party audit	16	12	16
Other	0	1	18

Other views expressed included:

- their projects were too small to be third party assessed
- an external standard would hinder the creativity of the staff
- there was no demand from customers.

Respondents without an external standard were asked if they would be considering one in the near future; Figure 7.7 illustrates the response. Those who answered 'Yes' were then asked which standard they would work towards. Of the 26 replies considering certification, only one (4%) suggested certification under TickIT.

7.4.10 The effect of business type and size for organizations using QA procedures

The responses came from a varied range of business types. Not surprisingly, the greatest response was received from software houses, because, as mentioned earlier, they could be considered positive to the subject. Quality assurance procedures were used throughout all industries (except research), but third party assessment remained very low except in the computer industries, where 16 software houses (59%) and five computer consultancies (56%) reported that they were third party assessed.

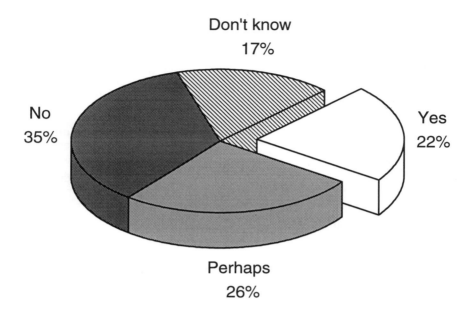

Don't know
17%

No
35%

Yes
22%

Perhaps
26%

Figure 7.7 Respondents considering external accreditation.

Substantially more responses were received from organizations that employed over 2,000 staff, but out of the 57 respondents in that size category only eight (14%) stated that they were third party assessed. Whereas, for organizations employing between 101 to 500 staff, 16 out of 34 (47%) had been third party assessed. These figures were not as anticipated, as their representation was inconsistent with popular belief that larger organizations were able to afford both the time and money for a third party audit. On closer examination, however, it could be seen that a very large majority of the computer companies within this sample fell within the two smaller size categories. This means that the figures must be viewed with caution, because it could be argued that if anyone should benefit by externally assessing their software, it would be the software industries.

In an effort to clarify the situation, the figures were re-examined, but this time those respondents who were software houses or computer consultants were removed. These figures offer a different perspective from those shown previously. Without the software supply companies included, the percentage of respondents whose quality practices within software development have been externally audited drops from 22% to 12%. Also, the percentage of smaller staffed organizations with third party certification drops quite dramatically from 17% and 47% to 0% and 6%, respectively.

This leads to a correlation coefficient of +0.9 between number of employees and percentage of accredited companies when software companies are excluded.

The number of staff employed on software development provided a better indicator of certification levels. In software houses, there is a higher percentage of staff directly employed on software development. As a consequence, the correlation coefficient for all responses calculated between staff employed on software development and uptake of certification is +0.78. Whilst the sample size prevents firm conclusions, the results suggest that company size is a critical factor in seeking certification.

7.4.11   Reasons for developers seeking or not seeking an external QA standard

Organizations whose software development was already assessed to an external standard gave their reasons for doing so as follows, in order of priority:

- commercial success
- to improve reliability
- to produce a system of known quality
- to satisfy users.

It was interesting that only 12% of the respondents with third party certification stated the reduction of development costs and increased productivity were of high consideration.

The major reasons for not seeking external certification were as follows, in order of priority:

1. Own QA procedure more 'appropriate'.
2. Time to implement new procedures.
3. Cost.

The most significant factor appears to suggest that these respondents believe their own quality practice is either sufficient or does not conform to the model contained within the ISO9000 standards. This perception seems to be unlikely to be true.

With regard to the TickIT initiative, 23% of respondents who were already externally assessed were not aware of it, and for the respondents who were not third party assessed, 70% were not aware. It would seem, therefore, that at the time of the survey, the TickIT initiative was preaching to the converted, yet failing to reach those sectors of industry where the need was greatest.

Since the survey was carried out at the end of 1991, further progress will undoubtedly have been made, particularly in the light of the 1993 campaign to reinforce the message of TickIT. There will also be a snowball effect as accredited companies insist on accreditation for their subcontractors.

Overall, the picture presented by this survey is of a patchy acceptance of the need for external accreditation and limited progress since the early surveys of Logica and Price Waterhouse, which were responsible for the establishment of the DTI's TickIT initiative in the UK.

7.5 Questions for discussion

1. How useful is ISO9000 to the development of a quality culture within software development?

    (a) What other factors lead companies to apply for ISO9000?
    (b) Which are the crucial factors in boosting ISO9000 uptake?

2. ISO9000-3 is presented not as a different standard but an amplification.

    (a) Do you agree with this presentation, or does ISO9000-3 alter ISO9000 significantly?
    (b) Do you think ISO9000-3 makes ISO9000 more relevant to software development?
    (c) What other elements of software development would you like to see covered in ISO9000-3?

3. The survey by Davies *et al.* was disputed by some TickIT enthusiasts at the time of publication as unrepresentative of the industry. The survey was defended as being a random sample of companies rather than a survey of large, enthusiastic but unrepresentative companies.

    (a) Did you think the findings seemed reasonable?
    (b) Do you think the criticisms made by those not using the standard were justified?
    (c) How would you boost the uptake of TickIT amongst the sceptics?

7.6 Further reading

Boehm, B. *et al.* (1978) *Characteristics of Software Quality.* TRW and North-Holland, New York.

Davis, C., Gillies, A.C., Smith, P. and Thompson, J.B. (1993) Current quality assurance practice amongst software developers in the UK. *Software Quality Journal* 2 (3), 145–61.

Edwards, H.M., Thompson, J.B. and Smith, P. (1989) Results of a survey of use of SSADM in commercial and government sectors in the United Kingdom. *Information and Software Technology* January/February, pp. 21-8.

ISO (1987) ISO9000–9004. Copies from BSI in the UK.

ISO (1991) ISO9000-3. Copies from BSI in the UK.

Logica (1988) *Quality Management Standards for Software.*

Medes, J.S., Smith, P. and Newton, M.J. (1987) A survey of the methods used in the development of technical software in the UK, *Proc 1st Int. Conf. on Reliability and Robustness of Engineering Software*, Como, Italy.

Naur, P. *et al.* (1976) *Software Engineering: Concepts and Techniques.* Petrocelli/Charter. New York.

Oppenheim, A.N. (1966) *Questionnaire Design and Attitude Measurement.* Open University Heinemann, London.

Price Waterhouse (1988) *Software Quality Standards: The Cost and Benefits.* A review for the UK Department of Trade & Industry.

Sinclair, M.A. (1975) Questionnaire design. *Applied Ergonomics* June pp73-80.

TickIT (1990) *TickIT: Making a Better Job of Software.* Guide to Software Quality Management System Construction and Certification Using EN29001.

TickIT (1991) *TickIT: Making a Better Job of Software.* Copies from the UK Department of Trade & Industry (DTI).

Chapter 8

Models and standards for process improvement

8.1 Chapter summary

One of the commonest complaints about ISO9001 is that it tends to fossilize procedures rather than encourage process improvement. As a consequence, a range of standards and models have been developed which seek to provide the benefits of quality standards whilst recognizing different stages of development and the need to improve.

Pre-eminent amongst these efforts has been the work of the Software Engineering Institute (SEI) from Carnegie Mellon University, resulting in the Process Maturity Model (PMM), which evolved into the Capability Maturity Model (CMM).

Other efforts to move standards beyond ISO9000 in the European arena have focused upon the ESPRIT programme, notably the SPICE, Pyramid and Bootstrap projects.

This chapter describes each of the principal approaches and considers the contribution they make to improving software quality.

8.2 The Capability Maturity Model

8.2.1 Introduction to the model

The basic premise underlying the SEI's maturity model is that the quality of a software product is largely determined by the quality of the software development and maintenance processes used to build it. The SEI maturity model is defined as a five-level framework for how an organization matures its software processes from *ad hoc*, chaotic processes to mature, disciplined software processes.

Gilchrist (1992) describes the levels, shown in Table 8.1.

The model is questionnaire-based. Questions are divided into 'essentials' and 'highly desirable'. To achieve a given level, an organization must attain 90% 'yes' answers to essential questions and 80% 'yes' answers to highly desirable questions.

The model is shown schematically in Figure 8.1.

Table 8.1 Five levels of the SEI CMM (after Gilchrist)

Level	Designation	Description
1	Initial	The organization has undefined processes and controls.
2	Repeatable	The organization has standardized methods facilitating repeatable processes.
3	Defined	The organization monitors and improves its processes.
4	Managed	The organization possesses advanced controls, metrics and feedback.
5	Optimizing	The organization uses metrics for optimization purposes.

8.2.2 Views of quality underpinning the model

The staged structure of the software process maturity framework is not new. It is based upon the principles outlined by the quality gurus: Shewhart, Deming, Juran and Crosby.

The software process is defined as a set of activities, methods, practices and transformations that people use to develop and maintain software and the associated products. The model assumes that as an organisation matures, the software process becomes better defined and more consistently implemented throughout the organization. This view may be contrasted with the ISO9000 model which assumes a relatively static quality management system and seeks to find evidence that required activities are carried out in a systematic fashion. Processes either meet ISO9000 or they don't: the result is conformance or non-conformance.

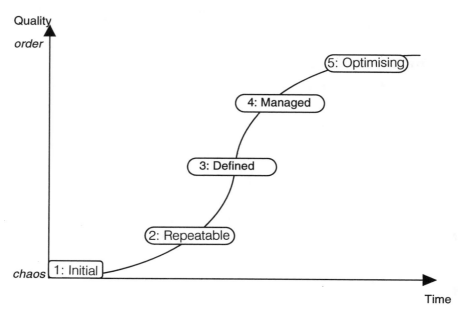

Figure 8.1 Schematic view of the Capability Maturity Model.

The maturity model seeks to measure how well these processes are carried out and may be traced directly to the work of Crosby (1979). He describes a quality management maturity grid (ibid., Chapter 3), which applies five stages to six measurement categories in subjectively rating an organization's quality operation. The five stages are:

- uncertainty, where management is confused and uncommitted regarding quality as a management tool;
- awakening, where management is beginning to recognize that quality management can help;
- enlightenment, when the decision is made to conduct a formal quality improvement programme;
- wisdom, where the company has the chance to make changes permanent (things are basically quiet and people wonder why they used to have problems);
- certainty, where quality management is considered an absolutely vital part of company management.

The six measurement categories are:

- management understanding and attitude, characterized as 'no comprehension of quality as a management tool' at uncertainty and 'an essential part of the company system' at certainty;
- quality organization status, characterized as hidden at uncertainty and a thought leader/main concern at certainty;
- problem handling, which are fought when they occur at uncertainty and prevented at certainty;
- cost of quality as percentage of sales, characterized as 20% at uncertainty and 2.5% at certainty;
- quality improvement actions, characterized as no organized activities at uncertainty and a normal and continued activity at certainty;
- summation of company quality posture, summarized as 'we do not know why we have problems with quality' at uncertainty and 'we know why we do not have problems with quality' at certainty.

Crosby's maturity matrix is summarized in Table 8.2.

Table 8.2 Quality maturity matrix (after Crosby, 1979)

	Attitude	Quality status	Problem handling	Cost as % of sales	QI actions	Posture
Uncertainty						
Awakening						
Enlightenment						
Wisdom						
Certainty						

As a precursor to the maturity model itself, Radice *et al.* (1985) working with Humphrey, identified 12 process stages, which were characterized by 11 attributes measured on a five-point scale. The process stages were stages in the lifecycle:

1. requirements;
2. product level design;
3. component level design;
4. module level design;
5. code;
6. unit test;
7. functional verification test;
8. product verification test;
9. system verification test;
10. package and release;
11. early support programme;
12. general availability.

The eleven attributes were:

1. process
2. methods
3. adherence to practices
4. tools
5. change control
6. data gathering
7. data communication and use
8. goal setting
9. quality focus
10. customer focus
11. technical awareness.

The five-point scale consisted of traditional, awareness, knowledge, skill and wisdom, and integrated management system.

Humphrey brought these concepts to the Software Engineering Institute in 1986, revised them to define maturity levels, and developed the foundation for current use throughout the software industry.

The origins of the maturity model itself lie in a request to provide the federal government with a method for assessing the capability of their software contractors.

In August 1986, the Software Engineering Institute (SEI), with assistance from the MITRE Corporation, began developing a process maturity framework that would assist organizations in improving their software process. In June 1987, the SEI released a brief description of the software process maturity framework (Humphrey, 1987), and, in September 1987, a preliminary maturity questionnaire (Humphrey and Sweet, 1987).

The 1987 SEI technical report *Characterizing the Software Process: A maturity framework* (Humphrey, 1987) described the software process maturity framework of the five levels in terms of the key actions needed to advance from one level to the next. These key actions were the first high-level expressions of what has become the key process areas in the CMM.

These actions are summarized in Tables 8.3 to 8.6, based on the analysis of Paulk (1995a). The model evolved through 1988 and 1989, particularly through the publication, *Managing the Software Process* (Humphrey, 1989), which documented a new version of the framework.

Since then, the model has continued to evolve, as shown in Table 8.7.

8.3 Individual levels of the CMM

At level 2 of the model, an organization is expected to have standardized methods enabling repeatable processes.

Table 8.3 Key actions for moving from maturity level 1 to level 2
Sources: (Humphrey, 1987; Paulk, 1995a)

Area	Required action
Project management	The fundamental role of a project management system is to ensure effective control of commitments. For software, this starts with an understanding of the magnitude of the job to be done. In the absence of such an orderly plan, no commitment can be better than an educated guess.
Management oversight	A suitably disciplined software development organization must have corporate oversight. The lack of management reviews typically results in uneven and generally inadequate implementation of the process, as well as frequent over-commitments and cost surprises.
Product assurance	A product assurance group is charged with assuring management that the software development work is actually done the way it is supposed to be done. To be effective, the assurance organization must have an independent reporting line to senior management and sufficient resources.
Change control	Control of changes in software development is fundamental to business and financial control as well as to technical stability. To develop quality software on a predictable schedule, the requirements must be established and maintained with reasonable stability throughout the development cycle.

The questionnaire asks whether:

- software tools are used to support documentation
- projects are tracked

- costing and sizing are performed
- change control is implemented
- standards are used
- reviews are taking place
- by level 3, the organization is expected to be monitoring and improving.

Table 8.4 Key actions for moving from maturity level 2 to level 3
Sources: (Humphrey, 1987; Paulk, 1995a)

Area	Required action
Process group	Establish a process group. This is a technical group with exclusive focus on improving the software development process. Until someone is given a full-time assignment to work on the process, little orderly progress can be made in improving it.
Process architecture	Establish a software development process architecture, which describes the technical and management activities required for proper execution of the development process. The architecture is a structural decomposition into tasks, which each has entry criteria, functional descriptions, verification procedures, and exit criteria.
Software engineering methods	If they are not already in place, introduce a family of software engineering methods and technologies. These include design and code inspections, formal design methods, library control systems and comprehensive testing methods.

Table 8.5 Key actions for moving from maturity level 3 to level 4
Sources: (Humphrey, 1987; Paulk, 1995a)

Area	Required action
Process measurement	Establish a minimum basic set of process measurements to identify the quality and cost parameters of each step.
Process database	Establish a process database with resources to manage and maintain it.
Process analysis	Provide sufficient process resources to analyse this data and advise project members on the data's meaning and use.
Product quality	Assess the relative quality of each product and inform management where quality targets are not being met.

Table 8.6 Key actions for moving from maturity level 4 to level 5
Sources: (Humphrey, 1987; Paulk, 1995a)

Area	Required action
Automated support	Provide automatic support for gathering process data.
Process optimization	Turn the management focus from the product to the process.

Table 8.7 Evolution of the CMM

Year	Version published
1987	Software process maturity framework (Humphrey)
1987	Preliminary maturity questionnaire (Humphrey and Sweet)
1987	Characterizing the software process: a maturity framework (Humphrey)
1989	Managing the software process (Humphrey)
1990	Draft version of CMM (v0.2)
1991	Version for discussion (v0.6)
1991	v1.0: Capability Maturity Model for software (Paulk *et al.*) 'Key practices for the Capability Maturity Model' (Weber *et al.*)
1993	v1.1: Capability Maturity Model for software, version 1.1 (Paulk *et al.*) Key practices for the Capability Maturity Model, version 1.1 (Paulk *et al.*)

The questionnaire asks about

- lessons learnt and transferred to new projects
- training programmes
- control of interfaces
- monitoring of subcontractors
- evaluation of new techniques.

At level 4, the questionnaire requires the organization to:

- operate a database for metrics data
- set measurable quality goals
- run a tool environment
- use a model for handling defects.

At level 5, the questionnaire asks the organization about optimization, specifically whether

- productivity is measured
- systems and components are reused

- old technology is replaced
- the software process is being improved
- errors are actively prevented.

The requirements of the latest version of the CMM (v1.1) for each level are summarized in Table 8.8.

For more detailed information, the reader is referred to the reference documents at the end of the chapter, notably Humphrey (1989).

Table 8.8 Overview of requirements of CMM v1.1 (after Paulk, 1995a)

Maturity level			
2	3	4	5
Requirements Management	Organization Process Focus	Quantitative Process Management	Defect Prevention
Software Project Planning	Organization Process Definition	Software Quality Management	Technology Change Management
Software Tracking and Oversight	Training Programme		Process Change Management
Software Subcontract Management	Integrated Software Management		
Software Quality Assurance	Software Product Engineering		
Software Configuration Management	Intergroup Co-ordination		
	Peer Reviews		

8.4 The role of the CMM

The role of the CMM is increasing. This may be attributed to a number of factors:

- the maturity of the model itself;
- the increasing general awareness of the need for externally recognized quality standards;
- the adoption of the model by key software purchasers, such as national departments of defence, some of whom (e.g. France and the US), have stated that all suppliers must reach a given level, usually 3, if they wish to tender for contracts.

Zopf (1994) has compared the ISO standards with SEI CMM. The comparison is shown in Table 8.9.

The CMM is attractive when compared to ISO9000, because it allows for improvement and evolution. It can also be used in conjunction with other quality standards. The approach can highlight defects as they occur and this can both improve quality and feed information into internal ISO assessment, highlighting potential non-conformances. The CMM prioritizes tasks for improvement and provides a matrix of strengths and weaknesses.

Paulk (1995b) places ISO9000 practices between levels 2 and 3 but argues that they are not directly comparable. He argues that the Capability Maturity Model for Software (CMM), developed by the Software Engineering Institute, and the ISO9000 series of standards, developed by the International Standards Organization, share a common concern with quality and process management. The two are driven by similar concerns and intuitively correlated.

The results indicate that, although an ISO9001-compliant organization would not necessarily satisfy all of the level 2 key process areas, it would satisfy most of the level 2 goals and many level 3 goals. Because there are practices in the CMM that are not addressed in ISO9000, it is possible for a level 1 organization to receive 9001 registration; similarly, there are areas addressed by ISO9001 that are not addressed in the CMM. A level 3 organization would have little difficulty in obtaining ISO9001 certification, and a level 2 organization would have significant advantages in obtaining certification.

However, Zopf argues that the higher levels of CMM (4 and 5) are expensive and may not be justified or affordable to customers. In this respect, the military origins of the CMM are demonstrated, where quality may be emphasized at any cost. Dunkelberger's (1989) OFC system described earlier in the book demonstrated a high cost, high quality military solution.

8.5 SPICE

With the increasing emphasis on software quality, there has been a significant investment in research into improving software quality. The European ESPRIT programme included a number of quality projects such as PYRAMID, METKIT and BOOTSTRAP:

- PYRAMID contributed a range of metrics, described in Möller and Paulish (1993).
- METKIT resulted in a set of training resources to assist companies in developing quality programmes.
- BOOTSTRAP developed a maturity model similar to the CMM model. This work was developed further with other international partners under the SPICE banner.

SPICE is a major international initiative to develop a Standard for Software Process Assessment. The project is carried out under the auspices of the International Committee on Software Engineering Standards, ISO JTC1, through its Working Group on Software Process Assessment/SC7/WG10. The SPICE standards cover software process assessment, improvement and capabili-

Table 8.9 Comparison of ISO9000 and SEI CMM (after Zopf, 1994)

	ISO9001	ISO9000-3	SEI CMM v1.0
Scope	Quality system	Notes for guidance for application of quality system to software development	Application of TQM to software development and maintenance
Goal	Quality and productivity improvement		
External purpose	Quality system certificate		Capability evaluation
Outcome	Yes/No		Levels 1–5
Identification of improvement needs	Internal quality audits		Process assessment
Results	Audit reports • observations of non-conformities • audit team's judgement on the extent of compliance • the system's ability to achieve defined quality objectives suggestion of corrective action for each observation		Final presentation • findings • strength/weakness profiles • demand of action matrix • points of main efforts • recommendation catalogue consolidated findings
Realization of follow-up actions	responsible person named for each observation		process improvement team
Follow-up checks	follow-up audits scheduled audits certification audits	self-assessment re-assessment	
Elements	Management responsibility Quality system Contract review Design control Document control Purchasing Purchaser-supplied product Product identification and traceability Process control Inspection and testing	Framework Management responsibility Quality system Internal audits Corrective action Lifecycle Contract review Purchaser's requirements spec. Development planning Quality planning Design and implementation	Level 2 Requirements management Project planning Project tracking Subcontract management Quality assurance Configuration management Level 3 Organization process focus Organization process definition

Table 8.9 (Continued).

ISO9001	ISO9000-3	SEI CMM v1.0
Inspection, measuring and test equipment	Testing and validation	Training programme
Inspection and test status	Acceptance	Integrated software management
Control of non-conforming product	Replication, delivery and install	Software product engineering
Corrective action	Maintenance	Intergroup co-ordination
Handling, storage, packaging and delivery	Support activities	Peer reviews
Quality records	Configuration management	Level 4
Internal audits	Document control	Process measurement and analysis
Training	Quality records	Quality management
Servicing	Measurement	Level 5
Statistical techniques	Rules, practices and conventions	Defect prevention
	Tools and techniques	Technology innovation
	Purchasing	Change management
	Included software product	
	Training	

ty. The driving force for SPICE has been largely from Europe and Australia, but it seems that over the next few years, work on the CMM is likely to be harmonized with the results of the SPICE working groups, and the CMM has been a major influence on the SPICE work to date.

Lightfoot (1995) in the SPICE documentation provided on the World Wide Web claims the following benefits to software suppliers:

- software suppliers will submit to just one process assessment scheme (presently numerous schemes are used)
- software development organizations will have a tool to initiate and sustain a continuous process improvement programme
- managers will have a means to ensure that their software development is aligned with, and supports, the business needs of the organization.

It is also claimed that it will help purchasers determine the capability of software suppliers and assess the risk involved in selecting one supplier over another.

SPICE is attempting to define a framework for conducting assessments together with guidance on how to use the framework for process improvement and process capability. The framework depends on an architecture that defines practices and processes needed for software development, maintenance, operation and support.

The overall structure is shown in Figure 8.2.

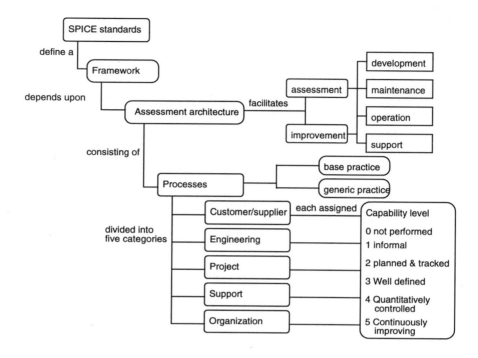

Figure 8.2 Overall structure of SPICE.

Table 8.10 Capability levels within SPICE

Level	Title	Definition
0	Not performed	General failure to perform base functions
1	Performed informally	Base functions generally carried out in an ad hoc manner. Identifiable products for the process
2	Planned and tracked	Base functions generally carried out in a planned manner. Performance verified. Work conforms to standards and requirements
3	Well defined	Base functions performed according to approved tailored standard documented processes
4	Quantitatively controlled	Detailed measures of performance collected and analysed. Prediction of performance. Quality of work is quantitatively known
5	Continuously improving	Quantitative goals based on business goals established. Continuous process improvement enabled by quantitative feedback of performance

The processes are classified into five categories:

- customer–supplier process category
- engineering process category
- project process category
- support process category
- organization process category.

Processes are considered to consist of essential activities known as base practices and additional activities known as generic practices.

SPICE differs from CMM in categorizing processes and capabilities by functional rather than organizational units. However, there are five capability levels which are not dissimilar to the CMM, with the addition of a level 0. The levels are defined in Table 8.10.

Capability within the SPICE context is measured by a conformant assessment, defined by Rout (1995), as one which:

- is conducted by an assessment team that meets the requirements defined in the standard
- uses an assessment process that meets or exceeds the demands of the standard
- is based upon a set of practices that meet or exceed the demands of the standard
- uses an assessment instrument that meets or exceeds the demands of the standard
- provides results in the form of a process profile, and
- has objective evidence that demonstrates that the above conditions have been met.

More detail of the SPICE assessment process is provided in Rout (1995). The SPICE standard is documented in seven documents, illustrated in Figure 8.3.

Work on the development and validation of SPICE is still in progress at the time of writing. SPICE validation is due to last until 1997. The final version may still be some way off. However, it seems likely that provided that standards can be harmonized with work carried out by the SEI on the CMM, that this represents the future of international standards for software process improvement. The biggest question mark will be the business case for investing sufficient resources to achieve the higher levels of capability.

This will ultimately be driven by customer demand and their acceptance of higher costs as a consequence.

8.6 Conclusions

The emergence of the CMM and the promise of SPICE have changed the role of standards in quality management. ISO9000 provided a way to gain external accreditation for a quality management system. However, it did not offer a mechanism for quality improvement. Indeed some practitioners have felt that it actually acted as a brake on improvement, setting in stone procedures implemented at the time of accreditation.

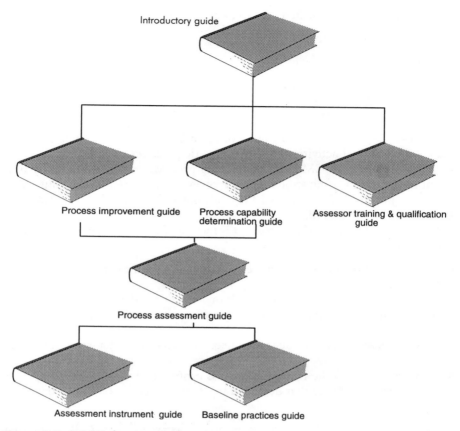

Figure 8.3 SPICE documentation.

The CMM and SPICE frameworks offer a path to process improvement. They do not exclude ISO accreditation, but do provide a mechanism for achieving better than ISO performance. They allow an organization to build an evolutionary path to the level of quality that they wish to achieve (Figure 8.4).

However, whilst the standards provide a framework, improvement will still only be achieved through the managed process of change outlined in Chapter 6. No standards can execute change. People execute change and must be persuaded of the benefits.

8.7 Questions for discussion

1. Compare ISO9000 with the Capability Maturity Model.

    (a) What advantages are there for the CMM?
    (b) Do you expect the CMM to replace ISO9000 as the primary standard for quality procedures? Give reasons for your answer.

2. Consider the benefits claimed for SPICE by Lightfoot.

    (a) How realistic are they?

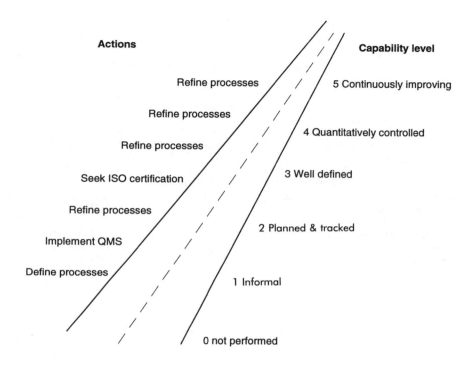

Actions   Capability level

Refine processes   5 Continuously improving

Refine processes

                       4 Quantitatively controlled

Refine processes

Seek ISO certification   3 Well defined

Refine processes

                   2 Planned & tracked

Implement QMS

Define processes   1 Informal

                   0 not performed

Figure 8.4 Evolutionary route to process improvement.

(b) How far are they pertinent to SPICE as opposed to CMM or ISO9000?
(c) Can you foresee any disadvantages?

3. Compare the capability levels within the CMM and SPICE.

(a) Are the levels comparable?
(b) Do you think harmonization is possible?
(c) What barriers are likely to prevent harmonization?

8.8 Further reading

Humphrey, W.S. (1987) *Characterizing the Software Process: a maturity framework.* Software Engineering Institute, CMU/SEI-87-TR-11, DTIC Number ADA182895.

Humphrey, W.S. (1989) *Managing the Software Process*, Addison-Wesley, Reading, MA.

Humphrey, W.S. and Sweet, W.L. (1987) *A Method for Assessing the Software Engineering Capability of Contractors*, Software Engineering Institute, CMU/SEI-87-TR-23, DTIC Number ADA187320.

Lightfoot, (1995) SPICE Home page on the World Wide Web: URL <http://www.esi.es/projects/SPICE.hmtl>

Paulk, M.C. (1995a) The evolution of SEI's Capability Maturity Model, *Software Process – improvement and practice*, pilot issue, **1**, 3–15.

Paulk, M.C. (1995b) How ISO9001 compares with the CMM, *IEEE Software*, **12 (1)**, 74–83.

Paulk, M.C. and Garcia, S.M. (1994) The impact of evolving the Capability Maturity Model to version 1.1, *Crosstalk: The Journal of Defence Software Engineering*, 7 (9), 7–11.

Paulk, M.C., Curtis, W., Chrissis, M.B. and Weber, C.V. (1991) *Capability Maturity Model for Software*. Software Engineering Institute, CMU/SEI-91-TR-24, DTIC Number ADA240603.

Paulk, M.C., Curtis W., Chrissis, M.B. and Weber, C.V. (1993) *Capability Maturity Model for Software, Version 1.1*, Software Engineering Institute, CMU / SEI-93-TR-24, DTIC Number ADA263403.

Paulk, M.C., Konrad, M.D. and Garcia, S.M. (1995) CMM versus SPICE architectures, *Software Process Newsletter*, IEEE Technical Committee on Software Engineering.

Paulk, M.C., Weber, C.V., Garcia, S.M., Chrissis, M.B. and Bush, M.W. (1993) *Key Practices of the Capability Maturity Model, Version 1.1*, Software Engineering Institute, CMU/SEI-93-TR-25, DTIC Number ADA263432.

Weber, C.V., Paulk, M.C., Wise, C.J. and Withey, J.V. (1991) *Key Practices of the Capability Maturity Model*, Software Engineering Institute, CMU/SEI-91-TR-25, DTIC Number ADA240604.

Zopf, S. (1994) Improvement of software development through ISO9001 certification and SEI assessment, Software quality: concern for people: *Proceedings of the 4th European Software Quality Conference*, 224–31, VDF, Zurich, ISBN 3 7281 2153 3.

Chapter 9

Case studies: from kitchens to software

9.1 Introduction to case studies

The three case studies described in this chapter are intended to illustrate different aspects of quality management and accreditation. They all concern organizations that have implemented quality management systems which have met the requirements of the ISO9000 standards. The results obtained have been rather different.

9.2 Total quality in the kitchen

9.2.1 Background

This is the story of a manufacturing company and a kitchen. The company is a large manufacturer of kitchen units based in the North-West of England in the UK. The company started life supplying kitchen units to large DIY retail outlets. In order to bid for contracts with certain large influential customers, the company applied for and received ISO9001 accreditation for its manufacturing operations. This enabled the company to bid successfully for a number of large contracts which, in turn, brought economies of scale, enabling the company to gain further bids by offering quality at a competitive price.

However, the market place available through retail outlets is limited, although large. The company decided to enter the contracts market, fitting kitchens to new housing developments, selling to large house-building companies. The company operation is no longer simply manufacturing. Each site deal requires negotiation regarding the range of units, finishes and fittings to be made available. In addition, the company must now employ fitters to fit the kitchens. In a time of economic recession, there is also an expanding market for taking over contracts from competitors going out of business. This brings particular problems when trying to match kitchens already fitted by competitors. In short, the company has now started to supply a bespoke product rather than simply 'shipping boxes'.

In such a situation, if the customer is to gain a perception of quality, it is necessary to apply quality management principles for all the company's operations, not simply manufacturing. Enter the customers, a married couple and the owner of a new house with a kitchen supplied by the company, requiring additional units to complement those fitted according to the developer's specification.

The story of a kitchen

The customers in question bought a new house with a kitchen supplied by the company. The company supplied a U-shaped set of units and worktop, with a sink under the window. At the left hand side of the kitchen, they provided wall cupboards, including an extractor over the hob. Over the other arm of the 'U', there were no wall cupboards (see the plan given in Figure 9.1).

In order to provide extra storage, the customers enquired whether matching wall cupboards would be available, to fit the dotted area shown in Figure 9.1. The builder replied in the affirmative and gave the name of the kitchen company who had supplied the original units. When the kitchen company was contacted, the telephonist had great problems determining which department the enquiry should be referred to. At first, the enquiry was referred to the wrong department. They said, 'Oh, you need contracts', but were unable to transfer the call. On ringing back, the telephonist was hard to convince that this was indeed an enquiry for contracts.

Once the call was eventually routed to contracts, the call was taken by a salesman. He was very positive in his response:

'We do not generally deal with the general public, although in cases such as these we are happy to supply extra units. However, we can only work by supplying an invoice and then receiving payment in advance. Once payment is received, the order can be despatched within ten days.'

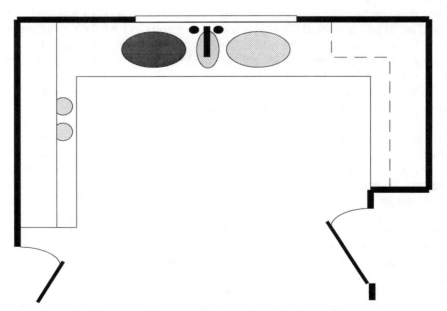

Figure 9.1 Plan of the customers' kitchen.

When asked to visit to ascertain the requirements, the representative replied that this would not be necessary as he had the plans for the original order in front of him. This was questioned vigorously at the time by the customers. 'Are you sure?' elicited the response, 'Oh, yes, what you need is ...' and the salesman reeled off a list of the units that he said would meet the customers' requirements. He gave an estimate over the phone, which was approved by the customers. He promised to send a written invoice by return of post. When he was asked about fitting, he replied that the units would come ready built, and could simply be 'hooked on the wall'. The agreed requirements specified that an open end unit would be supplied without gallery rails.

In spite of a certain scepticism at the apparently casual manner with which the order had been dealt, the invoice was awaited with eagerness, as the glasses and crockery intended to fill the cupboards were currently filling the customers' kitchen worktop.

After a week, no invoice was forthcoming. When the company was contacted, the enquiry was passed around between different departments. No one knew where the employee was who had given the original verbal estimate, and it was not clear who should be dealing with it. 'We don't generally do this sort of thing, you know' was the response.

However, a few days later, an invoice did arrive. It was a list of units, together with prices. A letter accompanied the invoice, confirming that upon receipt of payment, the order would be despatched within ten days. The letter was signed 'Yours sincerely/faithfully'. A small point, but another nail in the coffin of the customers' perception of quality. A cheque was despatched for the required balance.

Ten further days passed, and no units were received. Instead, a telephone call came, asking for a further £11.75 because the original order had 'been added up wrongly'. When asked for written confirmation because the original invoice showed no obvious error, the company employee replied that this would only delay things further as the order could not be processed until the full remittance had been received. In order to prevent further delay, a cheque for £11.75 was duly sent to the company.

Four weeks passed with no word from the company. The customers contacted the company by telephone. Once again, confusion reigned. The original contact was unavailable and no one knew anything about it. Once again, the phone system proved beyond the capability of some of the staff and the customers were cut off trying to reach another department.

The following day, another phone call was received by the one of the customers whilst at work:

'Oh yes, sir, the units are on the way to you at this very moment.'

This was a pity because, being in total ignorance of their delivery, there was no one at home to receive them. The company were unable to change the delivery arrangements, but fortunately the house builders agreed to receive and store the units until someone could get home to accept them. The units were placed in an adjacent garage.

Upon examination, a problem and an explanation emerged. The units were flat packed, not assembled as promised. They were supplied with gallery rails and the price of these gallery rails was £11.75! Upon telephoning the company they were told that customer service was closed, as it was after 5pm.

The next morning, the customers decided that the best solution was to return the incorrect units in person, and to sit outside the warehouse until a satisfactory solution was found. The units were placed in the car, and the car driven down to the warehouse. At this point, the matter was taken up by the warehouse manager. The first thing he said was that he had had the order ready 'to build and despatch for weeks', until he had received the order to send it out yesterday flat-packed. This he had done. He agreed to build the units and deliver them the following day. This was unfortunately not suitable, so a mutually convenient delivery date was set four days thence.

Once the assembled units were delivered another problem emerged. Unfortunately, the units delivered according to the original specification could not possibly make the required shape in the kitchen. The warehouse manager was contacted again. This time he just happened to be near the telephonist's desk when the call came in. He said he had been expecting a call as he had thought that the order did not contain enough parts to make a corner. He said that he would come down immediately and bring a selection of cupboards to complete their order, together with someone to assemble them.

He appeared within 20 minutes. The required cupboards were produced and assembled. The manager and his assistant left, satisfied that the job was at last completed satisfactorily. They did not adjust the bill to cover the extra units as they were not confident that the original estimate was correct anyway. They said that as more units had been supplied, this might provide some means of compensation. After an hour or two one of the customers walked into their kitchen with the units in the middle of the floor and noticed that the doors supplied did not match the originals. Although they were the same finish, they were not the same pattern. Another phone call was made and the warehouse manager promised to return with the correct doors, conceding that the mistake was his.

Once again, the units were assembled. Upon completion, the manager was heard to remark with a rueful grin, 'If you have any problems with your wardrobes, please ring someone else!' He also suggested that if help was wanted with 'hooking them on the wall', he could contact the fitter who was working on an adjacent property. Exhausted by the experience, the customer engaged the fitter. Fitting the job in between other jobs meant three days of the units sitting in the middle of the kitchen floor. However, when he finally came to fit the units the fitter found that 'hooking them on the wall' required:

- Levelling off the top of the tiles.
- Mitring coving and pelmet round 45 and 90 degree corners.
- Compensating for the fact that one of the doors had been wrongly hung.
- Constructing an end panel from a spare unit.
- Three hours' solid work for an experienced professional fitter.

The finished product is reported to look of a high quality!

9.2.2 *Conclusions*

This experience can provide many lessons for quality management (Figure 9.2). In particular, it highlights the problem of getting user requirements right, even though it is not in a software context.

The symptoms may be summarized as follows.

- A failure to provide an effective interface to the customer at first contact, i.e. the telephone system.
- Failure to establish customer needs.

They're ready built..just hook them on the wall...

You don't need a visit...I can tell what you need from the plans....

You need contracts that's not our department !

Figure 9.2 This is not quality!

- Failure to appreciate the consequences of the requirements.
- Failure to meet deadlines.
- No person taking responsibility at the start.
- Communication problems.

The root problems began because the salesman acting for the company thought he knew what the customers required and would not listen to them when they raised doubts. Right up until the fitter came to fit the units, problems arose because the personnel made assumptions about requirements which proved to be incorrect. Even the warehouse manager made errors because he did not realize that two doors opening at a corner will clash handles.

The second major problem arose because the human information system within the organization was very poor and incapable of facilitating proper communications. This was exacerbated by the fact that the distribution centre was situated 20 miles away from the sales office of the company.

The third problem was that only some of the people cared about the customers. The salesman did not care. The warehouse manager did care, but did not have enough information to provide what the customers required. The fitter cared because he knew he was getting paid directly by the customers. This highlights the need for the concept of internal customers, where everyone has a customer and everyone is a customer. A successful conclusion was reached eventually because enough people cared to make it happen. However, the aims of establishing a 'quality culture' and getting it 'right first time' were sadly lacking.

The story also highlights the limitations of ISO9001 accreditation. The company has ISO9001 accreditation for its manufacturing operations. However, if the administrative, sales and customer support procedures are not of the same standard, then the overall effect will not be quality. Further, the possession of ISO9001 proves that procedures exist and that should ensure that they are carried out. It will not and cannot ensure the existence of a quality culture where each and every employee cares about the quality of services and products provided.

The specification in this example is comparatively simple: only five kitchen units were involved. The need for a quality culture is much greater in more complex scenarios such as software projects. We shall now consider the story of a software house, which is trying to move towards the goal of a quality culture.

9.3 A software house: Sherwood Computer Services

Sherwood Computer Services are a software house, part of the wider Sherwood Group, whose principal business areas are disaster recovery, systems for government bodies and the financial services sector. The public services company is concerned with the supply of software and related services to local government. Its flagship housing management product is an integrated housing management system for local authorities, known as Threshold. The product is being marketed on the back of a large investment in quality, following lessons learned from the mistakes of the past.

The application of housing management is apparently ideal for computerization. There is a need for an efficient management information system and the cost of such a system should be readily recouped in greater rent revenues through greater occupation and more rapid collection. However, the computer systems provided in the past have often offered only partial solutions, dealing with one area of functionality such as rent accounting and arrears management, allocation of properties, the maintenance of property or the management of empty properties, known as voids. The ability to integrate discrete systems in these areas has often been lacking in the past.

Another problem in the supply of software to local government is the dependence upon the vagaries of central government decisions reflected in new legislation. This was seen most recently in the introduction of Community Charge or Poll Tax legislation (Hughes, 1990). The quality issues and solutions adopted by Sherwood Public Services may be seen against this background.

In 1979, a company was formed called Business Micro Systems Limited. This was later changed to LG Software to take account of the company's main business area, the supply of software to local government, hence the name. When the Government decided to give local authorities responsibility for housing benefit, BMSL decided to write a computer program to assist local authorities in its administration. The system was introduced in 1983. It was written in COBOL and ran principally on ICL mainframes running under the DME operating system, which was the major hardware platform within local authorities, the consequence of a 'made in Britain' purchasing policy in the 1970s. However, increasing use was being made of other equipment from Honeywell and IBM, as well as the alternative VME which was coming into use in some authorities. The system proved popular and became a market leader ahead of competition from ICL. Over a number of years, the client base expanded, from 50 or so in 1985 to a maximum of 90 by 1987. At the same time, the complexity of the software increased.

In 1985, the UK Government announced its intention to substantially revise the housing benefit rates to take effect from April 1988. The new rules would require a system of greater complexity. The Government continued to publish details of the new regulations up to and after the April 1988 introduction.

At first, LG Software decided that the new regulations could be accommodated within an upgrade of the software. This may well have been due to a communication breakdown between the management of the company and the development team. Management saw the job as an upgrade rather than a re-write. Deafness can sometimes be brought on by demands for higher budgets and longer timescales. The pricing and timescales were announced on this basis. This led to unrealistic pricing and unrealistic optimism about delivery. However, once work was under way, it became apparent that the new rules did indeed require a complete re-write of the software. The system was still required for delivery by Christmas 1987, in order to allow time for installation at all 90 sites before the April 1988 deadline. At this point, the project was now short on time and short on budget. With hindsight, most of the problems that followed stemmed from this error. Once the decision to upgrade rather than re-write was made, consequential problems were almost inevitable.

The project management techniques employed were not as sophisticated as they are today. PMW, a computerized project management tool, was just being introduced, and perhaps too little account was taken of the complexity of the required system. However, the techniques employed were typical of those in use at the time. The company failed to scale-up their techniques to meet their new needs.

The 1987 client base required the system to be made available in five environments:

- ICL: VME and DME
- Honeywell: DPS7 and DPS8
- IBM: System 38

The basic design was satisfactorily completed, making some use of structured analysis techniques such as SSADM. However, implementation of the design proved to be impracticable in the time available. The project was organized along traditional lines with analyst, programmers and an independent testing team.

The project plan required the system to be finished by January 1988 and on site for installation and acceptance testing. In spite of increased effort and greater use of contractors, by October 1987 it was realized that these deadlines would not be met. At this point, in an attempt to retrieve the situation, money was heavily invested, mainly in contractors. This actually reduced productivity as they took time to come 'up to speed'. Attempts to address one problem had merely created others. Similarly, testing was restricted because of the time constraints. This caused problems later on in terms of errors remaining in released software.

By 1 April, versions of the software with 80–90% of the promised functionality for ICL VME and DME, IBM and DPS regimes were available, including all the functions required immediately for 1 April. However, in order to release the software by 1 April, the curtailment of testing led to software with too many bugs, resulting in too many crashes.

Customer response was predictably angry. Litigation was threatened, although none materialized. Little cash was being received and sales of other applications were badly affected. At the same time, more money was required to fix the bugs in the software. By September, it was decided to cut the losses being incurred and transfer the customer base to the main competitor, ICL. Attempts were made to provide a continuing service to customers and ongoing support was provided on a non-upgrade basis for the LG benefit system. However, dissatisfied customers were encouraged to move to the use of HBIS, the comparable ICL product. Most moved over to ICL, but some remained with the now much better LG system. Some smaller customers moved to other systems.

The company had been acquired by the Sherwood group in 1987, but the management policy had been very much 'hands off' until the crisis had arisen. The parent group now took a greater interest. The company was re-launched under the name 'Sherwood Public Services'. Changes were made in senior management personnel. The new company was launched with a clear ethos enshrined in the Sherwood service charter:

'The Service Charter outlines Sherwood Public Services' commitment to quality products and services. The central element is a product and services guarantee. This guarantee means that services will be repeated if they do not meet customers' expectations. Ultimately, customers' money will be refunded if Sherwood fail to address problems effectively. The move to provide this guarantee was a well considered business decision. If deficiencies occur in our product or services, they cost us and the client money. We will not hide fault-fixing charters under maintenance costs. This means that we have the best possible structures to eradicate imperfections from our software and support services'.

(Sherwood company profile document, 1990)

Ever since April 1988, the company has faced the problem of convincing clients that it has learnt from its mistakes and the débâcle will not be repeated. The success of the immediate crisis management resulted in none of the threatened litigation actions being brought. However, it has taken longer to win back customer confidence.

Immediately after the re-launch, the money obtained from ICL for the Housing Benefit system customer base was made available for investment in the new company. The company looked towards a new product that would regain client confidence and distance Sherwood Public Services from its past. A new and distinctive product was needed which would be perceived as 'futuristic' and would hit the market at the right time to match changes in Government housing policy and trends towards departmental IT issues.

During the months of October 1988 to February 1989, work was carried out on a detailed investment appraisal. The appraisal document contained seven sections, a summary and detailed appendices providing support information. The seven sections covered market research, the product proposal, checkpoints, the competition, risk analysis, technical analysis and financial analysis.

Market research covered the size and state of the current market and trends for the future. It was backed by a major piece of market research carried out by Ealing School of Management.

The product proposal detailed the timing and pricing requirements, together with projected sales.

Checkpoints were provided in marketing and sales, development, client services, quality assurance and finance.

Competition looked at the competition from both other suppliers and from in-house developments.

Risk analysis was a major part of the appraisal, to minimize risk, particularly in the light of the length of time required before the product would start to pay back on its investment. Project management techniques were greatly enhanced compared with the earlier system and the project management workbench (PMW) computer-based tool was employed to achieve more realistic estimates of the required time. Further, the timescales came from the developers and were aimed at being realistic enough to provide a quality product.

The technical analysis detailed the requirements of the system, together with an evaluation of the hardware.

Finally, a financial analysis was presented which gave detailed projections for costs and income, together with details of the assumptions made.

The thoroughness of this analysis and the correctness of estimates made for a period of up to two years thence were essential to the success of the project.

The project was announced in January 1989 and the following distinctive points were made:

- It would be an integrated system, as shown in Figure 9.3, handling the principal housing management functions within one system built around a central relational database.

- It would be adaptable to changes in legislation through the use of a structured analysis and design methodology (SSADM) and a 4GL (INGRES, version 6).

- It would run under UNIX, facilitating its use as a departmental solution running on a variety of hardware platforms without the major problems experienced in 1987/88.

- Database integrity would be established and verified through the SSADM and a range of associated quality management procedures.

- The parent company would invest money from the deal with ICL into the development of Threshold in order to allow sufficient time for the system to be properly developed without the need to compromise any vital stages of the development.

- The product would be sold on the basis of quality. This 'quality' approach would be reflected in all aspects such as marketing and support as well as development.

The THRESHOLD project drew substantially upon the lessons of the past and experience gained in the company in SSADM and INGRES. Management were involved from the start to prevent any communication problems. The THRESHOLD development staff had gained credibility in the eyes of the management through their handling of the 1988 crisis. One of the highest risk areas concerned the use of the full SSADM methodology, together with the latest version of INGRES.

In the event, the use of SSADM was a popular choice with the development staff. It provided a solid base from which to work. It ensured consistency of working practices and quickly became the norm. In this sense, it aided cultural change towards the quality ethos sought by the company for THRESHOLD. The consistency of approach is also reflected in the documentation. A CASE tool was rejected as too high risk a strategy to adopt, particularly in the light of the limitations of the then current generation of CASE tools.

The desire to use the latest version of the INGRES 4GL did cause some concern. When development started, version 6.0 had not been released and development started in version 5.0 on a remote Pyramid machine. When version 6.0 was made available in an early form, some inevitable teething problems were experienced.

By February 1990, a Sequent computer had been acquired and version 6.3 of INGRES provided an excellent development environment. Targets had been set

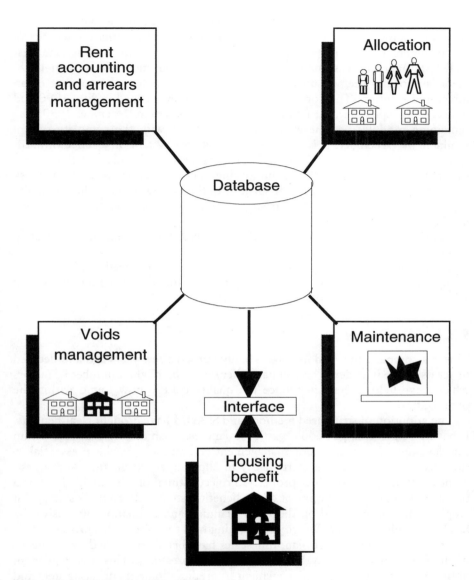

Figure 9.3 Schematic of an integrated housing management system.

and attained in both quality assurance and performance. Although development was identified as the highest risk area, support also gave grounds for concern. In order to address this area, a 'slot' system was proposed. Instead of 90 systems all going 'live' on one day, installation would be phased, limited to one a month at first. This was well received by potential customers. Components would be supplied over a period of time, the core database and rent accounting and arrears management modules first, followed by others over a 12-month period.

In spite of their best efforts, Sherwood experienced a number of problems. Sales were slow at first. This has been attributed to under-rating the scepticism of customers in the light of the events of 1988. In spite of this, the first THRESHOLD site was one of the sites that had been most unhappy in 1988. Some authorities seemed unready or unwilling to swallow the concept of an integrated solution. The core database was acceptance tested in July 1990 and delivered in September, the first modules being accepted in December 1990. The remaining modules became available during 1991, with the complete system available by December. It is intended to supply the system on a range of hardware platforms all running the UNIX operating system. Although porting is considerably easier than in 1988, it is interesting to note that it is not as trivial a task as the proponents of UNIX might suggest. In the interest of providing a quality support service, it is intended to support only three or four manufacturers' machines.

THRESHOLD has been available since 1990 and appears to be meeting expectations.

Once this change in working practices had been achieved, and new procedures clearly established, the company applied for ISO9001 accreditation in 1992 and received its certificate.

9.3.1 Conclusions

This is a company that had its fingers badly burned a few years ago and decided to set its house in order. The company themselves highlight a number of factors which have helped them introduce the quality culture now found within the organization.

The adoption of structured methods and SSADM have brought clear benefits. It has helped to change people's attitudes and establish quality practices within the development team. Senior management commitment has been essential to the success of the changes, particularly in allowing sufficient time and investment to develop the product properly. Project estimation was highlighted as a problem during the development of the benefit system and, from the start, great emphasis has been placed on thorough planning and estimation. Extensive use has been made of the PMW project planning tool to assist in this process.

Arising from the project plan, timescales have been determined by the needs of the development rather than by commercial pressures. This was dependent both upon effective project management to predict requirements accurately and senior management support to allow the development team to spend the required time and money.

An important factor has been a stable and experienced staff, with no contractors employed. This is easier to achieve when staff motivation, pride in their work and job satisfaction are high. This in turn promotes quality and any trend either to staff stability or the reverse tends to be self-sustaining. Should morale drop, staff stability falls and quality will tend to fall off. This in turn can be de-motivating and lead to further staff turnover.

With a stable workforce, the incentive to provide effective staff training in both quality management and technical matters is much greater. This in turn serves to motivate staff, and should encourage stability. Sherwood staff have received training in working practices, internal standards and team working.

The most recent innovation in the organization has been the introduction of team working practices. Teams have been established in the areas of development, marketing and support. Each team is largely autonomous and bears collective responsibility for the decisions made. Each member of staff has undergone personality profiling to ensure that as far as possible teams have a psychologically compatible membership. At the time of writing, the organization is still adjusting and it is too early to judge the success of this change. What it does reflect is the need for continual improvements. Total quality is striven for, but not arrived at.

It is worth comparing the practice with the theory. The company has certainly applied many of the ideas from quality management. An examination of current practice reveals that most of these ideas are currently implemented within Sherwoods. The approach adopted emphasizes many of the features favoured by Juran. For example, Sherwoods have adopted a team working policy to enable the formation of a quality culture within the organization by motivating and involving the staff in the management process. This actively reinforces the commitment of the whole staff, but devolves responsibility for management throughout the organization.

There remains room for further improvement, a point recognized by the organization. The first area for improvement is inter-group communications. For example, there is a feeling amongst the development staff that the marketing personnel do not consult them early enough when considering product enhancements. A further area for improvement is in the area of formalizing quality procedures. Whilst there is a clear commitment to quality in areas such as marketing, there does not appear to be the same formalization of procedures as in the development area. In areas such as support, targets have been set, but until the product goes 'live' at a significant number of sites, the procedures will not have been tested 'in anger'.

The Sherwood case study is intended to illustrate that total quality management is not about perfection, but about establishing a quality culture so that everyone in the organization is working towards improving the quality of service provided to customers.

The company did not use third party accreditation as an agent of change for its quality management practices. Instead, the accreditation process was viewed as simply another stage in the process, rather than as an end in itself. In practice, its main benefit to the company is to provide external credibility for the quality practices within the organization.

9.4 Does quality deliver benefits?*

The UK Post Office is still a public sector organization. However, it has successfully adopted many business practices and is in competition with commercial organizations in most of the profitable operations.

* The author is delighted to acknowledge the role of John Hemington in co-authoring this section.

The software operation of the Post Office is known as iT. The Post Office is effectively the sole customer of iT which is run as a distinct and separate operation. The introduction of quality practice into IT is known as Concept 2000.

As part of the project, an investigation has been carried out to consider whether there are clear business benefits to be had from an externally accredited quality management system (Hemington, 1994).

Intuitively one would expect that a project which implemented its planned approach would be more successful than one which produced plans but did not follow them, or than one which did not plan at all. It should be understood that the 'planned approach' is not static, but is modifiable in a controlled way. In order to test this hypothesis it is necessary to establish measures of success and compliance.

Once measures have been established, data can be collected for a sample of projects and the correlation can be calculated and tested for significance.

9.4.1 Metrics

The measures applied are:

- Compliance, which is derived through the application of the audit process.
- Achievement, which is derived through the weekly application of the progress monitoring process.

Compliance is calculated from the audit of a project. It equals 100 – the sum of non-conformance severities, where a severity in the range 1 to 5 is assigned to each non-conformity recorded. In the event that multiple audits are conducted on the project, compliance is the average across the audits. Compliance is in the range 0 to 100.

Achievement is calculated from data produced by the progress monitoring of tasks (Hemington, 1992). On a weekly basis each team member provides a return which states, for each assigned task, the percentage completion which has been achieved. This enables a calculation to be performed, using the task estimate, to establish the 'achieved hours' for the task. Summing the figures for all tasks, the total achieved/the total planned can be established, i.e. percentage achievement to date. If the latter is averaged over all the weeks for which progress monitoring is applied, this provides a very good measure of how closely to its plan the project is performing.

Achievement is generally in the range 0 to 100, although scores of greater than 100 are possible, indicating progress ahead of plan.

9.4.2 Data

The sample data was obtained from 14 projects which used the REDD (formerly CAIG) Quality System during the period 1990–93 (see Table 9.1).

Note that the projects are listed in chronological order, showing a generally positive trend in compliance and achievement scores. Three projects conducted during the period were excluded from the table, two small projects because they were not audited and one project because insufficient progress monitoring data was available.

Table 9.1 Project compliance and achievement scores

Project	Compliance	Achievement
1	47	61
2	95	95
3	76	94
4	67	80
5	83	65
6	44	70
7	44	70
8	91	79
9	87	97
10	83	90
11	85	88
12	88	82

The data is represented in the scatterplot of Figure 9.4.

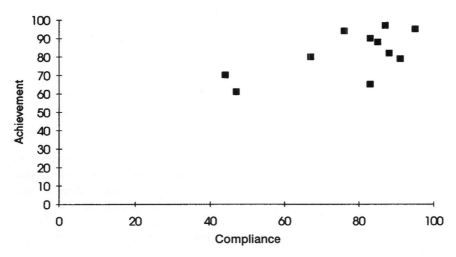

Figure 9.4 Scatterplot of compliance against achievement.

9.4.3 Results

Regression analysis of the sample data using Quattro Pro produces a correlation coefficient of 0.699. This is shown to be statistically significant, indicating that there is a relationship between compliance and achievement.

9.4.4 Implications for an existing quality system

It has been found that compliance with a planned approach has a positive impact on project performance. At the project level it is possible to take advantage of the correlation between compliance and achievement by establishing a linear fit which can be used to predict achievement levels, identify possible cost savings, and encourage higher compliance. The sample data yields a regression line with the profile in Table 9.2.

Table 9.2 Project compliance and achievement predictions

Compliance	Achievement	Prediction
47	61	75
95	95	90
76	94	90
67	80	83
83	65	77
44	70	79
44	70	79
91	79	83
87	97	91
83	90	88
85	88	87
88	82	84

Table 9.2 was calculated using a regression line of

Predicted achievement = 0.44 × compliance + 48.53.

The data can be used to bring pressure to bear on project managers to apply their plans, i.e. to conform to the quality system. A further use is to estimate losses incurred by not following plans; this in turn provides ammunition to bring about changes in attitude and priority at senior management level within an organization. Yet another use is to measure the effectiveness of the quality system itself; the realized benefits as a proportion of potential benefits would provide the metric.

For organizations considering introducing or extending the scope of a quality system, the relationship between compliance and achievement can be used to infer potential benefits. The reasoning is as follows.

If there is no quality system governing a project, one would expect the project to perform in a similar manner to a project which operates under a quality system but which does not follow its plans adequately. Therefore current achievement, where achievement is defined in a manner appropriate to the organization's working practice, may be related to low compliance and used as a basis for deriving achievement which would be likely from high compliance. The difference represents potential quality system benefits.

9.4.5 Estimating the benefits

The cost of low compliance

Difficulties in establishing agreements between iT and the Post Office businesses which are its customers mean that it is not possible to derive, for each of the projects in the sample above, a specific cost associated with the compliance/ achievement data. However, substantial data is available for the project with the lowest compliance, and this will be assumed to be representative for projects operating at that level of compliance.

This indicates that the project experienced the following overruns:

- effort: +70%
- timescale: +20%
- cost: +30%

Undoubtedly, part of the difficulty for the project related to scope changes which were not reflected in changes to plans. In terms of management control, failure to implement the plans was manifested in shortcomings in aspects such as applying walkthroughs, documenting design and planning for testing. As a consequence of the approach, work on the later lifecycle stages was started prematurely on unstable baselines, resulting in propagation of defects, high rework levels introducing further defects, etc. In short, quality was not planned in advance and built into the software.

Since the impact of scope changes remains unknown, it will be assumed that low implementation of plans accounts for 50% of the cost overrun, i.e. for 15% of project budget. Since the top-performing projects deliver at or very close to plan for effort, timescale and cost, the picture which emerges is of a performance differential between top compliance and lowest compliance of 15% in cost terms.

Past benefits

At the time, the area operating the quality system had a software development budget of about £3 million per annum. This suggests that the potential maximum benefit of the quality system, which would have been realized if all projects had operated at high compliance resulting in high achievement, was about 15% of budget, i.e. £450,000 per annum. Clearly, however, optimum performance for every project is a highly unlikely prospect.

The sample data has the following compliance profile:

minimum: 44
mean: 76
maximum: 95
range: 95 – 44 = 51
mean – minimum: 32
% of range attained on average: 32/52 = 63%

(Note that the observed maximum compliance of 95 is used in preference to the potential maximum of 100 since the audit which finds no non-conformities could be argued to be flawed.)

The above suggests that the REDD quality system may have delivered a benefit of 63% of its potential, i.e. £283,500 per annum. Since most of the work conducted under the quality system was on a time and materials basis, the benefits obtained will have been seen as capacity to undertake additional development activity for the Post Office businesses rather than as savings to those businesses.

Furthermore, 63% may be regarded as an effectiveness measure of the quality system.

Future benefits

Currently, the quality system is being rolled out to cover all software development activity within iT. This means expanding the number of users from about 50 to 250. The software development budget for the area is £28 million. This suggests a potential benefit of £4.2 million per annum. If just 50% of that potential could be realized it would represent a saving of more than £2 million per annum. Does such a saving seem plausible?

The Price Waterhouse report for the DTI (Price Waterhouse, 1988) addresses the question of the cost of quality. Its figures, based on a number of assumptions, indicate the potential for savings on failure costs of 5% to 10% of supplier turnover. For iT this would represent savings in the order of £1.4 million to £2.8 million, which is consistent with the £2 million suggested above.

A number of caveats must be made regarding the case presented above. These include the following.

• The analysis relies heavily on data for one project.
• The audit process is based on sampling, therefore compliance scores cannot be precise. In spite of this, the compliance scores which arose for the sample did reflect the quality manager's intuitive picture on relative project positioning on the basis of the audit reports which were produced.
• The progress monitoring used for this paper is conducted only for the 'constructive' phases of development, i.e. for design and unit code and test. Consequently quantitative progress figures are obtained from only part of the development process. (Monitoring of progress during later test phases is conducted, but relies on recording of test runs and fault occurrence, and so does not lend itself to the purpose of this paper.)

To improve the validity of estimates the approach could be improved to take account of:

- contract baselines
- faults/KLOC reported per system during the first six (or 12) months following delivery
- customer satisfaction measures.

9.5 Discussion

Having considered the potential benefits of operating a quality system, it is worth considering why such benefits appear to be so rarely achieved. This book has argued previously for the key role of people and the culture of the organization, through its critical effect on the operation of the quality system. Where the quality system and culture are congruent, the full potential benefit may be achieved. Where the match between the quality system and culture is poor, a negligible benefit may be achieved.

After potential benefits have been identified, the quality system should be designed so as to achieve an optimum match to the culture and to bring about any required changes in the culture.

Corporate culture is widely recognized as an important factor to be addressed when instigating organizational change. Yet in the area of quality, the question of culture tends to be closely associated with TQM initiatives and given little attention with respect to quality systems.

A quality system can only be successful if it is designed for the organization which it is to support. Design and implementation of a quality system must take account of the culture. This does not mean that existing values and norms need to be preserved at all costs. It does, however, mean that the elements which characterize a culture should be recognized, so that when interventions are made to introduce a quality system these can build on the positive elements while planned efforts are made to manage the culture away from the more negative elements.

The strategy may be termed 'fit and shift', in that the quality system should both fit onto the culture and bring a shift in those elements of the culture which need to be modified or discarded.

The quality system design needs to provide for multiple levels of information feedback so as to meet the requirements of ISO9001. A further consideration is to help establish a culture where the richness of the feedback can support the many levels of learning which it operates. ('Business deal with systems', Hampden-Turner, 1990). The quality system should be adaptable and flexible to mirror the adaptability and flexibility required of the organization in which it operates.

With the benefits potential already estimated as discussed earlier in the paper, the benefits being achieved should be tracked as a measure of the effectiveness of the quality system design. This will enable corrective action to be taken to establish a closer alignment between quality system and culture. It should also be recognized, however, that in some instances the culture may be such that the gap to be bridged to enable a reconciliation to the principles of ISO9001 may be too great.

9.6 Questions for discussion

1. Consider the service provided by the kitchen company.

    (a) What steps need to be taken to improve the service provided by the kitchen company?
    (b) Which of these fall under the scope of the quality management system?
    (c) What other procedures might be used to implement change?

2. Sherwood did not implement a CASE tool.

    (a) What advantages did this give them?
    (b) What potential benefits did they miss out on?
    (c) Which effect do you think was greater?

3. Consider the method of analysis used in the Post Office case study.

    (a) Do you think that it would convince a sceptical manager?
    (b) What other factors might you consider to support the case for a quality management system?
    (c) How might you explore the link between culture and success?

9.7 Further reading

Hemington, J. (1992) ISO9001: from requirement to reality, *Proceedings Third European Conference on Software Quality*, Madrid.

Hemington, J. (1994) Concept 2000: supplying quality software to the UK Post Office, *Proceedings Fourth European Conference on Software Quality*, Basle.

Chapter 10

Trends in quality: the future

10.1 Four key issues in quality

By way of conclusion, it is the purpose of this chapter to examine four key areas which will critically impact upon software quality in the next few years. They are:

- tools and methods
- process improvement
- standards
- meeting business needs.

10.2 Are CASE tools addressing the right issues?

CASE tools have been presented by some of the more irresponsible vendors and sectors of the press as the ultimate answer to quality, productivity and the universe. However, CASE tools were introduced to address very specific issues, namely to increase productivity and to reduce maintenance costs. This does not necessarily mean that the use of CASE tools will lead to uniform increase in all aspects of software quality.

There would also appear to be a disparity between the theory and the reality of the use of CASE tools by organizations.

The theory that maximum benefit in both quality and productivity is achieved by the wholesale adoption of fully-blown integrated CASE tools is not borne out in practice. This may be attributed to a number of reasons.

1. Limitations in technologies and tools.
   CASE tools still rarely deliver fully automated and reliable code generation (Figure 10.1). From a quality perspective, the ability to generate automatically a true representation of the design without the possibility of introducing errors at coding remains an attractive proposition. However, facilities are still very limited in this area.
   Automated code generation facilities may be missing for one of several reasons:
   - A front-end tool may be used which is not intended to provide these facilities.

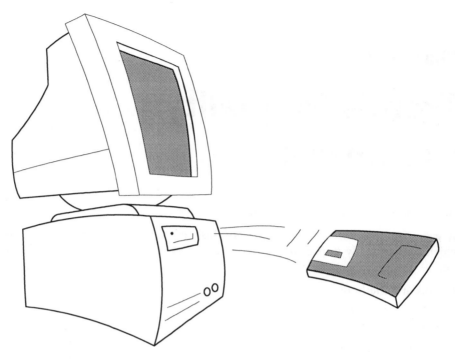

Figure 10.1 In most cases, computers do not generate their own code.

- Code generation is provided by a third party product which is not fully integrated with the rest of the tool.
- The code generation facilities prove to be difficult to use in practice.

All these problems have been experienced in the practical use of CASE technology (see, for example, Gillies and Smith, 1994). Without this 'missing' link the CASE tool loses one of its greatest advantages, the integrity of the design from inception to finished code.

2. Problems with existing systems
   Some companies have found that the integrated CASE tools are unable to provide systems which can be used alongside the existing systems. The theoretical solution of re-engineering old systems is superficially attractive, but has many practical problems.
3. CASE doesn't address the right issues
   However, the principal barrier to the positive impact of CASE upon the quality of systems is that it doesn't address the critical issues. CASE is targeted at improving the technical quality of a product rather than its fitness for purpose for business users.

   In order to consider the impact of CASE tools upon the overall quality of the final product, each criterion of quality may be examined in turn. The criteria to be considered are drawn from the model described in Chapter 4.

Two scenarios are considered. In the idealized case, we assume that an integrated CASE tool is used with full code generation facilities, automating the process from start to finish. In the 'real-world' scenario, the CASE tool is used for design only, with manual implementation of the generated design.

4. Maintainability

   One of the primary aims of the introduction of CASE tools is to reduce the costs associated with maintenance. This is achieved by a well-structured design and the automated production of software from the design, eliminating errors at implementation (the proverbial 'error-free' software). However, the practical experience of the use of CASE tools in the design phase alone shows fewer advantages. Further, any maintenance required of automatically generated code can only be carried out within the CASE environment as automatically generated variable names tend to make the source code unintelligible.

5. Reliability

   The reliability of code developed using CASE tools should again be enhanced due to the reduced number of errors arising from both carefully structured design and automatic implementation. However, practical use of current tools fails to gain full advantage through its use of manual coding, where errors can be introduced into the software.

6. Integrity

   The integrity of the software should be boosted by the use of CASE tools at both the design and implementation stages. Most tools offer assistance in normalization of data and checking that the code design is consistent. However, the greatest integrity is sacrificed if manual implementation of the design is employed as errors may still be introduced at the implementation stage.

7. Security

   The security of the software is dependent upon specific features built into the system. These are not generally specifically addressed within CASE tools and thus the impact of the tools on security is unlikely to be great.

8. Efficiency

   Code developed using CASE tools is unlikely to be efficient. If CASE tools are used only for design, then the program should be well structured. Structuredness of code conflicts with efficiency and thus the resulting code is likely to be inefficient. Automated code generation is likely to exacerbate these problems, since generated code cannot be manually optimized for performance.

9. Usability

   The impact of CASE tools upon usability is unlikely to be great. Most tools do provide some form of interface development aid, but these are not generally integrated with the underlying methodology at the heart of the development process. Thus the impact upon usability will be limited. Wider issues of usability beyond the provision of an attractive interface, such as user entry level requirements, are not considered.

10. Portability

   The portability of systems based upon the full integrated CASE process is severely limited, since the code generator is tied to a particular language and implementation, e.g. the IEF code generator produces COBOL code with DB2 database handling commands. This conflicts with the growth of open systems, based upon a variety of 4GL languages, all running under the UNIX operating system on various hardware platforms. The portability of designs generated by front-end tools is much greater, and such designs can be used to generate systems written in COBOL or 4GLs or even other 3GLs such as C. However, such designs do not actively promote portable source code which depends upon implementation without the use of hardware-specific features. They may therefore be regarded as neutral with respect to portability.

11. Adaptability

The adaptability of the software is closely linked with the maintainability of the code. Similar arguments apply, so that the greatest benefits will be achieved with the fully integrated approach and retrospective adaptation of generated code will require a return to the original design for modification, followed by regeneration of code.

12. Cost/benefit

CASE tools are designed to reduce software development costs by improving productivity and reducing maintenance costs. Against the benefits which can be expected, the cost of the tool must be weighed. In addition, there may be costs associated with training or re-training. The benefits will not be seen immediately as the gains in productivity will build up over time. Many organizations are quoting 'learning times' of the order of two years before full benefits are experienced. The use of CASE tools for design only will carry lower costs, since simpler and cheaper tools may be employed and re-training is likely to be less expensive. However, the longer-term benefits are likely to be correspondingly smaller.

13. Timeliness

The delivery time should be shorter using CASE tools than manual processes, improving the timeliness of the software. However, practical experience suggests that the gains occur in the implementation phase whether manual or automatic. Such gains are balanced by extra time spent in the design phase due to all the procedures required by the underlying methodology. The net effect tends to be neither beneficial nor detrimental. The timeliness should improve as the development staff become more familiar with the tools but, once again, this may take years rather than months.

14. Ease of transition

The experience of many organizations in making the transition from manual methods to CASE methods is unfortunately negative, both in terms of adoption of new development methods and in transition from old systems to new. One organization tried to implement a fully-blown integrated CASE procedure only to fall back to existing procedures because of staff problems in adapting to the new methods. Another organization is trying to put IEF in place, but is struggling to find a point where the transition can be made without fatal disruption to ongoing projects. The manager responsible indicated that 'IEF expects a greenfield site' and that he could not provide one. Compatibility of systems is a particular problem with automatic code generation systems.

15. User-friendliness

    The CASE tools do not provide tools or processes to study the impact of systems upon the end users in terms of their business objectives. Without this facility for examining the wider implications of the implemented systems, the effect upon this aspect of quality is likely to remain small and difficult to quantify.

    These effects are summarized in Table 10.1. The table shows the effect of the introduction of CASE technology in terms of a tick for a benefit and a cross for an adverse effect. The effects are graded according to strength: a single tick or cross for a lesser effect and a double tick or cross for a stronger effect. No effect is shown as a circle. The ideal case is compared with practical experiences gathered from organizations.

    The overall effect is positive when considering the technical aspects of quality and less positive when considering the wider implications of quality for the organization. Once again, quality improvements have focused upon improving the match to specification. It is also worth noting that many of the advantages of the CASE tools, particularly the use of 'front end' tools for design, are derived from the underlying methodology rather than the tool itself. Only when code generation is automated does the automation really start to pay dividends. Any break in the chain from inception to code provides a weak link and a potential loss in integrity. It may be compared with taking software from one system and typing it into another, rather than providing a direct communication link. It may not, therefore, be cost-effective for organizations to invest in current CASE tools.

Table 10.1 The effect of CASE in terms of quality criteria

Quality criteria	The ideal CASE	Practical implementation
Maintainability	✓✓	✓
Reliability	✓✓	✓
Integrity	✓✓	✓
Security	O	O
Efficiency	××	××
Usability	O	O
Portability	××	O
Adaptability	✓✓	✓
Cost/benefit	✓✓	✓
Timeliness	O	O
Ease of transition	××	O
User-friendliness	O	O

A better investment may be to focus upon gaining maximum benefit from a methodology using a manual system and simple computer aids such as drawing packages for constructing data modelling diagrams and prototype screen layouts.

If CASE tools are to bring genuine improvements in overall quality, they must be employed with care and thought within the context of an overall quality system.

10.3 Is process improvement appropriate for software development?

Process improvement is at the heart of most quality management procedures, whether they are known as total quality management (TQM), continuous quality improvement (CQI), or some other variant. However, it is not a panacea and there are issues which must be addressed if it is to be successfully applied to software development. There are differences between the manufacturing sector, where process improvement first developed, and the software development sector. Interestingly, up to five years ago, many authors argued that process improvement was a generic technique and was, therefore, universally transferable.

Much of the recent work on software quality improvement and quality standards, e.g. ISO9000-3, CMM and SPICE, has emphasized the distinctive elements of software development.

Some of the most distinctive features focus upon the role of the client in the software development process. One of the greatest strengths of the computer is its adaptability. In order to take advantage of this, much of the work carried out within software development is bespoke in nature. Clients play a much greater role in the development of software than is often the case with the manufacture of artefacts. Because of the adaptability of the computer and the rate of change of the technology itself, the needs of the user are likely to change rapidly and the software solution is expected to be able to respond to these changes without compromising the integrity of the product.

The nature of the product makes it more difficult to model for the purpose of discussing requirements. Whereas a physical model may be built for manufactured artefacts, the modelling techniques available to model data and code within software are more nebulous and less transparent to the user.

In order to apply the process improvement principles described in Chapter 7 to software development, we must address two types of issues: the process and the people. Inevitably, the two are inextricably linked.

Consider first the process. We have already seen that methodologies and CASE tools can bring advances in technical quality. However, it is also necessary to address the wider issues relating to user satisfaction. The development process required within a quality management system must be systematic and well understood. Most of the well-established methodologies, e.g. SSADM, IEM, SAM, place a strong emphasis upon gathering user requirements and verifying that the design process accurately reflects those requirements. However, this does not seem to produce the results desired by users. There seems to be a genuine need for an element of prototyping in a development cycle, as users cannot visualize software products in the way that they can visualize a manufactured artefact.

One approach is to take advantage of CASE tools and methods, but encompassed within an iterative loop. The requirements analysis phase of such methodologies is replaced by a broader iterative cycle, which aims to promote user involvement in the actual process of software development. Initial requirements are set by consultation with the users. These are not intended to be comprehensive or cast in stone. Rather they are intended to form the basis of a first system which may then evolve through evaluation by users. The purpose of the sequential methodology is to produce a faithful representation of the user requirements in the implemented code. This represents high 'match-to-specification' quality. However, if high overall quality is to be achieved, this specification must be prepared to evolve rather than remain static. This type of approach must be monitored by strict change control procedures in order to protect system integrity.

This approach may improve cost/benefit and timeliness through the early identification of problems in the resulting system. Even where this is not achieved, some of the system is delivered early. This will allow the user to start making use of the system or training users before the formal deadline. It is almost certain to improve clients' understanding of why any over-runs in time or budget may occur should this be necessary.

However, no procedures will effectively improve quality without a change in the organization and the people within it. Much of the work carried out within the process improvement area is concerned with changing people and organizations rather than just their production procedures. Many of these concepts transfer more easily between the manufacturing and computing sectors than the procedures themselves.

The principal barrier to quality in software development is the relationship between the client and the developer. At worse, this relationship is adversarial in nature and even in more enlightened environments, the client is generally regarded as a necessary evil. The result is limited user input into the development process. Given the vital importance of user requirements in software development, this is often disastrous for the long-term user satisfaction with the product, and the result is that it becomes another technical success that fails to be perceived as a quality product by the user.

Two issues must be addressed here. The first is the question of a rigid requirements specification, which has been at least partially addressed within the proposed procedure. However, the author's view has already been expressed that the use of diagramming methods and tools has a limited role to play in the solution, since a lack of tools is only a small part of the problem.

The second issue is an 'attitude problem'. Expert systems have shown that users can be involved in the system development process. Techniques such as knowledge elicitation (see Hart, 1989) can be used to obtain knowledge, ideas and expertise from non-technical personnel. There must first be a recognition on the part of the system developer that such personnel can make real and valid input to the system development beyond the traditional requirements analysis carried out at the start of the project. There is a further recognition that the involvement of users is not about 'telling people how to do their job' but about a fruitful partnership in search of a better product.

What is needed are different types of methods intended to establish a team approach and to change people's attitudes. The aim is to establish a state where the developers see the users, whether internal or external, as their customers and seek to genuinely meet their needs, and the users recognize that the developers are their customers in the sense that they must supply at the very least a problem definition. This means establishing the recognition that each group is critically dependent on the other, like the business analysis and software development groups described in Chapter 6. This will not be achieved overnight and certainly not by legislation. However, it should form a central part of any quality improvement programme.

The concept of quality circles can be used to further explore the problems that exist, and thereby achieve a consensus on the way forward. Quality circles should not simply be based around development teams but should include user representatives. The author's LOQUM technique (Gillies, 1994) is another technique developed to ensure that quality models take account of user views. In this way, solutions to problems should be acceptable to users and development teams should gain an understanding of the users' point of view.

Blank (1990) highlights five causes for resistance to change which may occur singly or in combination:

- insecurity
- a perception of change for change's sake
- prejudices because of bad experience
- conflict with self-interest
- communication problems.

Many of these issues can be tackled by education. The resistant person must see some benefit to overcome their resistance. This may be in the form of a better product, or more tangible benefits such as an easier life, a more enjoyable job, greater profitability reflected in job security or higher bonuses. Education should be concerned with explaining what quality is all about, how it may be achieved and what the benefits are to the personnel concerned. This may prove a greater problem within Western society than in Japan, where quality management ideas were originated. Western culture is more individualistic than Oriental cultures and Western sceptics will often want to see personal benefits. The idea of a 'quality culture' is essentially collective and this may not match the individualistic culture of Western society. Where quality management ideas have been most easily accepted in the UK manufacturing sector, it is often in geographical areas such as the North-East of England where a communal culture still exists and where high unemployment makes for a malleable workforce.

Quality is fundamentally a management problem. Without management commitment and belief, any initiatives to improve quality are doomed to failure. One of the biggest problems in management is to take a long-term view. Just as with CASE tools, the costs will initially outweigh the benefits. The primary reason for the Japanese success in quality in manufacturing is the recognition that quality is necessary for long-term profitability.

The conclusion must be that the adoption of total quality management practices within software development can have a beneficial effect on quality. However, the key to success is the management of organizational and cultural change. The characteristics of a successful transition to a 'quality culture' are:

- Personnel educated about quality and aware of its associated benefits.

- A co-operative rather than adversarial relationship with clients.

- A recognition of quality as user acceptability rather than conformance to specification.

- User involvement in all phases of software development.

- A commitment from management to a long-term view of profitability.

These will be achieved not by the adoption of specific methods but by successful management of change amongst the staff. Crucially, this depends upon achieving co-operation rather than confrontation (Figure 10.2).

10.4 What is the likely impact of standards?

The most common quality management standard remains the ISO9000 series of standards for quality management systems. We shall consider it first then consider emerging standards for process improvement such as CMM and SPICE.

The practice of quality management without an externally accredited QMS is at best inconsistent and, at worst, very poor. This is not the issue. The issue is whether the introduction of a quality system certified to ISO9001 is a cost-effective solution. The enthusiasm of the UK Government and the accompanying scepticism of some software suppliers have already been noted. If this scepticism is to be overcome, a number of problems remain.

Figure 10.2 Successful change depends upon changing conflict ... into co-operation.

10.4.1 The cost/benefit equation

The costs of a QMS and subsequent accreditation can be clearly documented, and are substantial. The benefits are less easy to quantify. Although maintenance costs are recognized as a major component of software costs, the attainable reduction is a matter of debate. The costs of such a system may alternatively be recouped by increasing prices. There is little hard evidence from customers that they are prepared to pay a premium for software produced by a process accredited to ISO9001. Even if they accept that quality is a good thing, there is an expectation that it is up to the supplier to get it right and bear the cost. Whilst there are cheaper sources of software which are not accredited, a quality premium may make the supplier uncompetitive.

The real problem is that the costs are clearly defined, but the benefits require a 'leap of faith'. Until the benefits are well documented in hard financial terms, many suppliers will resist investment until pushed by their customers.

10.4.2 The vital ingredient – staff

It is the author's view that a QMS will only work with the full co-operation of the staff. If the staff are ill-disposed towards the scheme, they will regard it as a bureaucratic nightmare that stifles creativity and produces mountains of paper that would have been more useful if they had remained as trees. The staff must believe that the system will both boost profitability and do their own personal job better.

Since many suppliers remain sceptical about the benefits of ISO9001, and are only applying for certification in order to satisfy customer demand, they face a problem convincing their own staff about the benefits. A QMS put in place as a marketing tool can easily be seen as a bureaucratic Big Brother, acting as if the customer were at the shoulder of the system developer all the time, joggling his or her elbow. A company which embraces quality management in the conviction that it will lead to better quality and higher profitability will surely have an easier job convincing their employees. Many large companies who supply the UK Government, who were required to put BS 5750 in place, are now spending a lot of money producing glossy brochures to convince the staff that quality is a 'good thing'.

10.4.3 Reducing administration

Another way to increase staff co-operation is to minimize the effort required to produce the reports and documentation which form an essential part of any quality system. This may be facilitated by the use of CASE tools. Many of these tools have extensive facilities for automatic generation of reports, or at least facilities to carry out many of the routine tasks required in document preparation.

However, administration and staff effort may also be reduced by designing the QMS around existing good practice. All organizations do some things well. The aim when designing a QMS should be to take advantage of existing 'islands' of good practice within the development lifecycle (Figure 10.3).

There are no universal solutions in quality, although the introduction of an accredited QMS will bring a number of advantages. It should ensure that quality management is both systematic and consistent. It should produce better monitoring of quality and, therefore, earlier detection of problems and errors. This in turn should reduce maintenance costs. It may also assist in marketing by allowing the company to project a 'quality' image.

However, these benefits come at a high financial cost, and there are a number of quality problems which these systems do not address:

- The emphasis in these systems is on conformance to specification. Fitness for purpose is less well served by these systems.
- User expectations are already high. These systems may raise unrealistic expectations, particularly in the area of adaptability, where testing requirements may make changes more expensive in terms of time and cost.
- Sometimes, users want 'quick and dirty' solutions. There is no scope for such compromise in these standards.
- The benefits are only likely to be realized gradually, so therefore return on investment may be slow at first.
- The benefits are likely to be least where good practice already exists.
- Some problems require an elegant as well as competent solution. There is little evidence that these systems will enhance elegance as well as competence.

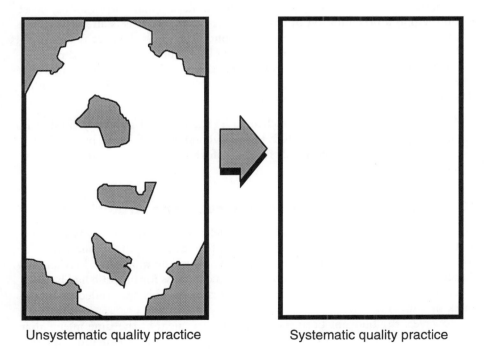

Unsystematic quality practice   Systematic quality practice

Figure 10.3 The aim of a QMS is to spread and systematize existing good practice (schematic).

Within their stated objectives, these QMSs can achieve good results. However, in order to maximize return on investment, it seems likely that unrealistic claims will be made in the name of marketing, and if this occurs, a backlash may set in.

The biggest potential argument against standards of this type in terms of maximizing quality is that ISO9000 tends to fossilize processes and act as a barrier to continuing improvement. This is the reason why new standards are being developed based upon continual process improvement rather than a static quality management system. CMM and SPICE are examples of this type.

Many of the benefits of ISO9000 also apply to these standards. Unfortunately, most of the counter-arguments in the bulleted list above also apply. The major difference between the different standards is that the newer standards do allow for continuous improvement and should therefore encourage implementation of better and improving procedures.

However, there are two drawbacks which may yet prove to be significant barriers to acceptance:

- Cost. Many organizations, particularly small to medium-sized companies, already regard the cost associated with ISO9000 to be beyond their means. The cost of achieving the higher levels of CMM or SPICE may prove to be prohibitive for all but a small group of the largest organizations.
- Imposition. Most standards gain acceptance because large and significant customers, e.g. government departments and multinational corporations, insist on them as a precondition of tendering for contracts. This is already starting to happen with CMM. However, such conditions generally specify a particular level of capability. Therefore, they are using the standard as a threshold, which does not encourage improvement once the required standard is reached. This reduces the significance of the CMM or SPICE to another static quality management standard.

Although CMM v1.0 was launched in 1991, it is still relatively limited in impact, especially in Europe. SPICE is due to complete validation by 1997. It is likely to be a number of years, therefore, before it is possible to state the true impact of standards of this type.

10.5 Beyond software quality: the need for a strategic view

In the 1970s, software quality was largely concerned with how well the software met the technical requirements contained in the specification, emphasizing the conformance to specification view of quality. Thus, the models of McCall and Boehm were conceived. In the 1980s, the idea of fitness for purpose had become much more important in software quality research. This was reflected in the work of Gilb and others.

However, the buoyant business conditions prevalent at the time meant that many organizations did not scrutinize their spending on information systems and consider whether the software systems they were purchasing were indeed fit for their intended purpose, and indeed whether they provided value for money.

In the 1990s, with more stringent economic conditions, many managers are starting to raise their expectations of the quality of their software systems. The honeymoon period for information systems would appear to be over; it now has to justify its existence in terms of a return on the resources invested, alongside other technologies. It should be remembered that software is not as different as we might like to think: Juran highlighted the issue of fitness for purpose within manufacturing back in the late 1940s.

At the same time, the way that information systems are implemented within the organization has changed. The present emphasis is on a strategic view of information and the systems used to process it, supporting the overall business strategy of the organization. These factors taken together suggest that the scope of software quality is likely to evolve into a more strategic view of quality. If software quality is seen as fitness for purpose, then a strategic view of software quality might treat quality as:

'the degree to which information provided by software systems fulfils its objective of enabling the business strategy to be achieved.'

The purpose of information systems is defined within the information technology (IT) strategy. This is required to meet the needs of the information strategy, which in turn should meet the needs of the business strategy. This view of quality is summarized in Figure 10.4.

Some work has been done in this area under the heading of IT effectiveness. However, whilst it has been clearly identified as a problem (NCC, 1989), there is a dearth of good solutions. The problems in providing solutions may be

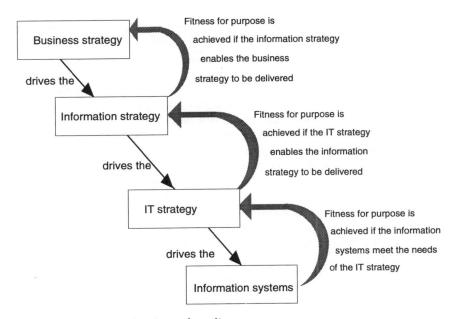

Figure 10.4 A strategic view of quality.

divided into two groups. The first set comprises those which are already familiar from the rest of the book:

- What criteria should be employed?
- Are the criteria universal, or should they be locally defined?
- How should they be measured?
- Is it possible to provide an overall measure of effectiveness?

Many of these issues were discussed as part of the NCC's IMPACT programme, intended to provide some answers to these problems. However, they do not yet seem to be effectively resolved.

The second problem faced by an organization seeking to investigate the match between IT and business strategies is to separate the impact of IT from other factors influential upon the success of the business strategy, e.g. management structure and style, competitive performance, external political and economic factors. IT effectiveness goes beyond software to include the totality of IT within an organization. It represents how effectively an organization is making use of the technology, and how this is reflected in the achievement of overall business objectives.

The issue of resolving the contributions from IT changes and management changes is particularly tricky. After all, IT changes not accompanied by management change are less likely to be effective. IT often has an enabling role to play in management changes. It could, therefore, be argued that this encouragement of management change is actually a valuable part of effective IT practice. If so, how can this can be quantified, and distinguished from other factors?

The consideration of IT effectiveness rather than simply software quality reflects a certain maturity in the technology. Traditionally, investment has been justified in terms of increased efficiency, e.g. 'how many people have we managed to make redundant?' However, with a much more sophisticated role for IT in today's commercial environments, the justification for investment rests upon more sophisticated arguments and forming part of an organization's strategic decision-making process. Many of the claimed benefits for IT do not appear explicitly on a balance sheet, e.g. better decision-making, better response time to customers, competitive advantage. There is a need to distinguish effectiveness from simple efficiency. IT efficiency is seen by the author as the ability of the IT function to enable the organization to reap short-term explicit financial benefits which should appear on the balance sheet. Examples would include savings in staff costs, increased production for the same staff cost and so on. IT effectiveness is concerned with more nebulous concepts such as competitive edge, company image and quality of decision-making. By their very nature they are much harder to measure. The distinction mirrors that between productivity and quality in more conventional software quality terms. Productivity is visible and quantifiable, whilst quality is much less so. Another distinction which may be made is that quality and effectiveness are long term, whereas productivity and efficiency show immediate benefits.

Answers to selected questions
Chapter 3

1.

	Passage 1	Passage 2
Fleisch–Kincaid index	16.8	14.6
Gunning–Fog index	18.8	16.7

2.

Group	Criteria	Metric	Weight	Product	PWF
	Usability	0.7	0.5	0.35	
Product	Security	0.5	0.5	0.25	
Operation	Efficiency	0.6	0.2	0.12	2/3
	Correctness	0.7	0.5	0.35	
	Reliability	0.4	0.4	0.16	
Product	Maintainability	0.8	0.4	0.32	
Transition	Adaptability	0.7	0.1	0.07	1/3
	Expandability	0.7	0.1	0.07	
Product operation weighted mean				0.42	
Product transition weighted mean				0.20	
PWF quality measure				0.35	

Chapter 6

2.

Module	'000 lines of code per module	No. of errors	QKZ2	QKZ2	
1	20	147	7.36	<3	1
2	23	183	7.96	3 to 6	2
3	22	186	8.45	6 to 9	8
4	24	265	11.05	9 to 12	5
5	30	276	9.21	>12	4
6	35	427	12.21		20
7	17	110	6.45		
8	23	205	8.90		
9	32	398	12.43		
10	34	544	16.00		
11	21	217	10.32		
12	12	38	3.20		
13	15	92	6.13		
14	32	435	13.59		
15	21	137	6.54		
16	23	212	9.23		
17	12	67	5.57		
18	18	162	9.00		
19	6	15	2.46		
20	21	206	9.82		
		Mean	8.80		
		Standard deviation	3.25		
		Correlation	0.91		

References

Ashworth, C. and Goodland, M. (1990) *SSADM: A Practical Approach*, McGraw-Hill, London.

Awad, E.M. and Lindgren Jr, J.H. (1992) Skills and personality attributes of the knowledge engineer: an empirical study, *Proceedings IAKE'92 Conference*, IAKE, New York.

Ayre, J., McFall, D., Hughes, J. and Delobel, C. (1995) A method for re-engineering existing relational database applications for the satisfaction of multimedia based requirements, *Conference Proceedings at the 6th International Hong Kong Computer Society Database Workshop*, 3–4 March 1995.

Barker, R. (1990) *CASE Method: Tasks and Deliverables*, Addison-Wesley.

Bissell, A.F. (1990) Multi-positional process evaluation: an example and some general guidelines, *Total Quality Management*, 1 (1), 95–100.

Blank, R.E. (1990) Gaining acceptance: the effective presentation of ideas, *Total Quality Management*, 1 (1), 101–14.

Boehm, B. (1981) *Software Engineering Economics*, Prentice-Hall, New York.

Boehm, B. *et al.* (1978) *Characteristics of Software Quality*, North-Holland, New York.

Box, G. and Jones, S. (1990) An investigation of the method of accumulation analysis, *Total Quality Management*, 1 (1), 115–23.

Brigham, F.R. (1975) Some quantitative considerations in questionnaire design and analysis. *Applied Ergonomics*, June, 90–6.

Brockelhurst, S., Shan, P., Littlewood, B. and Snell, J. (1989) Adaptive software reliability modelling, in *Measurement for Software Quality Assurance* (eds B. Kitchenham and B. Littlewood), Elsevier.

CCTA (1990) *SSADM Version 4 Reference Manual*, NCC–Blackwell, Manchester.

Chen, E.T. (1978) Program complexity and programmer productivity, *IEEE Trans. Soft. Eng.*, SE-4 (3), 187–94.

Chikofsky, E.J. and Rubenstein, B.L. (1988) CASE: reliability engineering for information systems, *IEEE Software*, 5 (2), 11–16.

Coats, R.B. and Vlaeminke, I. (1987) *Man–Computer Interfaces: An Introduction to Software Design and Implementation*, Blackwell, Oxford.

Computer Software and Applications Conf., IEEE, 499–504.

Constantine, L.L. and Yourdon, E. (1979) *Structured Design*, Prentice-Hall, New York.

Crosby, P.B. (1979) *Quality is Free*, McGraw-Hill, London.

Crosby, P.B. (1986) *Quality is Free*, McGraw-Hill, London (2nd edn).

Davis, C., Gillies, A.C., Smith, P. and Thompson, J.B. (1993) Current quality assurance practice amongst software developers in the UK, *Software Quality Journal* **2** (3), 145–61.

Davis, J.S. (1984) Chunks: a basis for complexity measurement, *Information Processing and Management Theoretical Computing Science*, 38, 145–71.

DeMarco, T. (1979) *Structured Analysis and System Specification*, Prentice-Hall, New York.

Deming, W.E. (1986) *Out of the Crisis*, MIT Center for Advanced Engineering Study, Cambridge, Mass.

Department of Defense (1985) STD 2167A standard.

DeYoung, G.E. and Kampe, G.R. (1979) Program factors as predictors of program reliability, *Proc. Comp. Software and Applications Software Conf.*, IEEE, 668–73.

Dickson, P. (1972) *Proc. Reliability and Maintainability Symposium*, IEEE.

Dreyfus, S.E. (1985) The nature of expertise, *IJCAI*, 85 (2), 1306 et seq.

Duda, R.O. and Reboh, R. (1984) AI and decision making: the PROSPECTOR experience in artificial intelligence in business (ed. W. Reitmann) 111–47, Ablex, NJ.

Duda, R.O. and Shortliffe, E.H. (1983) Expert systems research, *Science*, 220, 261–8.

Dunkelberger, K.A. (1989) OFC: a deliverable military planning aid, *Proc. Applications of AI VII Conference*, Orlando, SPIE 1095, 725–34.

Edwards, H., Thompson, J.B., and Smith, P. (1994) *The STePS Method*, McGraw-Hill, London.

Ernst and Young (1992) *The Landmark MIT Study: Management in the 1990s*, Ernst & Young, New York.

Fenton, N. and Pfleeger, S.L. (1996) *Software Metrics: A rigorous and practical approach* (2nd edn), International Thomson Computer Press, London.

Fergus, E., Hedley, D., Marshall, A., Veevers, A. and Hennell, M. (1988) The quantification of software reliability, *Proc. Software Engineering '88*.

Feuer, A.R. and Fowlkes, E.B. (1979a) Relating computer program reliability to software measures, *Proc. Nat. Comp. Conf.*, IEEE, 1003–12.

Feuer, A.R. and Fowlkes, E.B. (1979b) Some results from an empirical study of computer software, *Proc. 4th Int. Conf. on Soft. Eng.*, IEEE, 351–5.

Finkelstein, C. (1989) *An Introduction to Information Engineering – From Strategic Planning to Information Systems*, Addison-Wesley, Sydney.

Fisher, A. (1988) *CASE: Tools for software development*, Wiley, New York.

Fowler, F.J. (1988) *Survey Research Methods*, Sage Publications, USA.

Frühauf, K. (ed.) (1994) Software Quality: Concern for People, *Proceedings of the 4th European Conference on Software Quality*, VDF, Zurich, ISBN 3 7281 2153 3,

Funami, Y. and Halstead, M.H. (1975) *A Software Physics Analysis of Akiyama's Debugging Data*, Lafayette.

Gachnig, J., Klahr, P., Pople, H., Shortliffe, E. and Terry, A. (1983) Evaluation of expert systems: issues and case studies, in *Building Expert Systems* (eds F. Hayes-Roth, D. Waterman and D.B. Lenat).

Gane, T. and Sarson, C. (1977) *Structured Systems Analysis: Tools and Techniques*, McDonnell-Douglas, St Louis.

Garvin, D. (1984) What does product quality mean? *Sloan Management Review*, 4.

Gilb, T. (1977) *Software Metrics*, Winthrop (out of print).

Gilb, T. (1988) *Principles of Software Engineering Management*, Addison-Wesley.

Gilchrist, J.M. (1992) Project evaluation using the SEI method, *Software Quality Journal*, 1, 37–44.

Gillies, A.C. (1990) *Software Quality Workshop*, IT Institute, Salford: report available from the author.

Gillies, A.C. (1991) *The Humanization of the Software Factory, Information and Software Technology*, Special CASE edition, 33 (9), 1–6.

Gillies, A.C. (1992) Modelling software quality in the commercial environment, *Software Quality Journal*, 1, 175–91.

Gillies, A.C. (1993) LOQUM: locally defined quality modelling. *Total Quality Management*.

Gillies, A.C. and Hart, A.E. (1989a) Using knowledge-based ideas in image processing: a case study in human computer interaction, *Proc. BCS Expert Systems Conf. ES'88*, Brighton, UK, CUP.

Gillies, A.C. and Hart, A.E. (1989b) Using knowledge to enhance the scope and efficiency of image processing in fringe analysis, *IEEE/SPIE Applications of Artificial Intelligence VII, SPIE Proc. No. 1095*, Florida, USA.

Gillies, A.C. and Hart, A.E. (1992) On the use of graphical techniques to display profiles and quality, *Total Quality Management*, 3, (1).

Gillies, A.C. and Smith, P. (1994) *Managing Software Engineering*, Chapman & Hall, International Thomson Publishing, London.

Gong, H. and Schmidt, M. (1988) A complexity measure based upon selection and nesting, *ACM Sigmetrics*.

Gordon, R.D. (1979) Measuring improvements in program clarity, *IEEE Trans. Soft. Eng.*, SE-5 (2), 79–90.

Gunning, R. (1968) *The Technique of Clear Writing*, McGraw-Hill.

Halstead, M.H. (1977) *Elements of Software Science*, Elsevier.

Hampden-Turner, C. (1990) Corporate Culture for Competitive Edge, *The Economist Publications*.

Hansen, W.J. (1978) Measurement of program complexity by the pair (cyclomatic number, output count) *ACM SIGPLAN Notices*, 4, 29–33.

Hart, A.E. (1989) *Knowledge Acquisition for Expert Systems*, 2nd edn, Chapman & Hall, London.

Henry, S. and Kafura, D. (1981) Software structure metrics based upon information flow, *IEEE Trans. Soft. Eng*, SE-7 (5), 510–18.

Huda, F. and Preston, D. (1992) Kaizen: the applicability of Japanese techniques to IT, *Software Quality Journal*, 1 (1), 9–26.

Hughes, C. and Clark, J. (1990) CASE: the reality of current utilization, *Inf. Executive. J. Inf. System. Management*, 3 (3).

Hughes, L. (1990) 'Community charge: the Scottish Experience', *Proc. ITLG90 Conference*, Brighton, UK, HMSO, 3–5.

Humphrey, W.S. (1987) *Characterising the Software Process: A maturity framework*. Software Engineering Institute, CMU/SEI-87-TR-11, DTIC Number ADA182895.

Humphrey, W.S. (1989) *Managing the Software Process*, Addison-Wesley, Reading, MA.

Humphrey, W.S. and Sweet, W.L. (1987) *A Method for Assessing the Software Engineering Capability of Contractors*. Software Engineering Institute, CMU/SEI-87-TR-23, DTIC Number ADA187320.

Imai, M. (1986) *Key to Japan's Competitive Success*, McGraw-Hill.

Ince, D.C. (1988) *System Complexity*, Information Technology Briefings, Open University.

Ishikawa, K. (1985) *What is Total Quality Control? – the Japanese Way* (translated by D.J. Lu) Prentice-Hall, Englewood Cliffs, NJ.

ISO (1986) *Quality Vocabulary*, ISO8042.

ISO (1987) ISO9000–9004, from BSI in the UK. Reissued with minor modifications in 1994.

ISO (1991) ISO9000-3: *Notes for Guidance on the Application of the ISO9001 Standard to Software Development*, ISO.

Itakura, M. and Takei, H. (1994) Small group oriented KAIZEN in business software, *Software Quality Concern for People*.

Jackson, M.A. (1975) *Principles of Program Design*, Academic Press, London.

Jackson, M.A. (1983) *System Development*, Prentice-Hall, London.

Jacob, R.J.K. (1985) Designing expert systems for ease of change, *Proc. IEEE Symposium on Expert Systems in Government*, 246–51.

James Martin Associates (1988) *An Introduction to Information Engineering*, Texas Instruments.

Jorgensen, A.H. (1980) *A Methodology for Measuring the Readability and Modifiability of Programs*, BIT, 20, 394–405.

Juran, J.M. (1979) *Quality Control Handbook*, 3rd edn, McGraw-Hill, London.

Kafura, D. and Henry, S. (1981) Software quality metrics based upon interconnectivity, *Journal of Systems and Software*, 2, 121–31.

Kanji, G.K. (1990) Total quality management: the second industrial revolution, *Total Quality Management*, 1 (1), 3–12.

Kentger, R. (1981) cited in Watts, R. (1987) *Measuring Software Quality*, NCC Publications.

Kepner, C.H. and Tregoe, B.B. (1981) Entscheidungen vorbereiten und richtig treffen. Rationales Management: die neue Herausforderung, Verlag Moderne Industrie (in German, work cited in English in Watts (1987) *Measuring Software Quality*, NCC Publications).

Kincaid, J.P. *et al.* (1981) Computer readability editing system, *IEEE Trans. Prof. Comm.*, PC-24 (1), 38-41.

Kirkham, J.A. and Satiation, C. (1992) *An Analysis of the DTI SOLUTIONS Programme*. The ITI Papers, 3 (3), 25–31, IT Institute, University of Salford, Salford, Manchester M5 4WT.

Kitchenham, B. (1989a) Software metrics, in *Software Reliability Handbook* (ed. P. Rook) Elsevier.

Kitchenham, B. (1989b) Software quality assurance, *Microprocessors and Microcomputers*, 13 (6), 373–81.

Kliem, R.L. and Ludin, S.L. (1992) *The PEOPLE Side of Project Management*, Gower, USA.

Lantz, K.E. (1989) *The Prototyping Methodology*, Prentice-Hall, New Jersey.

Lehman, M.M. (1990) Uncertainty in computer application and its control through the engineering of software, *Journal of Software Maintenance*, 1 (1), 3–28.

Lightfoot, (1995) SPICE Home page on the World Wide Web, URL.

Logica (1988) *Quality Management Standards for Software*.

Long, J. and Dowell, J. (1989) Conceptions of the discipline of HCI: Craft, applied science, and engineering, *Proc. BCS HCISG Conf. People and Computers* V, 9–34, CUP.

Longworth, G. and Nicholls, D. (1986) *The SSADM Manual*, NCC-Blackwell, Manchester.

Low, C. (1992) TickIT, getting the message across, in Solomonides, C.M., Kirkham, J.A., Bowker, P. and Gillies, A.C. *SOLUTIONS Case Studies. The ITI Papers*, 3 (1), IT Institute, University of Salford, Salford, Manchester, M5 4WT.

Low, G.C. and Jeffrey, D.R. (1991) Software development productivity and back end CASE tools, *Information and Software Technology*, 33, 9, 616–24.

Maier, H.H. (1983) 'Die Prufung des Software-Qualitatsmerkmals Benutzungs-freundlichkeit', *QZ Management der Qualitatssicherung*, 1, 28 (in German, work cited in English in Watts, R. (1987) *Measuring Software Quality*, NCC Publications).

McCabe, T.J. (1976) A complexity measure, *IEEE Trans. Soft. Eng.*, SE-2, 4, 308–20.

McCall, J.A. (1980). An assessment of current software metric research, *Proceedings EASCON80*, IEEE, 333–3.

McCall, J.A. *et al.* (1977) Concepts and definitions of software quality, *Factors in Software Quality*, NTIS, 1.

McClure, C.L. (1978) A model for program complexity analysis, *Proc. 3rd Int. Conf. Soft. Eng.*, IEEE, 149–57.

Mills, H.D. (1980) *IBM Systems Journal*, 4.

Mohanty, S.N. and Adamowicz, M. (1976) Proposed measures for the evaluation of software, *Proc. Symposium on Computer Soft. Eng.*, MRI, New York Polytechnic, 485–97.

Musa, J.D. (1975) A theory of software reliability and its applications, *IEEE Trans. Soft. Eng.*, SE-1, 312–17.

Myers, G.J. (1976) *Software Reliability: Principles and Practice*, Wiley, New York.

Myers, G.J. (1979) *The Art of Software Testing*, Wiley, New York.

Naur P. *et al.* (1976) *Software Engineering: Concepts and Techniques*, Petrocelli/Charter, New York.

NCC (1989) *The Impact Programme*, details from NCC, Oxford Road, Manchester, UK.

NCC (1990) *PRINCE Manual*, NCC–Blackwell, Manchester.

Oakland, J. (1989) *Total Quality Management*, Heinemann.

OED (1990) *The Concise Oxford English Dictionary*, 9th edn, OUP.

Oppenheim, A.N. (1966) *Questionnaire Design and Attitude Measurement*. Open University/Heinemann, London.

Ottenstein, L.M. (1981) Predicting numbers of errors using software science, *Proc. ACM Annual Conf.*, ACM, 157–67.

Oviedo, E.I. (1980) Control flow, data flow and program complexity, *Proc. Computer Software and Applications Conf.*, IEEE.

PACTEL (PA Computers and Telecommunications) (1985) *Benefits of Software Engineering Methods and Tools*, Department of Trade and Industry, London.

Paige, M. (1980) A metric for software test planning, Proc.

Parkinson, J. (1990) Making CASE work, in *CASE on Trial* (eds K. Spurr and P. Layzell), Wiley, New York.

Parnas, D.L. (1979) Designing software for ease of extension and contraction, *IEEE Trans. Soft. Eng.*, SE-5, 128 et seq.

Paulk, Mark C. (1995a) The evolution of SEI's Capability Maturity Model, *Software Process – improvement and practice*, pilot issue,1, 3–15.

Paulk, Mark C. (1995b) How ISO9001 compares with the CMM, *IEEE Software*, 12, No. 1, 74–83.

Paulk, Mark C. and Garcia, Suzanne M. (1994) The impact of evolving the Capability Maturity Model to version 1.1, *Crosstalk: The Journal of Defence Software Engineering*, 7, **No. 9**, 7–11.

Paulk, Mark C., Curtis, Bill, Chrissis, Mary Beth and Weber, Charles V. (1991) Capability Maturity Model for Software, *Software Engineering Institute*, CMU/SEI-91-TR-24, DTIC Number ADA240603.

Paulk, Mark C., Curtis, Bill, Chrissis, Mary Beth and Weber, Charles V. (1993) *Capability Maturity Model for Software*, version 1.1, Software Engineering Institute, CMU/SEI-93-TR-24, DTIC Number ADA263403.

Paulk, Mark C., Weber, Charles V., Garcia, Suzanne M., Chrissis, Mary Beth and Bush, Marilyn W. (1993) *Key Practices for the Capability Maturity Model*, version 1.1, Software Engineering Institute, CMU/SEI-93-TR-25, DTIC Number ADA263432.

Paulk, Mark C., Konrad, Michael D., and Garcia, Suzanne M. (1995) CMM versus SPICE architectures. *Software Process Newsletter*, IEEE Technical Committee on Software Engineering.

Perry, W. (1987) *Effective Methods of EDP Quality Assurance*, 2nd edn, Prentice-Hall.

Peters, T. (1988) *Thriving on Chaos*, Macmillan.

Peters, T. and Waterman, R. (1982) *In Search of Excellence*, Harper & Row.

Price Waterhouse (1988) *Software Quality Standards: the Costs and Benefits*, Department of Trade and Industry, London.

Price Waterhouse (1990) *Information Technology Review* 1989/90, Publications Office, Price Waterhouse, 32 Bridge Street, London SE1 9SY, p. 19.

Price Waterhouse (1992) *Information Technology Review* 1991/92, Publications Office, Price Waterhouse, 32 Bridge Street, London SE1 9SY, p. 7.

Radice, R.A., Harding, J.T., Munnis, P.E. and Philips, R.W. (1985) A programming process study, *IBM Systems Journal*, 24, No. 2.

Rector, A. (1989) Address to local research seminar.

Remus, H. and Zilles, S. (1981) Prediction and management of program quality, *Proc. 4th Int. Conf. on Soft. Eng.* IEEE, 341–50.

Rock-Evans, R. (1991) *CASE Analyst Workbenches: a Detailed Product Evaluation*, Volume 4, Ovum Ltd, 7 Rathbone Street, London W1P 1AF. ISBN 0 903969 41 6, p. 47.

Rout, T.P. (1995) SPICE A Framework for Software Process Assessment, *Software Process Improvement and Practice*, pilot issue, 57–66.

Rumelhart, D.E. and McClelland, J.L. (1986) *Parallel Distributed Processing* (Vols 1 and 2) MIT Press: Cambridge, Mass.

Salford University Business Services Limited (1991) *Software Engineering Solutions: Final Report*, Department of Trade and Industry, London.

Schmitz, P. *et al.* (1975) Ein Kombinationsverfahren für Rangfolgeentscheidungen Schriftreihe des Rechenzentrums der Universitaat zu Koln, vol. 23 (in German, work cited in English in Watts, R. (1987) *Measuring Software Quality*, NCC Publications).

Simpson, H. (1986) The MASCOT method, *Software Engineering Journal*, 5, 103–20.

Sinclair, M.A. (1975) Questionnaire design. *Applied Ergonomics*, June, 73–80.

Solomonides, C.M., Kirkham, J.A., Bowker, P. and Gillies, A.C. (1992) *SOLUTIONS Case Studies*. The ITI Papers, 3 (1), IT Institute, University of Salford, Salford, Manchester M5 4WT.

Sommerville, I. (1989) *Software Engineering*, 3rd edn, Addison-Wesley.

Spikes Cavell (1993) Software methodologies, *Computing*, 8 April, 20–1.

Sprouls, J. (1990) IFPUG. *Function Point Counting Practice Manual* Release 3.0, IFPUG, Westerville, OH, USA.

Stacey, R.D. (1990) *Dynamic Strategic Management for the 1990s*, Kogan Page.

Stobart, S.C., Thompson, J.B. and Smith, P. (1990) An examination of the benefits and difficulties that the implementation of a software development environment can present within the DP industry, *Int. Conf. on System Development Environments and Factories*, Berlin.

Stobart, S.C., Thompson, J.B. and Smith, P. (1990) An analysis of the use of commercial CASE tools. *4th Int. Workshop on CASE*, California.

Stobart, S.C., Thompson, J.B. and Smith, P. (1991) CASE: software development, *IEE Computer-Aided Engineering Journal*, 8 (3), 116–21.

Stobart, S.C., Thompson, J.B. and Smith, P. (1991) The use, problems, benefits and future directions of CASE in the UK. *Information and Software Technology*, 33 (9) 629–36.

SUBSL, ed. Gillies (1991) *Case Studies in Software Engineering*.

Taguchi, G. (1981) *On-line Quality Control During Production*, Japanese Standards Association, Tokyo.

Taylor, J.R. (1989) *Quality Control Systems*, McGraw-Hill, London.

Thayer, T.A. *et al.* (1977) *Software Reliability Study*, TRW-SS-76-03, IEEE Computing Society.

TickIT (1991) *TickIT: Making a Better Job of Software*, Department of Trade and Industry, London.

Torsun, I.S. (1987) PAYE: A tax expert system, in Research and Development in Expert Systems III, *Proceedings ES'86*, 69–80, CUP.

Warnier, J.D. (1981) *Logical Construction of Systems*, Van Nostrand Reinhold, New York.

Watts, R. (1987) *Measuring Software Quality*, NCC Publications.

Weber, C.V., Paulk, M.C., Wise, C.J. and Withey, J.V. (1991) *Key practices for the Capability Maturity Model*, Software Engineering Institute, CMU/SEI-91-TR-25, DTIC Number ADA240604.

Woodward, M.R. *et al.* (1980) Experience with path analysis and testing programs, *IEEE Trans. Soft. Eng.* SE-6 (6) 278–86.

Yasuda, K. (1989) Software quality assurance activities in Japan, in *Japanese Perspectives in Software Engineering*, Addison-Wesley.

Yau, S.S. and Collofello, J.S. (1979) Some stability measures for software maintenance, *Proc. Computer Software and Applications Conf.*, IEEE.

Yin, B.H. (1979) Software design testability analysis, *Proc. Computer Software and Applications Conf.*, IEEE, 729–34.

Yin, B.H. and Winchester, J.W. (1978) The establishment and use of measures to evaluate the quality of software designs, *ACM Software Engineering Notes*, 3 (5), 45–52.

Yourdon, E.N. (1989) *Modern Systems Analysis*, Prentice-Hall, New York.

Zolnowski, J.M. and Simmons, D.B. (1979) A complexity measure applied to Fortran, *Proc. Computer Software and Applications Conf.*, IEEE.

Zopf, S. (1994) Improvement of software development through ISO9001 certification and SEI assessment, Software quality: concern for people: *Proceedings of the 4th European Software Quality Conference*, 224–31, VDF, Zurich, ISBN 3 7281 2153 3.

Further reading

Bader, J., Edwards, J., Harris-Jones, C. and Hannaford, D. (1988) Practical engineering of knowledge-based systems, *Information and Software Technology*, 30 (5).

Baugh, P.J, Gillies, A.C. and Jastrebski, P. (1993) An expert database system for business planning, *Information and Software Technology*, 35 (3), 131–7.

Beynon-Davies, P. (1987) Software engineering and knowledge engineering: unhappy bedfellows? *Computer Bulletin*.

Bleazard, G.B. (1976) *Program Design Methods*, NCC–Blackwell, Manchester.

Born, G. (1988) *Guidelines for Quality Assurance of Expert Systems*, Computing Services Association.

Buxton, J.N., Naur, P. and Randell, B. (eds) (1969) Software engineering techniques, *Proc. NATO Conference* (Rome, 1969), published by the Scientific Affairs Division, NATO, Brussels.

CCTA (1983) Central Government Mandatory Standard No. 18, Parts 1–6, Central Computer and Telecommunications Agency, London.

Chisholm, S. and Gillies, A.C. (1994) A snapshot of the computerisation of general practice and the implications for training, *Auditorium*, 3 (1).

Cupello, J.M. and Mishelevich, D.J. (1988) Managing prototype knowledge/expert system projects, computing practices, *Communications of the ACM*, 31 (5).

Curtis, B. (1990) Managing the real leverage in software productivity and quality, *American Programmer*, 3, No. 7, 4–14.

Cutts, G. (1987) *Structured Systems Analysis and Design Methodology*, Paradigm Press, London.

Dahl, O.-J., Dijkstra, E.W. and Hoare, C.A.R. (1972) *Structured Programming*, Academic Press, New York.

Davis, C., Gillies, A.C, Smith, P. and Thompson, J.B. (1993) Current quality assurance practice amongst software developers in the UK, *Software Quality Journal*, 2 (3), 145–61.

Edwards, J.S. (1991) *Building Knowledge Based Systems – towards a methodology*, Pitman.

Eva, M. (1992) *SSADM Version 4: A User's Guide*, McGraw-Hill, London.

Gillies, A.C. (1992) Measuring software quality in the commercial environment, *Software Quality Journal*, 1 (3).

Gillies, A.C. (1994) LOQUM: locally defined quality modelling, *Total Quality Management* 5 (3), 71–5.

Gillies, A.C. (1994) On the usability of software for medical audit, *Auditorium*, 3 (1).

Gillies, A.C. (1995) The computerization of general practice: an IT perspective, *Journal of Information Technology*, 10 (1).

Gillies, A.C. and Baldeh, Y. (1995) 20 years on from MYCIN – the lessons that should have been learnt in methods, co-operative decision-making and validation for medical applications, *Romanian Journal of Applied Medical Informatics*, 1(1), 1–10 .

Gillies, A.C. and Hart, A.E. (1992) On the use of graphical techniques to describe profiles and quality, *Total Quality Management*, 3 (1).

Gillies, A.C., Smith, P. and Lansbury, M. (1994) 'The validation of KBS: current practice and agents for change', *Journal of AI, Cognitive Science and Applied Epistomology*.

Gomaa, H. (1986) Software development for real-time systems. *Comm. of the ACM*, 29 (7), 657–68.

Hall, P.A.V. (ed.) (1990) *SE90: Proceedings of Software Engineering 90*, Cambridge, UK.

Hekmatpour, S. and Ince, D. (1988) *Software Prototyping, Formal Methods and VDM*, Addison-Wesley, London.

Hemington, J. (1992) ISO9001: from requirement to reality, *Proceedings Third European Conference on Software Quality*, Madrid.

Hemington, J. (1994) Concept 2000: supplying quality software to the UK Post Office, *Proceedings Fourth European Conference on Software Quality*, Basle.

Hickman, F.R. (1989) *The Pragmatic Application of the KADS Methodology*, The Knowledge-Based Systems Centre of Touche Ross Management Consultants.

IEEE (1983) *IEEE Standard Glossary of Software Engineering Terminology*, IEEE Standard 729–1983, IEEE, Washington, USA.

Ince, D. (1991) *Software Quality and Reliability: Tools and Methods*, Chapman & Hall, London.

Jones, G.W. (1990) *Software Engineering*, Wiley, Chichester.

Juran, J.M. (1988) *Juran on Planning for Quality*, Macmillan, New York.

Macro, A. and Buxton, J. (1987) *The Craft of Software Engineering*, Addison-Wesley, London.

Mair, P. (1987) Integrated project support environments, *Electronics and Power*, 33 (5), 317–23.

Martin, J. (1982) *Program Design Which is Probably Correct*, Savant Research Studies, Carnforth.

Martin, J. and Finkelstein, C. (1981) *Information Engineering*, Savant Research Studies, Carnforth.

Mellor, S.J. and Ward, P.T. (1986) *Structured Design for Real-Time Systems*, Yourdon Press, New York.

Moller, K.H. and Paulish, D.J. (1993) *Software Metrics*, Chapman & Hall, London.

Naur, P. and Randell, B. (eds.) (1969) Software engineering: report on a conference sponsored by the NATO Science Committee (Garmish, Germany, 7–11 October, 1968) published by Scientific Affairs Division, NATO, Brussels.

Olphert, C.W., Poulson, D.F. and Powrie, S.E. (1990) ORDIT: the development of tools to assist in organizational requirements definition for information technology systems, *Conference Proceedings Computer, Man and Organization* II, 9–11 May, Nivelles, Belgium.

Paulk, Mark C. and Konrad, Michael D. (1994) An overview of ISO's SPICE project, *American Programmer*, 7 (2), 16–20.

Porter, D. (1992) *Towards the Common KADS Method*, Touche Ross Management Consultants.

Price Waterhouse (1988) *Software Quality Standards: The Costs and Benefits*, Price Waterhouse Management Consultants, London.

Radice, R.A., Harding, J.T., Munnis, P.E. and Philips, R.W. (1985) A programming process study, *IBM Systems Journal*, 24 (2).

Ratcliff, B. (1987) *Software Engineering: Principles and Methods*, Blackwell, Oxford.

Spurr, K. (1989) CASE: a culture shock, *Computer Bulletin*, 1 (5), 9–13.

Stamps, D. (1987) CASE: cracking out productivity, *Datamation*, 1 July, 55–8.

Stevens, W.P, Myers, G.J. and Constantine, L. (1974) Structured design, *IBM Systems Journal*, 13 (2), 115–39.

Thompson, J.B. (1989 and 1990) *Structured Programming with Cobol and JSP*, Vols 1 and 2, Chartwell Bratt, Bromley.

Thompson, J.B. and Edwards, H.M. (1990) Analysis and design methods for computer based information systems – the impact of the post-1992 single European market, *European Trade and Technology Conference ETT'90*, Sunderland, UK.

Warnier, J.D. (1977) *Logical Construction of Programs*, Van Nostrand Reinhold, New York.

Index

accreditation 143, 148–152, 155,
    157–165, 183, 188, 212
  second party 143
  third party 143, 152, 155,
    157–165
adaptability 6, 18, 22, 32, 49, 52,
    206, 208
AQAP 145
automation 14, 32, 55, 72, 84, 206
availability 4, 46, 47, 48–9

BAA (Business Area Analysis) 82
Blank 210
Boehm 17, 18, 21, 22, 27, 31, 32,
    34, 36, 45, 54
Box 111
Brockelhurst 56
BS5750
  See also ISO9001/EN29001 144
BSD (Business System Design) 82

CASE 13, 14, 56, 74, 80, 83–87,
    89–92, 203, 212, 214
clarity 22
CMM 167–177, 179
code generation, automatic 87,
    203–208
comparability 33
complexity 12, 18, 33, 35, 37, 38, 58,
    69, 74, 87, 95, 128–130, 196
constraints 4, 7, 13, 48, 50, 51, 74,
    77, 190
COQUAMO 34, 53–56

COQUAMO-1 54–55
COQUAMO-2 54–55
COQUAMO-3 54–56
corrective action 55, 110, 150, 153,
    162
correctness 12, 18, 20, 23, 24, 26,
    33, 34, 36, 192
cost benefit 206, 212
critical factors 3
Crosby 12, 13, 45, 102–106, 108,
    109, 118
cyclomatic number 35, 38

dataware 48
decision table 80
DeMarco 78, 80, 101
Deming 45, 102–104, 107, 109, 123
descriptive metric
  See also metrics 31
design specification 7, 48, 80
DFD (Data Flow Diagrams) 78
Dickson 48
direct measurement 22, 24, 29, 57,
    207
documentation 22, 34, 49, 73, 74,
    77, 80, 84, 95, 98, 107, 110,
    125, 127, 147–151, 192, 212
DoD (US Department of Defense) 6,
    34, 143
DTI (Department of Trade and
    Industry) 131, 145, 155, 165

ease of transition 25, 207

economy 3, 4, 32
effectiveness
    See also IT effectiveness 18, 35,
        36, 49, 58, 87, 108, 151,
        155, 215–217
efficiency 19, 23–27, 33, 34, 41, 61,
    64, 205, 207, 216
ELHs (entity life histories) 79
EN29001 155
E-R (entity relationship) modelling
    87–88
error detection 34
error prediction 34
evolutionary development 45, 46, 96
Excelerator 84–86
expandability 22, 36
expectation 5, 212

Fenton 56–59
fidelity 48
fitness for purpose 12, 102, 104, 120,
    129, 214
flexibility 6, 53
Ford Escort 4–5, 14

Garvin 11, 15, 53
Gilb 45–53, 66, 94, 95, 130
Gillies 6, 129, 204, 210
Gordon 35
Gunning 34

Halstead 34
Hansen 35
Hart 209
hierarchical models 16, 17, 21, 24,
    25
histograms 111
Hughes 189

ICASE (Integrated CASE) tools 85, 87
IEF(Information Engineering Facility)
    85–87, 206
IEM (Information Engineering
    Methodology) 70, 82–86
IEW (Information Engineering
    Workbench) 85
insecurity 97

integrity 19, 20, 37, 48, 49, 72, 85,
    89, 124, 192, 204, 205, 207
interoperability 99
inverse 18, 22–24
ISD (Information Systems
    Development)
    See also methodology 70, 136
Ishikawa 109, 110, 111, 112
ISO (International Standards
    Organisation) 5, 106, 142–147,
    152–155, 165–166, 175
ISO9000–3 145–147, 152–154
ISO9001 144–147, 152–154
ISO9002 144–147, 152
ISO9003 144–147, 152
ISP (Information Strategy Planning)
    82, 83
IT (Information Technology) 6, 10,
    22, 29, 31, 99, 125, 127, 129,
    145, 152–155, 191, 196, 215,
    216
    effectiveness 60, 214–216

Jackson 79
Juran 12, 102–105, 107, 109, 195
Jorgensen 35

Kaizen 137–8
Kepner-Tregoe method 39
Kincaid 34
Kitchenham 3, 34, 52, 53

Lantz 69, 101
Logica 165
logical design 74, 77
LOQUM 129, 135, 137, 210

maintainability 4, 18, 20–25, 31–33,
    35–38, 47, 49, 52, 56, 131,
    205, 207
management of change 117
manufacturing view 13
market research 190
McCabe 35, 36
McCall 17–22, 31, 32, 36, 38, 214
methodology 12, 13, 69–74, 81–85,
    106, 109, 131–134, 205–208

METKIT 175
metrics 29, 30, 31–34, 36–40
Mills 95
Mini 3, 4, 14
mini-specification 80
models of quality 16, 143
modifiability 21
modularity 23, 35
Mohanty 35
MTTF (Mean Time To Failure)
    34–35, 52
Musa 35
Myers 18, 35

Oakland 107, 108, 11, 119
OED (Oxford English Dictionary) 4

Paige 36
PAPI 58, 60
Pareto analysis 110, 112
Perry 18, 22–24, 27
physical design 74, 76, 77, 79
    control 79
polarity profiling 40
portability 23, 33, 36, 37, 205
predictive metric 31
Price Waterhouse Consultants 125,
    131, 165, 200
product operation 19, 40
    revision 19, 40
    transition 19, 40
product-based view of quality 11, 12
production 6, 82–84, 87, 110, 115,
    139, 205, 216
productivity 50, 52, 55, 58, 84, 85,
    138, 165, 190, 203, 206, 216
project estimation 80
PWF (Phased Weighting Factor)
    38–40

QIP (Quality Improvement
    Programme) 106, 109
QIT (Quality Improvement Team)
    118, 135
QMS (Quality Management
    Standard) 14, 106–110, 117,
    125, 130–132, 143–144, 212

quality
    assurance 27, 56, 70, 74, 80,
        125–128, 131–134, 137, 193
    audit 115, 152, 153
    chain 120
    circle 107, 117, 118, 135
    control 103, 125, 133, 152
    criteria 4, 13, 18, 21–24, 26, 29,
        36, 38, 45, 56, 207
    culture 109, 117, 120, 122, 130,
        135, 136, 152, 187, 210
    drivers 54
    factors 53
    measurement of 22, 29, 45
    of software See software quality
    overall measure of 17, 22, 24,
        216
    standards 144–155
    See also BS5750, ISO9000/3,
        ISO9001, accreditation
    views of 7, 9, 11, 14, 53, 74

rapid prototyping 130
RDA (Relational Data Analysis) 79
readability 34–37
records of achievement 17
relationships 22–24, 36, 38, 87, 110
reliability 4, 10, 12, 18, 19, 32–37,
    39, 47, 52, 55, 58, 73, 85, 205
Remus 34
requirements analysis 7, 12, 73, 77,
    79, 94
requirements specification 13, 77, 80,
    134
reusability 23, 24, 33, 55
Rolls-Royce 3–5, 11, 13

SAM (Structured Analysis
    Methodology) 80, 84
scatter diagrams 111, 113
Schmitz 40
security 10, 23, 39, 49, 205
simple scoring 38
software
    engineering 13, 33, 45, 69, 89, 90,
        94, 124, 128, 139, 170
    factory 6, 115, 116

quality 5, 6, 14, 21, 29, 31, 60, 98,
    115, 117, 130, 143, 203, 216
SPC (Statistical Process Control) 104,
    107, 109–111, 113
specification 4, 6, 13, 73, 77, 80, 89,
    115, 184, 209
SPICE 175–180, 211, 214
SSADM 74–80, 132, 190, 192, 194
standardization 33, 131
strategic view of quality 214, 215
structure charts 80
structuredness 31–32, 69

Taguchi 111
Taylor 133
TD (Technical Design) 82
Telon 85
testability 25, 135
TickIT 154–156, 160–161, 165
timeliness 206, 209
Total Quality Management (TQM) 13,
    102, 106–108, 113, 201, 208
traceability 146, 149
training 46, 52, 96, 104, 105, 110,
    118, 132, 134, 135, 151, 206
transcendent 11

UNIX 194

usability 23, 25, 33–37, 39, 43, 47,
    49, 52, 56, 58, 72, 205
usefulness 14
user-based view of quality 12
user requirements 7, 37, 73, 74, 77,
    94, 113, 115, 127, 129, 187,
    208

validity 33, 36, 152
value-based view of quality 11, 14, 53
viability 48
views of quality 7, 9, 10, 11–13, 53,
    113
    See also user-based, value-based,
        manufacturing, transcendent
        and product-based views of
        quality

waterfall model of the software
    lifecycle 7, 12, 13, 73, 74, 92,
    98
Watts 18, 21, 22, 32, 33, 38, 39, 44
weighted scoring 38, 39
Woodward 36
workability 47, 48

Yasuda 113, 114, 117
Yin 35